SCENIC DRIVING

ATLANTIC CANADA

NOVA SCOTIA, NEW BRUNSWICK, PRINCE EDWARD ISLAND, NEWFOUNDLAND & LABRADOR

CHLOË ERNST

gpp®
travel

Guilford, Connecticut

To buy books in quantity for corporate use or incentives, call **(800) 962-0973** or e-mail **premiums@GlobePequot.com**.

All photos by Chloë Ernst.

Editor: Kevin Sirois
Project Editor: Lynn Zelem
Layout: Joanna Beyer
Maps: Design Maps Inc.

ISBN 978-0-7627-6481-5

Printed in the United States of America
10 9 8 7 6 5 4 3 2 1

CONTENTS

The Scenic Drives

New Brunswick

Nova Scotia

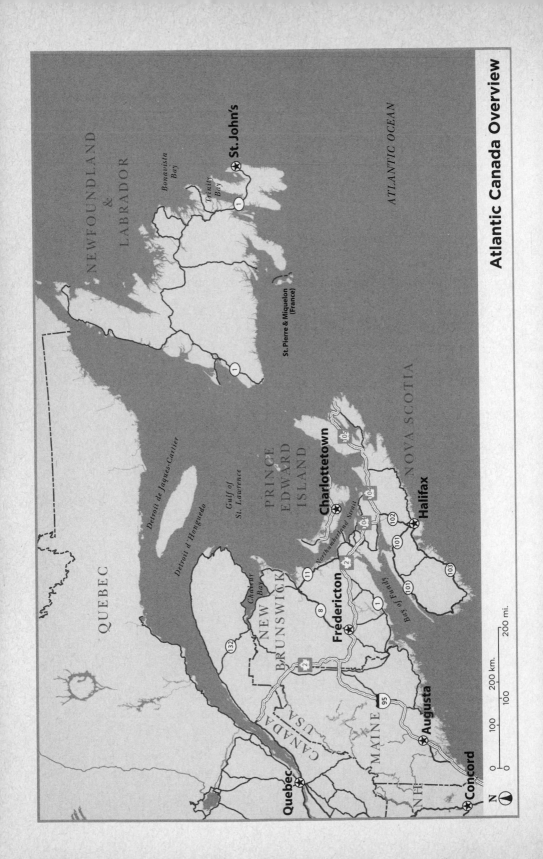

Atlantic Canada Overview

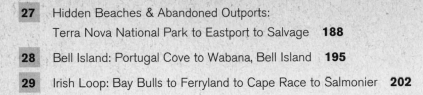

Trans-Canada Highway	═══════ [2] ═══════
Interstate	═══════ (95) ═══════
Featured Trans-Canada Highway	═══════ [2] ═══════
Provincial Highways	─────── (58) ───────
Featured Provincial Highway	─────── (58) ───────
Local Road	───────────────
Featured Local Roads	───────────────
Capital	✪
Drive Locator	⓫
Featured Town	○
Nonfeatured Town	○
Point of Interest	■
River, Creek, or Drainage	∼∼∼∼∼∼∼
Lake or Ocean	⬮
State/Province/National Border	─ ─ ─ MAINE ─ ─ ─
National Park, National Forest, Provincial Park	[🌲]

Map Legend

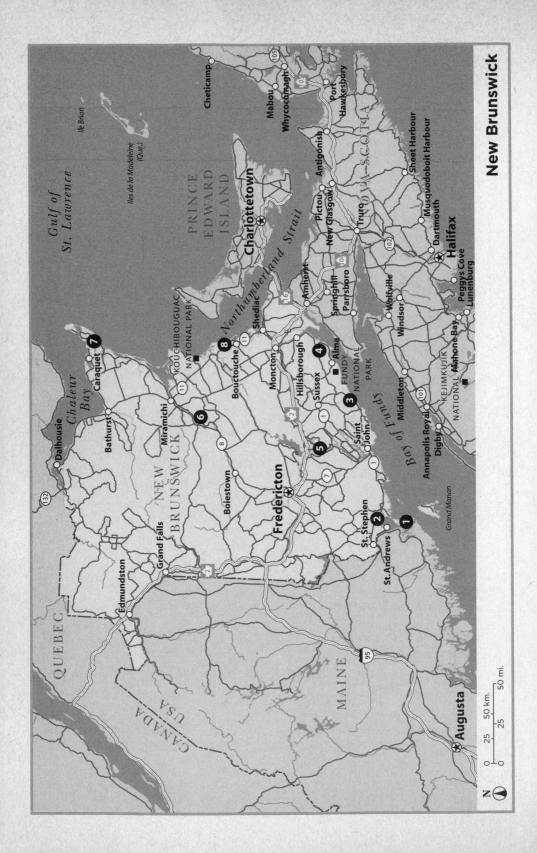

New Brunswick

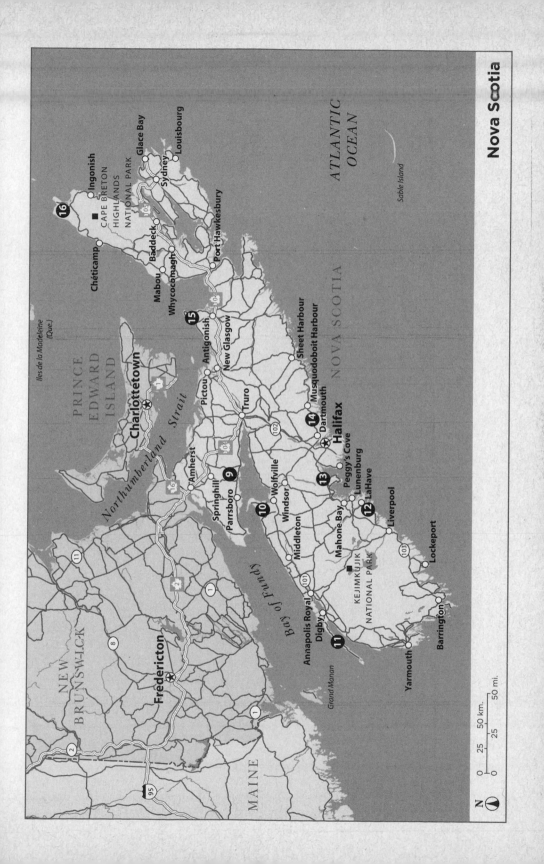

Nova Scotia

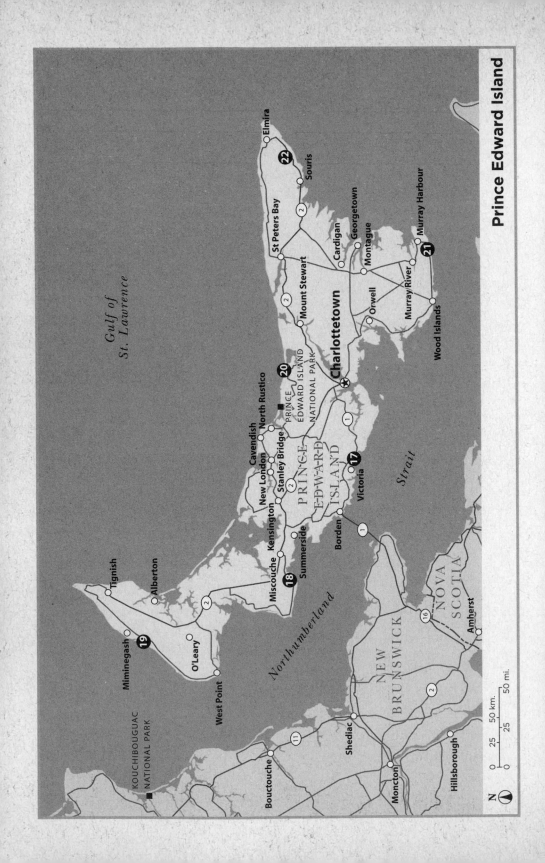

Prince Edward Island

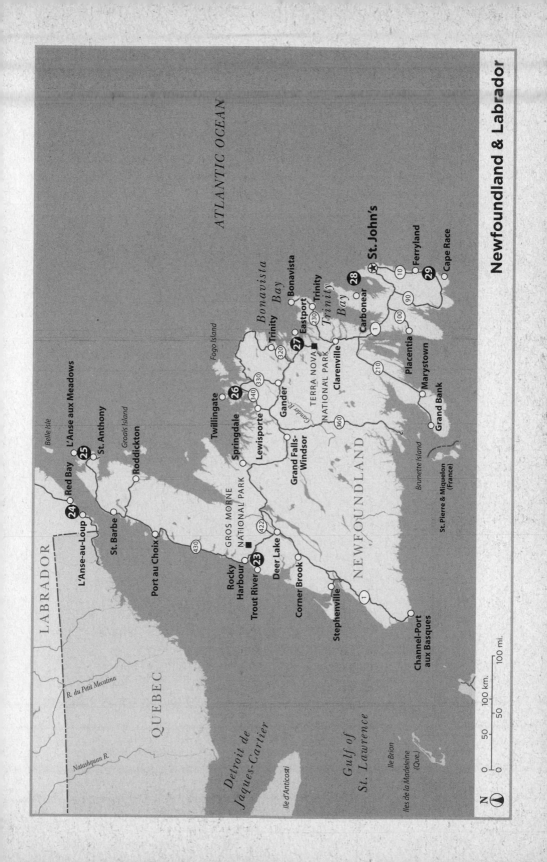

Newfoundland & Labrador

ABOUT THE AUTHOR

Be it riding the Tancook ferry, timing the Fundy tides, or learning an island fiddle tune, Chloë Ernst has always enjoyed exploring the Atlantic Canadian coast. She grew up sailing among Mahone Bay's treasured islands, where her family roots go back to the 1750s.

Chloë earned an honors degree in journalism and Spanish from the University of King's College in Halifax, Nova Scotia. After writing for the *Bridgewater Bulletin* and interning at *Saltscapes* magazine, she moved to Vancouver, British Columbia.

The travel writer has published guidebooks and articles with Frommer's, the *Toronto Star,* and online magazines. She also has written *Day Trips from Seattle* (2010), published by Globe Pequot Press.

Look for updates on her mostly Canadian travel adventures at www .chloeernst.com.

ACKNOWLEDGMENTS

Plates of lobster legs in Prince Edward Island, sailing out to the herring festival on Tancook Island, passing through New Brunswick by train, or watching the sunrise on the Argentia ferry—these are just a few of my treasured Atlantic Canada travel memories. My family often spent vacations in Nova Scotia until we moved to the South Shore when I was 10.

Now having completed this guide that I hope will take other travelers to similar places, I feel immensely grateful for everyone who helped me rediscover this region I love so dearly.

To editor Kevin Sirois and the staff at Globe Pequot Press, I offer my thanks for your help, dedication, and expertise.

To the tourism associations and proprietors around the four Atlantic Provinces, thank you for providing quality resources and excellent service. In every province I met gracious locals (and their dogs), asking about our out-of-province plates or just stopping to chat. Thanks for the friendly greetings.

To my parents, thank you for the support and love and, most of all, for welcoming me home.

My thanks to neighbors and friends who shared their homes and stories of their travels with me, including the Ernsts, the Campbells, the MacCaulls, the Swinamers, the Abdullahs, Molly Kleiker, Jason Meisner, and Julie McHugh. To Rosario and Victor, I am grateful for your generous understanding.

A special thank you to Ian and Jaki for your kindness and warmth.

Lastly, my gratitude goes once again to Matti. Your love and constant support is so appreciated. In the slightly cheesy but nonetheless wonderful words of Anne Shirley from *Anne of Green Gables,* thank you for being a kindred spirit.

INTRODUCTION

The Atlantic Provinces seem to cover only a small section of Canada—that is, until you're driving along their coastlines. Ocean treasures are abundant: fishing outports in Newfoundland and Labrador, docked schooners and beaming lighthouses in Nova Scotia, the depth of the Fundy tides in New Brunswick, and red sandy beaches in Prince Edward Island. But Atlantic Canada—drawing its name from its location on and susceptibility to the Atlantic Ocean—also spans farmlands, river valleys, and great swaths of forest. Histories intertwine ancient First Nations communities, Viking explorers, Basque whalers, French cartographers, Acadian farmers, English merchants, outport fishermen, and entrepreneurial businesswomen.

Atlantic Canada's rich history and achingly beautiful coastal scenery, which seems like home even to those "from away," are even more engaging when you take the slow road.

In this guide, 29 scenic drives take the long way around to stop in end-of-the-road communities and little-visited places in New Brunswick, Nova Scotia, Prince Edward Island, and Newfoundland and Labrador. But we don't shun the favorites either: The Cabot Trail in Cape Breton, the Irish Loop on the Avalon Peninsula, and the *Anne of Green Gables* route near Cavendish are rightful treasures.

Scenic Region: New Brunswick

If you are arriving in Atlantic Canada by land, the forests of New Brunswick will likely be your first experience. Escape the monotone of the highway to explore the province's greatest treasures that lie mostly in the coastal regions: the world's highest tides in the Bay of Fundy, vibrant Acadian towns on Chaleur Bay, and the Reversing Falls of the Saint John River.

New Brunswick is Canada's only officially bilingual province, and seeing French-only signs or being greeted *en français* adds a new dimension to traveling here. Saint John and Moncton, the largest cities, are close to the Bay of Fundy. Fredericton, the capital, sits inland along the Saint John River. Because enjoying some of the province's best attractions (such as the Hopewell Rocks and Ministers Island) rely on the tides, New Brunswick is the only province where your list of essentials includes a tide table.

When the tide recedes, walk on the muddy Bay of Fundy bottom at Hopewell Rocks, New Brunswick.

The provincial history starts with First Nations, primarily the Mi'kmaq and the Maliseet, who have fished, hunted, and lived along the rivers and coasts for generations. Metepenagiag First Nation west of Miramichi is known as the village of 30 centuries. The French explorers and cartographers Jacques Cartier (in the 1500s) then Samuel de Champlain (in the 1600s) visited New Brunswick's coastal areas. French settlers followed, building dikes to reclaim farmland and naming the three Maritime Provinces "Acadia." Into the 1700s, the region seesawed between British and French control.

When Britain took final control, they issued a deportation order in 1755 for the Acadians—those French that has settled in the 1600s—unless they swore allegiance to the British crown. Many were exiled from the region, imprisoned, or taken to France and US regions such as Louisiana. Some Acadians escaped deportation and moved north to settle the Acadian Peninsula along Chaleur Bay.

During the late 1700s and 1800s, Loyalists fleeing after the American Revolution, Irish escaping the potato famine, and Scotts departing the Highlands all arrived in New Brunswick. In 1784 the area north of the Bay of Fundy became the colony of New Brunswick and then part of the Dominion of Canada in 1867.

The Fundy coast from the Maine border to the Nova Scotia border is the primary scenic region. The Saint John Reversing Falls, Fundy National Park, and the Hopewell Rocks are all stunning attractions formed by the world's highest tides, which reach up to 16 meters (53 feet) in the head of the bay. Along the Northumberland Strait, discover the Acadian heritage of the province. In this proud region, Acadian flags—the French flag with a five-point gold star—adorn everything from lobster pots to benches and boats. Inland, rivers and culture-rich cities break the deep green of the province's great forests.

The province shares its longest border with Quebec, has an international crossing to Maine, faces Nova Scotia across the Bay of Fundy, and links with Prince Edward Island via the Confederation Bridge.

Scenic Region: Nova Scotia

Lighthouses, fishing wharves, and historic streets come close to summing up Nova Scotia. Heritage inns, live music, and easily spotted wildlife abound as you explore a province almost encircled with coastline. Stop at beaches, parks, and viewpoints to slow down and admire the sights.

Traditionally Mi'kmaq territory, Nova Scotia saw John Cabot land on its Cape Breton shores in 1497. French settlers, the Acadians, built dikes and farms here as they did along the New Brunswick coast during the 1600s. Most visitors will base themselves in the current provincial capital, Halifax. But the French established

From the Cape George Point Lighthouse, Nova Scotia, look out to the shores of Cape Breton and Prince Edward Island.

the first permanent European colony in what was to become Canada at Port Royal on the Bay of Fundy in 1605.

After an unsuccessful Scottish settlement in the 1620s, the region changed hands many times over the following century. A 1710 conquest and the 1713 Treaty of Utrecht put Acadia in British power, leaving Cape Breton and Prince Edward Island in French hands. As in New Brunswick, British control led to the deportation of the Acadians starting in 1755.

The coastal access, fisheries, farmlands, forests, and other natural resources made Nova Scotia a desirable territory. And the 7,500 kilometers (4,660 miles) of coastline feature in every scenic drive in this region.

All of mainland Nova Scotia is ringed with fishing villages, giving way to a central region of farms and forest. Becoming the provincial capital in 1749, today Halifax is known for its live music and museums—although a historic British fort still watches over the port city.

Connected to the mainland by only a causeway, Cape Breton Island differs widely in its culture. Moose roam the wilds of the Cape Breton Highlands, and a rare few locals still speak in Gaelic tongues. Fiddle music, Highland dancing, and lively ceilidhs add vibrancy to the industrial backdrop in Sydney, the second largest city in Nova Scotia.

The province shares the Bay of Fundy with New Brunswick and has ferry service to the latter as well as Prince Edward Island and Newfoundland. The route from Yarmouth to Maine ended in 2009.

In Nova Scotia, it's truly the rural roads that take you to the local events, small communities, accessible islands, and endless beaches that make the province so precious.

Scenic Region: Prince Edward Island

Farmland and golf courses cover the grassy acres of Prince Edward Island, or PEI. An easy province to navigate, where driving clear across the island takes less than four hours, PEI is a long-time favorite for summer road trips. The highest point on the island sits at only 142 meters (466 feet) elevation, but the scenery rolls in every direction to a sandy coastline. The picturesque landscape transitions from potato rows, hay fields, and grazing pastures to red cliffs, golden sands, and calm salt waters.

The Mi'kmaq were the island's first residents. Much later than elsewhere in Atlantic Canada, French settlement started in the 1720s with a colony at Port-la-Joye. Acadians were deported with the Great Upheaval, and the British changed the region's French name of Île St-Jean to St. Johns Island. A surveyor divvied the land into 67 lots and 3 royalties in the 1760s, and lotteries allocated land to mostly absentee landlords in England. With influxes of Scottish and Irish settlers in the 1800s, the rich soils allowed for rapid population expansion despite the feudal

The Marconi station at the Cape Bear Lighthouse was the first in Canada to receive the Titanic *distress call.*

system and lack of definitive land ownership—a problem that would not be fully resolved until after Confederation.

In 1864 the Charlottetown Conference, held at Province House in Charlottetown, seeded the idea of Canada. But the island, by then renamed Prince Edward Island, held out from joining the dominion until 1873—when it was pressured by the high cost of building a provincial railway. Part of the Confederation carrot was maintaining a year-round link to the mainland: For centuries it was the ferries and, as of 1997, the Confederation Bridge.

Today the two largest cities, the capital Charlottetown and Summerside, both face the Northumberland shore to Nova Scotia and New Brunswick. The entire island is scattered with rural communities, connected with twisting coastal routes, straight roads paralleling the original lot divisions, and earthy red farm lanes.

In Prince Edward Island it is the places between that form the province's most scenic regions.

Unlike the other three Atlantic Provinces, the far extremes of the province—North Cape, West Point, Wood Islands, and East Point—are close enough to be easily explored, be it by scenic drives or the Confederation Trail. The railway, decommissioned in 1989, forms this recreational path network that spans the full length of the island.

Farmlands are abundant, and late summer is a wonderful time to drive past the crop fields. Beaches encircle the green island, ranging in hues from white to golden to red.

Museums of oddities contrast the pastoral scenery, introducing everything from the world-famous Malpeque Bay oysters to houses built from glass bottles to Irish moss seaweed pie.

Scenic Region: Newfoundland & Labrador

Newfoundland and Labrador, Atlantic Canada's most visually stunning province, requires a special effort to visit. But going the distance to this easternmost part of Canada rewards unfathomably with rugged beauty, inaccessible coast, and friendly locals who will still wave to you on the highway.

Two ferry routes from North Sydney, Nova Scotia, and an international airport in St. John's, Newfoundland, provide the first link to the province locals call "the Rock." Paved main routes, small coast-hopping ferries, and dirt-road highways provide access to the communities, even to remote Labrador—a vast, empty, and stunning region that stretches north to border Quebec and Nunavut.

The coastline measures nearly 30,000 kilometers (18,640 miles), more than any other Canadian province (although that of the Northwest Territories and Nunavut dwarfs this number). Summer icebergs, Atlantic puffins, whale pods, and caribou herds show the pure natural wonders of the province. The history spans extinct Beothuks, exploring Vikings, Basque whalers, French fishermen, and English colonizers and merchants. Archaeological digs throughout the province uncover these ruins with amazing occurrence, be it the Colony of Avalon in Ferryland, John Guy's settlement in Cupids, Beothuk villages in Boyd's Cove, or a 7,500-year-old Maritime Archaic (a native culture) burial mound at Point Amour, Labrador.

In the unclaimed wilderness (of which there is a lot), hiking trails lead to ancient fossils, and inland fjords are diminutively called ponds.

St. John's, the largest city, lies on the Avalon Peninsula to the east of the province. But it is in the great bare stretches of highway in Labrador and the barrens of the Irish Loop where the truly arresting beauty can be found.

Newfoundlanders are a unique, friendly bunch and even boast their own dictionary to decipher the local dialect.

The human history here stretches back thousands of years and the geological history hundred of millions more. Artifacts of the Maritime Archaic and Paleo-Eskimo people are still found in digs. The extinct Beothuk lived on the coast most recently, and Inuit still live in Labrador. Vikings set up a small settlement in L'Anse aux Meadows about 1,000 years ago. Basque whalers visited the Labrador coast in the 1500s to hunt bowhead and right whales and render the blubber into oil. French fishermen harvested the sea bounty off the coast in the 1600s, as did the English. From 1907, Newfoundland was the Dominion of Newfoundland under the British Crown. This ended when Newfoundland joined Confederation in 1949, but you'll still see the colors of Newfoundland's unofficial flag flying.

Known as the Pink, White, and Green, the flag is said to symbolize peace between the Irish and English. An anthem written by Archbishop Michael Howley in 1902 describes it thus:

> The pink the rose of England shows,
> The green St. Patrick's emblem bright,
> While in between the spotless sheen
> St. Andrew's cross displays the white.

The current Newfoundland flag became official in 1980.

Once-abundant cod and other fish stocks have diminished, forcing those in small fishing-supported communities—often called outports—to move to larger centers. But some outports remain, with their fishing stages, docked vessels, and saltbox houses. It makes a coastal out-of-the-way drive in Newfoundland almost like time travel.

Geology

Shifting tectonic plates and recent ice ages have carved, pushed, and formed a diverse landscape in Atlantic Canada, a region that once abutted Africa. But the geology of each province is distinct, from the soft red soils of PEI to the jutting rocks of Newfoundland.

The Appalachian Mountains stretch up the coast into Newfoundland, defining much of New Brunswick. While the formation of the Bay of Fundy as a tidal funnel is perhaps the best-known geological wonder, a visit to Grand Manan, an island off the Fundy coast, reveals a contrasting scenery of sedimentary and volcanic rocks.

In Nova Scotia a fault runs from Cobequid Bay off the Bay of Fundy to Chedabucto Bay near Cape Breton. It divides the province into two geological regions: the Avalon Zone to the north and the Meguma Zone to the south. For much of geological history, the two existed on different super continents before ending up on one. Become a Nova Scotian rock hound with visits to the Joggins Fossil Cliffs between Amherst and Parrsboro, a coal-mine tour in Glace Bay, or a shoreline walk in Arisaig Provincial Park.

Prince Edward Island offers scant fossils, but the island was once connected to the mainland until sea levels rose. The island sits on a shallow ocean shelf, creating lots of coastal lobster habitat.

Get below the surface with Newfoundland geology at the Johnson Geo Centre near Signal Hill. Sunk into the hillside, exhibits show the evolution of the province nicknamed "the Rock." The most unique rock-spotting places in the province are the fossils at Mistaken Point at the tip of the Avalon Peninsula, and the Tablelands in Gros Morne, where exposed mantle and an ancient ocean bed provided evidence for the theories of plate tectonics.

Natural World

Unfortunately most of the creatures you'll see on Maritime roads will be road-kill—mostly raccoons, porcupines, and skunks. These species along with black bears, deer, coyotes, and moose are most commonly spotted in the Maritimes (defined as just New Brunswick, Nova Scotia, and Prince Edward Island).

Newfoundland has fewer small mammal species than the Maritimes, with no raccoons or skunks, as well as no snakes. Moose, however, seem to make up for the lack of smaller beasts and are a factor in many fatal road collisions.

Whale-watching tours provide excellent access to the breaching sea mammals, while bird watching in all four provinces is the most accessible wildlife experience. Along the shorelines, migratory sandpipers and piping plovers feed and nest. Newfoundland has burgeoning colonies of gannets at Cape St. Mary's and Atlantic puffins at Witless Bay. Jays, woodpeckers, and birds of prey make for more great sightings throughout the provinces, especially in national parks.

Heed advice about endangered and threatened wildlife. Don't feed animals, thereby desensitizing them to humans and cars.

Outdoors Advice

Head out prepared. On the coast, which is to say the majority of Atlantic Canada, fog rolls in without warning. In summer, the severe weather is limited, but autumn hurricanes are becoming increasingly common this far north. In winter, snow can halt all travel for days.

Even on short hikes over marked trails, take the essentials: water, food, rain gear, maps, and a compass. Advise someone of your route and expected return time. Also, be prepared for bugs: from the early-season black flies and no-see-ums to the summer-long mosquitoes. Long sleeves, pants, and a good bug repellant will save much grief (and scratching).

If you must take a souvenir while beachcombing, look for sea glass, a lobster trap rib, or a fishing buoy. You're not only finding a unique beach treasure, but also collecting garbage from the shoreline.

Fishing requires a license, although for some activities like clam digging you need only observe the daily limit. Check with a local visitor bureau or park ranger for exact regulations, as well as any health-related shellfish closures (like red tide) for that area.

Emergencies & Preparedness

Most, if not all, areas now use 911 as an emergency number. While a cell phone can be useful in emergencies, there is no guarantee that cellular service will be available in all areas. While this is especially true for remote and wilderness areas, there are areas with irregular or no coverage in these drives.

For those on a road trip, an auto-plan membership can provide assistance in areas where services are limited. But it's no substitute for checking gas, fluids, tires, mechanics, and the weather before departing.

HOW TO USE THIS GUIDE

This scenic driving guide is unconcerned with checklist travel: that is, making sure you visit everywhere in a given area. It's about taking things slowly, going to the end of the road and back, and traversing new landscapes. The drives are spread out evenly over the four Atlantic Provinces, and I've focused on highlighting favorite historical sites, picturesque parks, protected natural areas, and friendly communities where you'll meet people like nowhere else.

Each drive includes the text with navigation directions and descriptions plus a map and a photo. Some drives also offer side trips, or options to explore further. You'll find contact information for attractions, parks, and visitor bureaus, separated by drive, in Appendix A at the end of the book. Rarely do I give hours for attractions, although the vast majority of places in the region open daily from June to September.

I only occasionally list specific restaurants or accommodations. In most areas your options will number in the dozens. The tourism offices in all four provinces produce an annual magazine-like travel guide that lists accommodations, campgrounds, festivals, and attractions. Some also include shops, art galleries, and selected restaurants. Contact details for main provincial tourism offices are listed in Appendix B.

Any listed prices are in Canadian dollars. And while they were current at the time of printing, they may have since changed.

A detailed and current road map, however, is most essential supplement. Look for one that lists route numbers for tertiary highways and rural roads, not just major highways. Handy extras are maps that pinpoint the location of attractions and parks. (Disclaimer: None that I've used are fully accurate or regularly updated, so be warned!)

Generally, most roads in Atlantic Canada can be called highways or routes interchangeably. In general I've delineated the two, referring to major thoroughfares as highways and local roads as routes.

Exploring all the scenic drives outlined in this guide will take you to the most spectacular spots in Atlantic Canada. But unless you are lucky enough to be on a two-month vacation, driving all in the same go is just about impossible. Choose a few to provide the groundwork of a trip or to use as a weekend-getaway or day-trip guide.

A cliché but a deserving one nonetheless: Be sure to take a sense of discovery as you turn onto an unknown route—perhaps it leads to a quiet beach, seafood canteen, friendly artist's studio, or something unknown.

NEW
BRUNSWICK

Fundy Island–Hopping

Campobello Island to Deer Island

General Description: This 55-kilometer (34-mile) island drive teases with water views, winding roads, and ferry rides. The attractions number only a few on Campobello and Deer Islands, but they are excellent ones: a former president's 34-room summer cottage, an island lighthouse, and a tidal whirlpool. Shorebirds and whales frequent the coast, drawn by a rich ecosystem freshened daily by the Bay of Fundy's powerful tides. Watch for this wildlife from the isolated beaches, hiking trails, or on a boat tour.

Special Features: Roosevelt Campobello International Park, Herring Cove Provincial Park, Head Harbour Lightstation (East Quoddy Lighthouse), Old Sow Whirlpool, free ferry to Deer Island, bird watching, hiking, golfing, beaches, whale watching, sailing.

Location: The Fundy Islands lie near the Maine–New Brunswick border in Passamaquoddy Bay. The Lubec, Maine–Campobello, New Brunswick, border crossing is about 85 kilometers (52.8 miles) from St. Stephen, New Brunswick.

Driving Route Numbers & Names: Route 774, Herring Cove Road, Route 772.

Travel Season: The summer season, with its warmer ocean temperatures and whale sightings, has been a favorite for centuries. Part of the Atlantic Flyway, the islands welcome migratory birds like sandpipers and endangered piping plovers in August. Late spring (May and June) and early autumn (September and October) are considered

shoulder seasons but are still lovely in the Maritimes, bringing slightly cooler days and mostly clear skies. The ferry from Deer Island to Campobello Island runs only late June to mid-September.

Camping: Campsites close to a beach and hiking trails are tucked in Herring Cove Provincial Park on Campobello Island. Full-service sites for RVs as well as no frills tent sites mean the campground easily accommodates a range of campers. The amenities stack up: laundry facilities, water, washrooms, showers, and even a 9-hole golf course. Deer Island has a private campground on the southern point, near the ferry dock to Campobello and Eastport.

Services: As both of these Fundy Islands have small populations, you won't find many services on either Campobello Island or Deer Island. Campobello offers the better services, including a grocery store, restaurants, library, and post office. But there is no gas station, so you'll have to fill up across the border in Lubec, Maine, or continue on to Deer Island. For accommodations, have the pick of a heritage inn or vacation cottages. Deer Island does offer dining options close to the Letete ferry dock as well as a gas station in Fairhaven.

Nearby Points of Interest: St. George–Canal Beach, St. George Falls, Canal Covered Bridge, Grand Manan Island and ferry.

Time Zone: Atlantic time zone (GMT minus 4 hours).

The Drive

This 55-kilometer (34-mile) scenic drive slots into a few different itineraries. It can be part of a loop around Passamaquoddy Bay, an out-and-back ferry trip from

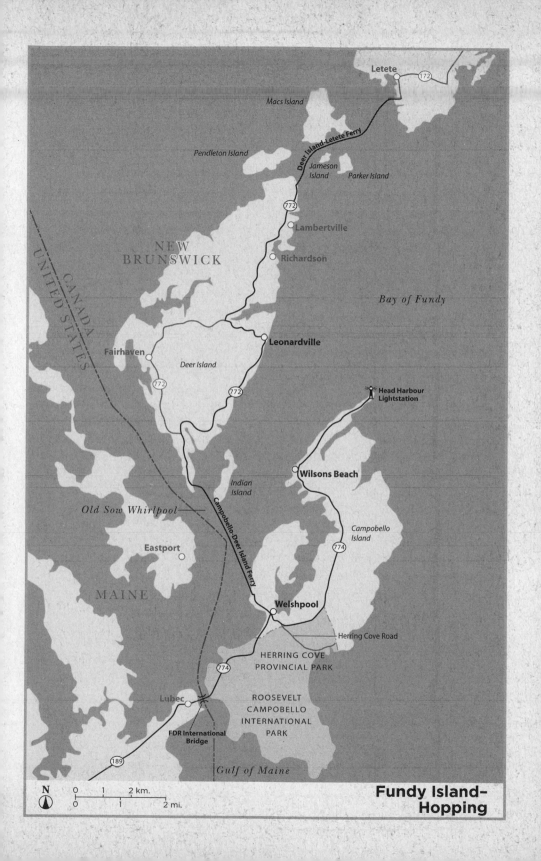

Letete

172

Macs Island

Deer Island–Letete Ferry

Pendleton Island

Jameson Island

Parker Island

772

○ Lambertville

NEW
BRUNSWICK

○ Richardson

Bay of Fundy

CANADA
UNITED STATES

● **Leonardville**

Fairhaven ○

Deer Island

⚓ **Head Harbour
Lightstation**

772

772

● **Wilsons Beach**

*Indian
Island*

Old Sow Whirlpool

Campobello–Deer Island Ferry

Eastport ○

*Campobello
Island*

774

MAINE

● **Welshpool**

Herring Cove Road

**HERRING COVE
PROVINCIAL PARK**

774

**ROOSEVELT
CAMPOBELLO
INTERNATIONAL
PARK**

Lubec ○

**FDR International
Bridge**

189

Gulf of Maine

N

0   1   2 km.
0   1   2 mi.

**Fundy Island-
Hopping**

Letete (thereby staying in Canadian waters), or an alternative to the border crossing at Calais–St. Stephen. We treat it here as a through trip from the border crossing at **Lubec, Maine,** to the New Brunswick mainland.

In Maine, follow US 1 to the junction with Route 189. Cross the river at Whiting and head east to the international border. The **FDR International Bridge** connects the US peninsula to Canada's Campobello Island. Dubbed a "friendly" border crossing in the tourism brochures, you'll still need proper documentation (a valid passport or passport card) to enter Canada. In addition to crossing an international border, you also move into the Atlantic time zone, which is an hour ahead of Eastern Standard Time.

Driving over the bridge, watch for the classic red-capped **Mulholland Lighthouse** on the left. To visit the lighthouse, turn left after the bridge on Narrows Road. To the right of Route 774—which runs the length of Campobello Island—an island visitor center is located in a lighthouse-style building.

About 1.5 kilometers (0.9 miles) past the border on Route 774, make a left turn to head down to the shore at **Friars Head.** Trails, a picnic area, and observation deck provide access to and views of the shoreline at **Friars Bay.** Stop here, or continue on to **Roosevelt Cottage** less than a kilometer farther along Route 774 for similar views and more shoreline access.

Roosevelt Cottage

A clearly sign-posted, left-hand turn to **Roosevelt Campobello International Park** leads to the rust-red, three-story cottage where Franklin D. Roosevelt spent his summers as a boy, young father, and the 32nd president of the United States. Thirty-four rooms, 18 bedrooms, and 6 bathrooms make the house more than a small summer getaway.

Admission is free to the visitor center and house where, from late May to Canadian Thanksgiving (the second Monday of October), the Canadian and American interpreters give the history of the property and family. The house is run as an international historic site, as a symbol of the Canada-US friendship. Rooms still contain the Roosevelt's furniture in pristine condition, from the wicker furniture in the living room to the toys in the playroom.

Roosevelt first visited the island with his parents in 1883 when he was one year old. FDR's mother, Sara Roosevelt, purchased the property from Mrs. Hartman Kuhn in 1909 because it neighbored her own. When she died, Sara Roosevelt left her son the then much-smaller cottage.

Eleanor and Franklin Roosevelt visited the cottage in the summers from 1909–1921, spending the warm season without electricity or telephone. Besides hiking and visiting the beach, the Roosevelts spent long hours sailing in Passamaquoddy Bay.

Roosevelt Cottage, Campobello Island, New Brunswick.

Roosevelt added a wing to the cottage in 1915 to accommodate his growing family.

Large grounds include gardens, an icehouse, the foundation of the Roosevelt's old cottage, and a beach on Friars Bay. A highlight is seeing the Roosevelt master bedroom. In this pretty room, which has a rather small-looking bed by today's standards, Franklin Roosevelt Jr. was born in 1914; it is also where FDR became ill with polio in 1921.

Campobello Island

The Roosevelt Cottage was just one part of a vast summer industry on the island. In the late 1880s, a group of businessmen from New York and Boston built large hotels here and promoted **Campobello Island** as a summer destination. Summer cottages followed, and the vacation buzz lasted for about 30 years before taking full-summer holidays became impossible for many workers. Only a few of these summer cottages, and none of the large hotels, are left.

With the construction of the FDR International Bridge in 1962, Campobello has once again become a popular summer destination.

Historically the Passamaquoddy First Nation was the first to live in the area. Prior to foreign influx, they hunted and fished in the bay.

French and then British settlers began arriving in the mid-1700s. The island population grew steadily after Captain William Owen's arrival in 1770. Crops and fisheries sustained communities in Welshpool and Wilsons Beach.

To continue the scenic drive and explore these historic communities, drive northeast on Route 774. The road heads through the forested island to a three-way intersection. The left route takes you directly to Welshpool and the Deer Island ferry, but for now continue exploring Campobello by turning right toward Herring Cove and Wilsons Beach.

Shortly after the intersection, make a right on Herring Cove Road and follow signs for the provincial park. At **Herring Cove Provincial Park,** a 1.6-kilometer (1-mile) dark-sand-and-pebble beach looks out on **Grand Manan Island.** Watch for ferries making the passage from Blacks Harbour on the New Brunswick mainland to the largest of the Fundy Islands. A 9-hole golf course, restaurant, and campground at the park revive the feel of Campobello as a summer destination.

Back on Route 774 head northeast again for a forest drive that cuts through the middle of the island. Occasionally the trees break to reveal rocky coves and fishing wharves. At **Harbour de Lute,** across from Schooner Cove Road, the views improve. The harbor mouth features cragged cliffs, island views, abandoned boats, aquaculture ponds, and the older wooden homes of **Wilsons Beach.**

The road turns here to follow a narrow peninsula. To the right is Head Harbour, and to the left is Head Harbour Passage. The land signals an end near East Quoddy Head as it narrows enough to allow water views on both sides.

At the northern end of Lighthouse Road, the photogenic **Head Harbour Lightstation** sits on its own island. Also known as **East Quoddy Lighthouse,** you can walk out to the island at low tide or take a boat at high water. The Friends of Head Harbour Lightstation maintain the lighthouse, charging a fee to visit the island or climb the lighthouse tower. If you only have time for a quick stop before the ferry, the no-charge observation area provides a panoramic shot but limited views of the actual lighthouse. You'll see the keeper's quarters but not the iconic lighthouse—its white tower flashed with a bold red cross.

Return on Route 774 past the provincial park, this time bearing right to **Welshpool.** Just before the ferry terminal, turn down the steep decline of Welshpool Wharf Road. The small village lanes include a historic bed-and-breakfast as well as a library built in 1898. The library introduces Campobello history with exhibits including photos, quilts, and even a carriage.

From June through mid-September, the **Campobello–Deer Island ferry** runs hourly during the daytime. Contact **East Coast Ferries** (www.eastcoastferries.nb .ca) for a full schedule. In 2010, the fare ran $16 for a vehicle and driver, or $3 for passengers, plus fuel surcharges. The company also runs a ferry from Deer Island to Eastport, Maine. While taking the 20-minute crossing from Campobello to Deer Island, keep an ear out for island gossip and an eye out for whale pods.

Great views of **Eastport, Maine,** a small city on Moose Island, are another scenic highlight of the ferry journey. See the grand old brick buildings that line the waterfront. A church spire rises above the town that once thrived on its sardine canning factories.

Tidal Whirlpool

The quick crossing to Deer Island passes between Eastport and Indian Island. The tidal forces make for a different ferry ride—a ferry engine swings out to compensate for the power of the tidal flow.

About 3 hours before high tide, the **Old Sow Whirlpool** forms as the largest tidal whirlpool in the Western Hemisphere. Taking different forms, the roiling turbulent waters sometimes form a large funnel as the rising tide pushes around Indian Island and over the ocean floor. There's even a certificate available from the Old Sow Whirlpool Survivors' Association for those who pass through the whirlpool and live. But asking a ferry deckhand about Old Sow is definitely the preferred approach.

Nearing the end of the sailing, look to the left of the ferry dock to where **Deer Island Campground at Deer Island Point** provides great views of the whirlpool, Passamaquoddy Bay, and occasionally whales. There's also a small navigation light on the end of the grassy point.

Deer Island

Visiting **Deer Island** is more about the drive than any single destination. Follow Deer Island Point Road to Route 772, which heads left to Fairhaven or right to Chocolate Cove and Leonardville. While Fairhaven has restaurants and a gas station, I prefer the more coastal route around the eastern shore of the island.

Turning right toward Chocolate Cove, follow Route 772 as it passes tiny coves and fishing wharves. At low tide the fishing weirs appear as a tangle of nets, lines, and posts. Used to catch herring, the weirs make for great coastal photos at low water. Also along the shore, see the aquaculture ponds used to raise Atlantic salmon.

At **Leonardville** more fishing weirs, wharves, historic homes, and the Leonardville Light show the working community's connection to the saltwater. Fishing boats and floats dot the shoreline, and piled nets edge the road.

The road climbs back up from the shoreline toward the head of Northwest Harbour. Here the road branches left to Fairhaven or right to the ferry. Marshlands, hilly terrain, and historic buildings trim the drive.

The road twists sharply through the communities of **Richardson, Lords Cove,** and **Stuart Town,** feeling more like a country lane as it winds around veranda-fronted houses. To the east the **Bay of Fundy** is clogged with rocky islands.

Just before Richardson you cross the 45th parallel—halfway between the equator and the North Pole.

Along the shore of the island on Northern Harbour Road, an ocean pen that can hold 3 million crustaceans rates as the world's largest lobster pound. The holding area stores lobsters before they are shipped or processed.

At the ferry terminal to Letete on the New Brunswick mainland, a small cafe/diner serves snacks and sells gift items. The free 20-minute crossing curves around a dozen islands before docking on the far shore.

There are more than two dozen Fundy Islands, of which Campobello and Deer are the second and third largest.

Via Letete, Route 172 connects to Highway 1 to continue a coastal drive along the Bay of Fundy.

Side Trip: Grand Manan

Grand Manan, the largest of the Fundy Islands, is not accessible directly from Campobello or Deer Islands. Grand Manan is a rugged spot, with small fishing communities, coastal trails, and excellent bird watching. Artists—both locals and visiting—take inspiration from the offshore whale pods and tidal-carved rock formations.

Perhaps the most unique island attraction, however, is the **Grand Manan Whale and Seabird Research Station.** Scientists and volunteers get hands-on with observations and research projects on common terns, right whales, and harbor porpoises.

Besides fishing, there is a local dulse processing plant. The Atlantic seaweed is collected at low tide, sun dried, and then packaged as a salty snack.

Fishing weirs along the coastline of Deer Island, New Brunswick.

Drive the Ocean Floor

St. Andrews to Covenhoven via Bar Road

General Description: The book's shortest drive covering just 8 kilometers (5 miles) round-trip, it is also the most unique: A road accessible only at low tide leads to an abandoned summerhouse that looks more like a English country estate than the former home of a railway man. Walk the grounds of Covenhoven to see the windmill, bathhouse, and tidal swimming pool. It's the perfect vantage over Port Chamcook Harbour and the island-studded expanse of Passamaquoddy Bay.

Special Features: Atlantic Salmon Interpretive Centre, Ministers Island Historic Site—Covenhoven summerhouse, bathhouse, windmill, barns, carriage house, livestock, walking trails, horse rides, clam digging.

Location: Southwestern New Brunswick, on the Fundy coast. St. Andrews lies across the St. Croix River from Maine; the closest border crossing is about 30 kilometers (18.6 miles) away at St. Stephen.

Driving Route Numbers & Names: Bar Road, Carriage Road.

Travel Season: Visit the summerhouse in its best season, when lawn picnics, horse rides, and clam digging are possible. The attraction retains a longer season than most local attractions. Tours run from May through mid-October, although visitors should contact the island for the exact, tide-dictated schedule.

Camping: Perhaps the prettiest location for a campground I've seen, the Kiwanis Oceanfront Camping sits at the tip of St. Andrews overlooking Passamaquoddy Bay. The oceanfront sites are geared toward RVs, and tent sites are tucked to the back of the campground. Facilities include showers, washrooms, Internet, laundry, a playground, and a kitchen shelter.

Services: St. Andrews offers the basics plus a lovely selection of historic inns, waterfront restaurants, and adorable shops. The town's Main Street is a heritage district and a picturesque spot to enjoy an afternoon on a patio. There are grocery stores, public washrooms, and a gas station to serve the community and visitors. While there are medical clinics in St. Andrews, the closest hospital is in St. Stephen.

Nearby Points of Interest: Kingsbrae Garden, Ross Memorial Museum, Fairmont Algonquin Hotel and golf course, St. Andrews Blockhouse National Historic Site, St. Croix Island International Historic Site.

Time Zone: Atlantic time zone (GMT minus 4 hours).

The Drive

An adventurous drive, this 8-kilometer (5-mile) loop heads off the paved road and over a low-tide sandbar to arrive at an uninhabited summerhouse. The island lies to the east of the holiday haven of **St. Andrews,** once a railway resort town.

Off Highway 1, take exit 39 to follow Route 127 toward St. Andrews. A same-numbered route also cuts down from Highway 1, exit 25, and arrives on the west

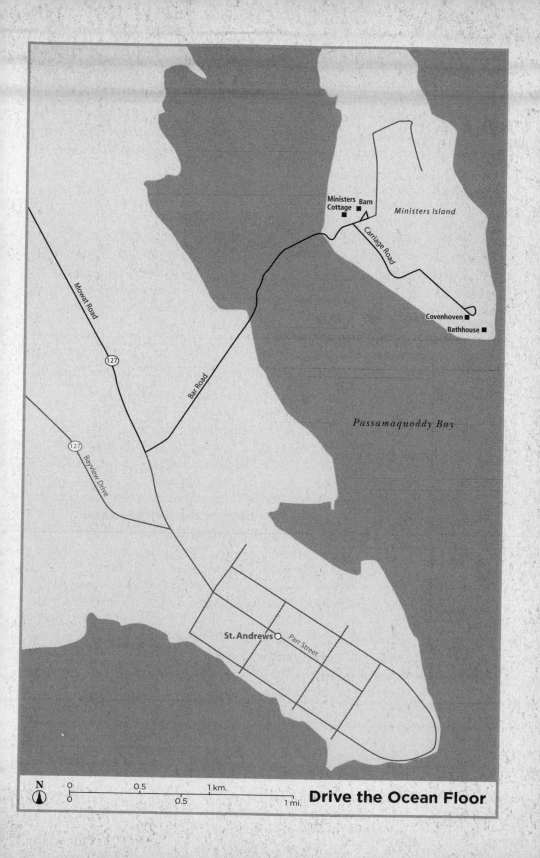

Ministers Cottage

Barn

Ministers Island

Carriage Road

Covenhoven

Bathhouse

Mowat Road

127

Bar Road

127

Bayview Drive

Passamaquoddy Bay

St. Andrews

Parr Street

N

0   0.5   1 km.

0   0.5   1 mi.

Drive the Ocean Floor

side of town. If that is your route, cross the peninsula on Ghost Road, Clarke Road, or Cornelia Street, and then follow Route 127 south to Bar Road.

On the way to Ministers Island from exit 39, you pass the **Atlantic Salmon Interpretive Centre,** at 24 Chamcook Lake No. 1 Rd. off Route 127. Nature trails and an in-stream salmon aquarium allow you to interact with the riparian and river habitats. Cultural exhibits tell the intertwined histories of humans and salmon.

About 17 kilometers (10.6 miles) from Highway 1 exit 39, turn left off Route 127 to follow Bar Road down to the shoreline. This drive will yield plenty of animal sightings; watch for deer on this wooded road.

If you're uncomfortable dodging rocks and potholes or driving on uneven surfaces, it may be best to park here on the St. Andrews side and take the shuttle to Ministers Island. While you'll be less independent, you will avoid possible rock hazards on Bar Road. That being said, on any given summer weekend, dozens of vehicles of all sizes drive across to explore. Proceeding slowly is essential.

Bar Road

Across a 750-meter (0.5-mile) sandbar that is accessible only at low tide, you travel from St. Andrews to **Ministers Island.** The Ministers Island website (www .ministersisland.ca) posts a schedule for accessing the island by vehicle, and the hours change daily with the tides. Allow plenty of time to explore the island; otherwise, subject to the rush of the Bay of Fundy's high tides, you could be stranded for hours.

There's no single route across the sandbar. Marked in part with large stones, the shaley ground offers a number of paths that change as the water scours the surface. Clam diggers may be parked along the sandbar, fishing for bivalve mollusks in the thick mud.

As the road approaches Ministers Island, a gatehouse sits to the right where you'll pay a pricey-but-worthwhile admission fee. Leading up from the shore a steep gravel road forks left to the barn and right to the summerhouse, Covenhoven.

Most of the island is a mix of forest and bucolic farm fields. Taking the right fork, follow the gravel road—Carriage Road—through an idyllic English countryside. Stone walls, grazing sheep, and mature hardwoods transport visitors to a British landscape. Look out over the green pastures to see llamas, cows, horses, and goats all grazing.

Trail rides on Ministers Island, New Brunswick.

Covenhoven House

The towers, wings, and windmill of **Covenhoven** cut impressive silhouettes on Ministers Island. Sir William Van Horne was a railroad baron who rose from a telegraph operator in Illinois to president of the Canadian Pacific Railway as it built its coast-to-coast railway. Van Horne watched as the last spike was hammered into the ground in Craigellachie, British Columbia, thus finishing the railway five years ahead of schedule.

Built in the 1890s and designed by architect Edward Maxwell with heavy input from Van Horne, Covenhoven has 50 rooms, 11 bathrooms, and 11 fireplaces. Banquet-sized dining rooms, endless bedrooms, playrooms, kitchens, and drawing rooms were all elegantly furnished in Van Horne's time.

A painter, amateur architect, and livestock breeder, Van Horne incorporated his many interests into this summerhouse. Adding wings and completing renovations to the mansion, the most treasured, perhaps, was the nursery he added for his only grandchild, William. In his grandchild's room, Van Horne painted a scene of Dutch boys and girls playing that still livens the nursery walls.

After the deaths of Van Horne in 1915 and his wife Lady Van Horne in 1929, the property was left to their unmarried daughter Adaline. In 1941, upon Adaline's death, the property was bequeathed to a niece and later sold. It became a provincial historic site in 1977, the start of its long road to protection and restoration.

Featuring a wooden-shingle style slightly reminiscent of national park lodges, the multiwing house now sits empty. Explore the house independently or with a guided tour. Walking through the rooms, you'll note that some are partially furnished while others have nothing but peeling wallpaper and crumbling plaster. Simple exhibits pale in comparison to the empty upstairs rooms, which have so many doors and bathrooms that one can quickly get lost.

At the back of the house, you'll see the windmill that pumped water into the house and a small building where carbide gas was produced and piped into the house for lighting.

From the front porch, where there are patio tables with a panoramic view, walk down to the round bathhouse on the shore. A handsome circular stone tower overlooks **Passamaquoddy Bay.** Van Horne used the bathhouse as a painting studio and displayed his fossil collection in the glassed-in top floor. A curved staircase leads down to a changing area and then out to the shoreline where a tidal swimming pool is sunken into the rock.

Looking out over blue water and verdant hills, it's easy to imagine why first the Passamaquoddy First Nation and later Van Horne were enchanted into taking up residence here.

A network of hiking and biking trails surrounds the property, and the large grassy lawns are dappled with fruit trees and historic monuments.

Van Horne's summerhouse, Covenhoven, on Ministers Island, New Brunswick.

The Barn and Ministers Cottage

Return on the gravel road to the main fork, just uphill from the junction with Bar Road. This time turn right toward the barn.

Built by unemployed shipbuilders, with each floor covering 771 square meters (8,300 square feet), the finely smoothed curves, shingled grain silos, and huge footprint of the barn stand out. It towers larger than the house.

Admire the ribbons awarded to Van Horne's prized Clydesdale horses and herds of Dutch Belted cattle. A few sweet ponies are available for trail rides.

Beyond a retreat and artistic haven for Van Horne, the property was very much a working farm. Crops, livestock, heated greenhouses, and a creamery meant the island boasted great self-sufficiency. Van Horne had milk, produce, and other farm foods couriered by train to his winter residence in Montreal.

Near the barn you'll spot the blue-trimmed stone cottage built by Rev. Samuel Andrews in 1790. Andrews was the island's namesake minister, although the Passamaquoddy called the island Qonasqamqi Monihkuk, meaning "sand point island." A Loyalist Anglican minister, Andrews came to the area from Connecticut in 1786.

From the cottage, drive down the gravel hill, over Bar Road, and to the mainland. Route 127 leads south to St. Andrews and to a T-junction at Harriet Street. There is a nearby visitor information center that can direct you to the attractions, but the pretty railway-resort town is also small enough to explore impromptu.

Side Trip: St. Andrews and St. Croix

Better explored on foot than in a vehicle, **St. Andrews** is a quintessentially cute seaside town. The national historic district includes the thoroughfare of Water Street where large inns, fine restaurants, and lush gardens line the main route. Around the town lies a seeming week's worth of attractions.

At 188 Montague St. in the heart of the historic district, the **Ross Memorial Museum** features a decorative art collection in a heritage house. The almost-palatial brick home was constructed in 1824 for Loyalist Harry Hatch, his wife, and 11 children. An art collection donated by Henry and Juliette Ross can be viewed throughout the two-story mansion.

Nearby on Frederick Street, visit the **Old Gaol** with its grim 1832 conditions, and the **Charlotte County Courthouse,** which is still used for trials. The **Sheriff Andrews House** at 63 King St. continues the locked-down theme. Sheriff Elisha Andrews owned the house, built in 1820. He was the son of Rev. Samuel Andrews of Ministers Island.

Concerned over their proximity to the American border, local residents raised funds to construct the fortification at **St. Andrews Blockhouse National Historic Site** during the War of 1812, when Great Britain and the United States were at arms. The blockhouse surveys the St. Croix River, and, in summer, guides revive those nervous days of the border watch.

Close to the grand Fairmont Algonquin hotel, **Kingsbrae Garden** provides a day of botanical explorations for gardeners. Trim flower borders, neatly pruned bushes, and labyrinth-like paths have earned it a nod as one of the 10 best public gardens in Canada. More than 50,000 trees, shrubs, and flowers are carefully planted over 11 hectares (27 acres).

West of St. Andrews, follow Route 127 along the St. Croix River to **St. Croix Island International Historic Site.** Located on the international border and accessible only by ferry, the island was the site of North America's first attempted French settlement. The French explorer Pierre Dugua, with Samuel de Champlain aboard, arrived here in 1604. The site was later abandoned in favor of Port Royal, Nova Scotia (see Drive 11).

3

Fundy Trail Parkway

St. Martins to Big Salmon River

General Description: In this 25-kilometer (15.5-mile) scenic drive, we preface the developed lookouts of the Fundy Trail Parkway with sea caves and two covered bridges in St. Martins. Along the parkway itself, the viewpoints number more than a dozen. Cross a suspension bridge, learn about shipbuilding, find an old foundation of a long-gone community, visit a sea captain's burial ground, and hike to waterfalls. A haven for walkers, runners, and cyclists, the wooded coastal trail parallels the smoothly paved roadway, and then surpasses the road to connect through to Fundy National Park farther northeast.

Special Features: Two covered bridges, St. Martins sea caves, Quaco Museum, 16 lookouts, guided hikes, a tide-carved pillar or "flowerpot" rock, suspension bridge, Hearst Lodge, Melvin Beach, Pangburn Beach, Big Salmon River, walking, running, hiking, and cycling.

Location: On the Fundy coast, south-central New Brunswick.

Driving Route Numbers & Names: Main Street, Big Salmon River Road, Fundy Parkway.

Travel Season: Summer brings the clearest days for a drive, but the sea caves and lookouts along this coast are interesting and make for stunning photographs year-round. In autumn, the leaves turn glowing fall colors, giving the drive new life at the end of its season. The Fundy Trail Parkway is open Victoria Day weekend (May) through Canadian Thanksgiving (second Monday in October).

Camping: While there is no camping available along the Fundy Trail Parkway, find family-oriented campgrounds in St. Martins and Bay View.

Services: St. Martins has gas stations, craft shops, and restaurants. For medical services, Saint John lies less than an hour to the southwest along Route 111. The selection of ocean-side accommodations includes cottages and bed-and-breakfasts, as well as the inland Hearst Lodge off the Fundy Trail Parkway.

Nearby Points of Interest: Quaco Head Lighthouse, covered bridges; in Saint John: Reversing Falls, Carleton Martello Tower National Historic Site, Irving Nature Park, Rockwood Park, City Market, museums, and galleries.

Time Zone: Atlantic time zone (GMT minus 4 hours).

The Drive

Hairpin bends, tidal beaches, and forest trails make the **Fundy Trail Parkway** a delightful journey along the Bay of Fundy coast. The first phase of the roadway opened in 1998, and the full paved scenic route is expected to be finished in 2013. A multiuse trail parallels the road and connects to **Fundy National Park** along the coast.

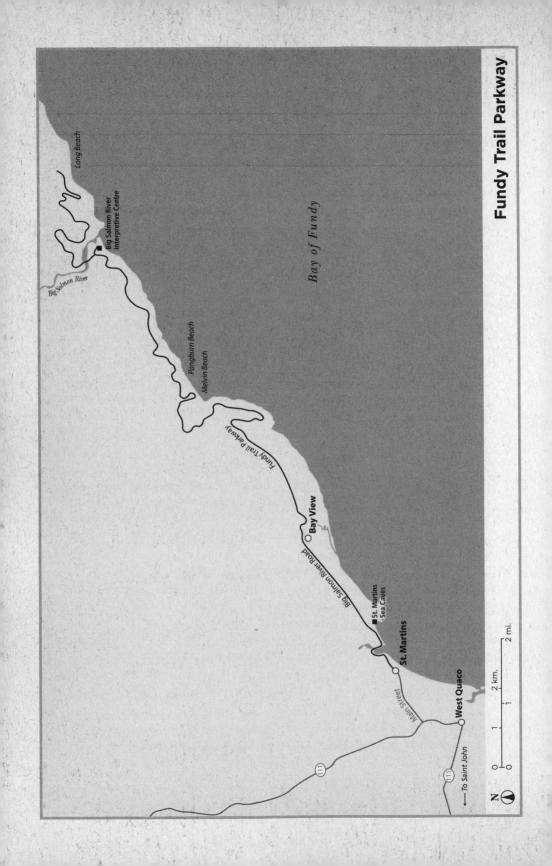

Fundy Trail Parkway

Bay of Fundy

Long Beach

Big Salmon River Interpretive Centre

Big Salmon River

Pangburn Beach

Melvin Beach

Fundy Trail Parkway

Bay View

Big Salmon River Road

St. Martins Sea Caves

St. Martins

Main Street

West Quaco

111

111

To Saint John

N

0   1   2 km.
0   1   2 mi.

To reach the parkway, first head to **St. Martins.** From Saint John, follow Route 111 for about 45 kilometers (28 miles) east past the airport. Or, drive Highway 1 to Sussex before taking exit 198 to connect with Route 111.

St. Martins

A busy Main Street of canteens and accommodations leads northeast toward the Fundy Trail Parkway. Not on the waterfront but with views of the **Bay of Fundy,** the heritage homes and an occasional abandoned house stand alongside craft shops and galleries. The **Quaco Museum** at 236 Main St. has a small selection of excellent exhibits, including a feature on shipbuilding and a hand-cranked foghorn.

The Mi'kmaq were the area's first settlers and named the locale Goolwagagek, meaning "haunt of the hooded seal."

Loyalist soldiers founded the town in 1783, and St. Martins was once a center for shipbuilding with hundreds of ships being launched from the slipways here. But, like many places in Atlantic Canada, with the advent of metal-hulled ships, the demand for wooden sailing boats disappeared.

The town hosts its annual **St. Martins Old Home Week Festival** in July—welcoming new visitors and old-timers for a weekend of parade, theater, music, and tours.

Drive northeast on Main Street toward the Fundy Trail Parkway. As the road meets the Irish River, it follows a cove. Fishing boats are tied up to a wharf in front of a covered bridge. The bridge, built in 1935, crosses the Irish River. Turn right to the parkway, or continue up the river along Main Street to cross on a second covered bridge dating to 1946. Nearby, a tourism information booth dispenses brochures and advice from a lighthouse-style building.

Big Salmon River Road follows the coastline to an impressive frame: the **St. Martins Sea Caves,** surrounded by beach, forest, and ocean. Often people will be exploring the mouths of the gaping caves, giving a sense of their great size even from a distance. The sea caves are carved into the red cliffs by the tide and are accessible around low tide—just walk across Macs Beach after checking the tide table with the visitor information center.

From the sea caves, the road cuts through farmland and past homes for about 6.5 kilometers (4 miles). At Little Beach the road forks right toward the parkway admission gate.

Fundy Trail Parkway

The paved **Fundy Trail Parkway** provides a low-speed way to see the Bay of Fundy coastline. Ultimately the route will connect to Fundy National Park,

A covered bridge near St. Martins, New Brunswick.

farther east along the coast. Along the way more than a dozen lookouts feature scenic stopping places. Day-use parking lots allow walkers, runners, and cyclists to explore the coastal multiuse trail independently and safely. A shuttle bus stops at each of the lookouts and provides options to those interested in a shorter walk: You can walk ahead then catch a shuttle back to your vehicle.

It's possible, but not necessary, to stop at all the lookouts. In fact, stopping at every one can be tiring. I recommend picking four to six that are located near beaches, hikes, waterfalls, and services that suit your interests and needs. Two absolute musts to add to your list are the Big Salmon River Interpretive Centre and the final lookout over Long Beach.

At **Fox Point** the first lookout gives views of the coastline to the west, out to **Quaco Head Lighthouse.** But I prefer the second observation area at **Fownes Head,** where a short trail leads to views of a "flowerpot" rock—a tree-topped pillar of rock, sliced from the coastline by the tides. Look northeast to the dramatic bluffs and cliffs of the Fundy coast.

Inland a guided walk to the **Sea Captain's Burial Ground** will reveal the area's shipbuilding history. Other guided walks, organized through the Big Salmon River Interpretive Centre, go to the old community schoolhouse and Hearst Lodge.

The next stop at **Melvin Beach** provides more great views as well as staircase access to the pebbly shore. At low tide only, walk to the sandier **Pangburn Beach.** At high tide, explore inland to **Fuller Falls**—a pretty waterfall where cable stairs (which are similar to a rope ladder, although less steep) lead down to an observation deck. Both beaches and Fuller Falls connect to a parking area and **Bradshaw Lookout** via the multiuse trail.

At **Black Point Lookout,** spectacular views include Pangburn Beach, Melvin Beach, and cliffs that separate the two at high tide. **Hearst Lookout** gives big ocean views across the Bay of Fundy to Nova Scotia from its high altitude. **Pejebescot Lookout** also provides a nice perspective of the coastline. At **Davidson Lookout,** which has picnic tables, look east on a clear day to see Nova Scotia and Isle Haute off Cape Chignecto.

After Davidson Lookout the road descends a hill, and your gaze will widen over tidal flats, river, and forest. At the stop sign, turn right to the **Big Salmon River Interpretive Centre,** or continue straight on the Fundy Parkway drive. My preference is to complete the scenic drive, then return to Big Salmon River to walk the trails, see the remains of the old community, and cross the suspension bridge.

Continuing straight after the stop sign, drive over Big Salmon River. Look left to see the suspension footbridge. Talus slopes and quarry-like cliffs flank the roadway, which has been cut into the bedrock. The rock strata reveal a tumbled ancient creation—the solid grays, browns, reds, and purples forming a geological mosaic.

While **Cranberry Brook Lookout** provides views of the interpretive center as well as secluded picnic tables, I prefer to continue to the **Interpretive Centre Lookout** where you can look out on broad **Big Salmon River,** the **Mitchell Franklin Vehicle Bridge,** and **suspension footbridge. Big Salmon River Lookout** delivers majestic views of the river delta and the ocean it feeds.

Stop briefly at **Hairpin Lookout** to see the turn you're about to make: a tight bend around a point that has been sliced flat to make way for the road. Driving slowly around the turn, keep your eyes on the road and let your passengers enjoy the views. It's then just meters to **Long Beach Lookout**—the final viewpoint. At the time of my visit, the road was barricaded at Long Beach Lookout, although the paved road continued beyond; the plan is to open final sections of the route by 2013.

Long Beach, about 150 meters (492 feet) below the cliffs, stretches out to Tufts Point. Smooth, golden sands edge the coastline, made all the sweeter by its inaccessibility. As admission to the parkway is good until evening (check exact times with parkway staff), it is tempting to stay here watching the tides until sunset.

Big Salmon River

Back at the **Big Salmon River Interpretive Centre,** which shows a short film in French and English about the area, browse the photos and exhibits on display. Primarily covering the history of the community at Big Salmon River, the exhibits tell how the logging-company town developed over a century from the mid-1800s to the 1940s.

More than 20 families lived here in the 1920s, gathering at the community hall for social functions. The men worked for the sawmill, which provided electricity. The children attended classes at the schoolhouse; in 1910 the teacher at the school was just 16 years old.

But when the sawmill burnt down in 1933, the loss crippled the town's industry. Walking down from the large parking lot at the stop sign to the interpretive center takes you past the old foundation of the schoolhouse—one of the few remaining signs of the community.

From the interpretive center, walk along **Big Salmon River** to watch for birds and water life. Then follow the river upstream to where the 84-meter (275-foot) suspension footbridge spans the banks and provides a fun diversion.

The interpretive center is also the departure point for the 2.8-kilometer (1.7-mile) hike to the overnight accommodations at **Hearst Lodge.** Built by newspaperman William Randolph Hearst, the outdoorsy lodge serves lunch and dinner. And just as Hearst visited the lodge to entertain and play outdoors more than 60 years ago, you can, too, today.

Side Trip: Saint John

With large industrial factories within its limits, New Brunswick's largest city doesn't make the best first impression. But park along the sometimes roughly paved city streets and explore the **Saint John** downtown district on foot. First browse the vendors at Canada's oldest market, the **Saint John City Market** in its historic location on Charlotte Street. Close to the marina-side market square, find quality museums such as the **New Brunswick Museum** with its collections of art and geology exhibits, or the **Loyalist House,** which hosts tea with the city's mayor in summer.

Sea caves near St. Martins, New Brunswick.

Within a short drive of the downtown, view natural tidal-bore rapids at the **Reversing Falls** viewpoint on Bridge Road, the seabirds and ocean-side trails in the **Irving Nature Park,** or a campground and canoe lakes in **Rockwood Park.**

To get a better sense of these contradicting forces of nature and industry in Saint John, head up to the **Carleton Martello Tower National Historic Site** on Whipple Street and survey the city from the best viewpoint.

4

Hopewell Rocks

Hillsborough to Fundy National Park

General Description: Connecting the Fundy coast's iconic attractions, this scenic drive visits the flowerpot-shaped Hopewell Rocks, the rocky point at Cape Enrage Interpretive Centre, and the ocean-side playground of Fundy National Park. Over just 80 kilometers (50 miles), the road covers a diverse landscape that includes forest, river, marsh, and ocean. Opportunities for bird spotting on the mud-flat beaches are a highlight, as is watching the tide come in.

Special Features: Steeves House Museum, New Brunswick Railway Museum, Albert County Museum, Hopewell Rocks, Sawmill Creek Bridge, Bank of New Brunswick Museum, Shepody National Wildlife Area, Cape Enrage Interpretive Centre, Fundy National Park, bird watching, saltwater swimming pool, hiking.

Location: Southeastern New Brunswick, near Moncton, on the Fundy coast.

Driving Route Numbers & Names: Route 114, Route 915, Cape Enrage Road.

Travel Season: The tides run in every season, but spring through autumn is the most pleasant time to kayak the high tide, hike wooded trails, or walk the muddy ocean floor. Spring and fall bring migratory birds such as the sandpiper to the tidal beaches. In summer, undoubtedly the busiest season, room rates increase while availability decreases. It is also when the national park is most crowded. If you plan to spend time outdoors, black flies are vicious May through mid-June, while mosquitoes hone in for most of the warm season. Most attractions stay open summer long.

Camping: Camp at the end destination, Fundy National Park, where a campground at Pointe Wolfe is secluded and equipped with showers, washrooms, fire pits, and a telephone. As the location is unserviced, RV sites with hookups are available at park headquarters and Chignecto North. Beyond the basics, both also have kitchen shelters, playgrounds, dump stations, and laundry.

Services: Stock up in Moncton, Alma, or Sussex on gas and snacks. On the scenic drive, Alma and Hopewell both feature dozens of motel rooms and seafood restaurants. More overnight options include bed-and-breakfasts with a friendly charm, independent vacation homes, and beachside cottages.

Nearby Points of Interest: Magnetic Hill, heritage museums, local galleries, and shopping, all in Moncton.

Time Zone: Atlantic time zone (GMT minus 4 hours).

The Drive

This 80-kilometer (50-mile) scenic drive never strays far from the water—first following the Petitcodiac River and then the Bay of Fundy coastline. Museums, natural oddities, bird-watching beaches, and plenty of outdoor activities from golfing to boating all make the trip stand out.

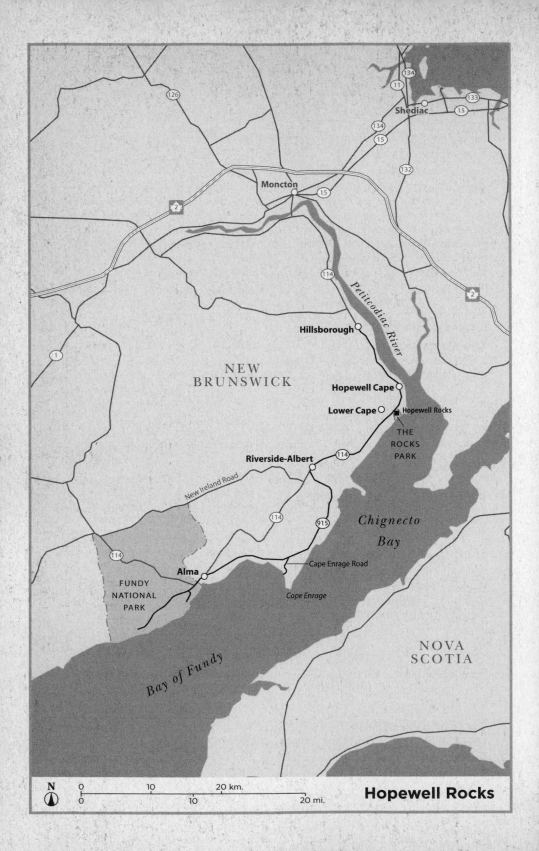

Hopewell Rocks

From downtown **Moncton,** take Bridge Road to Route 114 and follow the busy route as it crosses the Petitcodiac River to Riverview. Heading southeast, Route 114 is a residential area through to Hillsborough, about 35 kilometers (22 miles) from Moncton.

In the riverside town of **Hillsborough** you'll find a cluster of museums and restored heritage buildings.

The **Steeves House Museum,** at 40 Mill St., honors a Father of Confederation, William Henry Steeves. Born in this historic mansion when it was a much smaller cottage, Steeves found his wealth in lumber and shipping. He represented Albert County at the Charlottetown Conference in 1864. Today the heritage house shows antique furniture and gorgeously detailed quilts sewn by Steeves's relatives.

On Main Street, the **New Brunswick Railway Museum** displays a large collection of artifacts and railway cars. Climb aboard to see the interiors or visit the replica station.

From Hillsborough along the banks of the Petitcodiac River, meadows lead down to marshes. From 1700 to the 1760s, Acadians farmed the pretty riverside lands, using dikes to reclaim the ground from the tides. German immigrants arrived in 1767 to continue farming the fields.

Hopewell Rocks

From Hillsborough, drive 13 kilometers (8 miles) along Route 114 and the Petitcodiac River toward the Hopewell Rocks.

Before you reach the Flowerpot Rocks, the Memramcook and Petitcodiac Rivers converge around Fort Folly Point.

In this former center of Albert County, the **Albert County Museum** at 3940 Rte. 114 is an overlooked gem. Nine historic buildings in their original locations retell the tales of this shire town, or county seat. From murders to war stories, learn the area's history with guided visits to the records office, courthouse, and jail. The most recent addition is the **R. B. Bennett Commemorative Centre,** honoring Canada's 11th prime minister, who hailed from Albert County.

Toward Lower Cape, watch on the left for the signs for the **Hopewell Rocks** at 131 Discovery Rd. Pull into the vast parking lot—probably one of the largest you'll see at any Atlantic Canadian attraction—and walk down to the interpretive center. There, find a restaurant, washrooms, and exhibits covering the area's geology, Mi'kmaq legends, and wildlife. Check the tide tables and walk the 15-minute forest trail to the famed rock towers topped with greenery, also known as the **Flowerpot Rocks.** The interpretive center can provide details on the shuttle service for those who have limited mobility.

Although it's nice to see the tidal-carved pillars at both high and low tide, don't miss the chance to walk through the curious shapes when the tide is out. Arches, aliens, and animals all make great photos. A photo tip: While the scenery looks beautiful empty of other visitors, be sure to take a few pictures with people next to the Hopewell Rocks to capture the scale. Throughout the park discover lookouts, hiking trails, and beaches to enjoy on a longer visit.

From Hopewell Cape continue west along **Shepody Bay.** The spit of land across the water is Cape Maringouin, New Brunswick, with the Joggins fossil coast of Nova Scotia behind. This shoreline features marshy meadows that fill twice daily with tidal saltwater, only to be completely drained about six hours later. This scenery changes vastly between tides with the water's range at the Hopewell Rocks measuring about 14 meters (45 feet).

At Hopewell Hill take an easy detour along "Old Route 114" to the now decommissioned 1908 **Sawmill Creek Covered Bridge.**

Cape Enrage

Follow Route 114 for 5 kilometers (3 miles) to **Riverside-Albert.** The enchanting riverside farming community features a tearoom and old **Bank of New Brunswick Museum,** now the local heritage and tourism information center. The town hosts the mid-September weekend **Albert County Exhibition & Fair** with a pageant, draft horses, and entertainment.

As the road bends left at Crooked Creek, Route 915 spurs toward the coast and Cape Enrage while Route 114 continues inland. Either route is lovely.

A shorter, faster option, Route 114 passes through the **Shepody National Wildlife Area.** With marshland surrounded by rolling hills and the **Shepody River No. 3 covered bridge** at Midway Road, it is an equally scenic alternative but with no must-stop attractions.

Along Route 915, the road draws closer to the coast through Harvey, New Horton, and Little Ridge. At Cape Enrage Road, make the left turn and follow signs to Cape Enrage. You're now alongside **Barn Marsh Island**—faintly separated from the mainland by Barn Marsh Creek. Follow the road to its end, where the light station at **Cape Enrage** has been beaming since the 1840s. Besides the views across Chignecto Bay, enjoy rappelling and rock climbing, or just browse the art and crafts gallery. Nearby, visit **Waterside Farms Cottage Winery** at 2008 Rte. 915 for fruit-wine tastings as well as tours.

Explore the coast at Hopewell Rocks to see tide-carved pillars and cliffs, New Brunswick.

Fundy National Park

From Cape Enrage, Route 915 rounds Rocher Bay to **Alma,** where flat tidal beaches are feeding grounds for seabirds such as migratory semipalmated sandpipers and endangered piping plovers. Restaurants advertising fresh lobster and seafood line the main street. When you are coming into town, an information and activity center in the town building on the right can provide accommodation suggestions and brochures.

Just through town, visit the **Fundy National Park** visitor center and park headquarters on Upper Salmon River for trail maps. Point Wolfe Road leads into the park, providing access to the golf course, saltwater swimming pool, and waterfall hikes. The road is not a coastal one, rather heading through thick forests and over the Point Wolfe covered bridge to reach dozens of hiking trails. The Fundy Circuit links seven of these trails to form a 50-kilometer (31-mile) loop. For a shorter challenge, try the 0.6-kilometer (0.4-mile) boardwalk trail to Point Wolfe Beach, with its telescope and wildlife interpretive panels, or the 1.5-kilometer (0.9-mile) loop to Dickson Falls, where a tiered waterfall tumbles over mossy rocks.

Fundy National Park, which was designated in 1948, is now a haven for the endangered peregrine falcon. The bird of prey was reintroduced to the park after being displaced. Other species to watch for in the park include bears, moose, raccoons, deer, and coyotes.

From the park headquarters, Route 114 cuts inland through the forest, passing a boat rental at **Bennett Lake** and another visitor center at **Wolfe Lake.** In the center of the park, the **Hastings Auto Trail** provides an option to leave the paved surface and see the forest from your vehicle.

From the park boundary, it's about 22 kilometers (14 miles) to Highway 1 for journeys east to Moncton or west to Sussex and Saint John. For a spectacular September event, visit Sussex during the **Atlantic Balloon Fiesta**—during which dozens of hot-air balloons float like Christmas ornaments in the sky.

Saint John River

Grand Bay to Fredericton to Lower Prince William

General Description: One of Canada's prettiest river drives, a journey along the Saint John River includes small cable ferries, a military base, and a power-generating dam. Escape the well-traveled Fundy coast to head inland and discover historical districts, art galleries, and the provincial capital. Over 200 kilometers (124 miles) along the Saint John River, this journey travels from coastal to pastoral.

Special Features: Queens County Court House Museum, Queens County Museum, Grand Lake Protected Natural Area, Gagetown Military Museum, Canadian Military Engineers Museum, cable ferries on Saint John River, Kings Landing Historical Settlement, Mactaquac Provincial Park, Mactaquac Dam. In Fredericton: Historic Garrison District, York Sunbury Museum, School Days Museums, New Brunswick Sports Hall of Fame, Beaverbrook Art Gallery, Legislative Assembly of New Brunswick, Government House.

Location: From New Brunswick's largest city (Saint John) to its capital (Fredericton), this drive travels through the province's south-central region.

Driving Route Numbers & Names: Route 177, Route 102, Route 715, Route 105.

Travel Season: In spring, watch the river as it swells with snowmelt. Summer brings boating, swimming, fishing, and other outdoor activities for a languid vacation. The fall foliage of the Acadian forest along the Saint John River makes the area an autumn favorite.

Camping: Camp at Mactaquac Provincial Park at the northern end of this drive, where a golf course and beach add interest to the basic amenities. Both tent sites and pull-through RV sites are available.

Services: Saint John and Fredericton lack no services. En route, find gas stations and basic supplies in Grand Bay, Gagetown, and Oromocto. For heritage inns and quality restaurants, Fredericton tops my list as the best in the province. Plus you can check in with the city's visitor center to obtain a free parking pass.

Nearby Points of Interest: In Saint John: Reversing Falls, Carleton Martello Tower National Historic Site, Irving Nature Park, Rockwood Park, City Market, museums, and galleries. Farther northwest along the Saint John River: Crabbe Mountain Ski Area, Grand Falls Gorge, Hartland covered bridge (the longest in the world), and Covered Bridge Potato Chip Company in Waterville.

Time Zone: Atlantic time zone (GMT minus 4 hours).

The Drive

Branded as the **Fiddlehead Drive**—fiddleheads being the spring shoots of the ostrich fern that are readily foraged, cooked, and eaten in the Maritimes—this 200-kilometer (124-mile) scenic route follows the beautiful banks of the **Saint John River.**

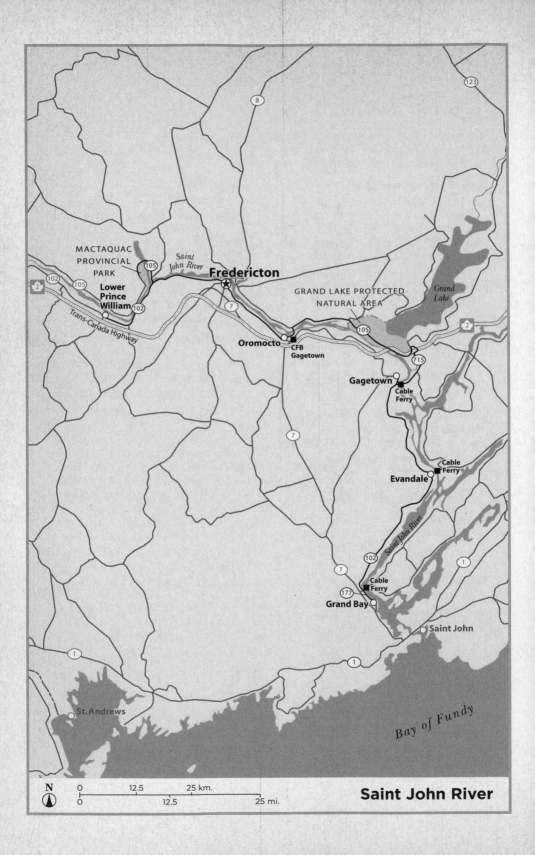

MACTAQUAC
PROVINCIAL
PARK

*Saint
John River*

Fredericton

GRAND LAKE PROTECTED
NATURAL AREA

*Grand
Lake*

105

2

**Lower
Prince
William**

102

105

102

Trans-Canada Highway

105

7

Oromocto

CFB
Gagetown

715

Gagetown

Cable
Ferry

7

Cable
Ferry

Evandale

Saint John River

1

102

7

Cable
Ferry

177

Grand Bay

○ **Saint John**

8

123

2

1

○ St. Andrews

Bay of Fundy

N

0   12.5   25 km.

0   12.5   25 mi.

Saint John River

Take Highway 7 to exit 90, then from Grand Bay follow Route 177 to the junction with Route 102, which traces the west bank of the river toward Fredericton. Marshlands and rolling hills surround the Saint John River. The first of three cable ferries on this scenic drive runs from Hillandale, a neighborhood of Westfield, to Hardings Point on the Kingston Peninsula.

Keeping close to the riverbank you can see up Long Reach where mid-river islands and sandy beaches break up the river. The large **Kiwanis Oak Point Campground** provides clear views at its pull-through RV sites. Here, the gorgeous wide views end as the tangle of river tributaries begins.

Cable Ferries & Historic Gagetown

A second cable ferry crosses the river at **Evandale.** Part of the New Brunswick highway system, the cable ferries charge no toll to vehicles. Feel free to take one across, explore some riverside roads, and return again to the Fiddlehead Drive.

Long Island and Upper Musquash Island change the path of the river as it forms a series of lakes. Passing Queenstown and the swamps of Otnabog, the road curves inland to Pleasant Villa.

About 2 kilometers (1.2 miles) before the Gagetown turnoff, find a third cable ferry running to Lower Jemseg. Because the Fiddlehead Drive crosses to the east bank of the river here, first head into the historic village of **Gagetown** to discover the quaint main street and heritage homes before returning to the ferry dock.

The seat of Queens County, Gagetown offers provincial historic buildings and history-steeped homes. The 1836 **Queens County Court House Museum** at 16 Court House Rd. is one of the oldest justice buildings in the province. Having meted verdicts into the 1960s, today the building is filled with antique decor and a genealogy research center. **Tilley House** at 69 Front St. was home to a former premier and Father of Confederation Samuel Tilley; it now houses the **Queens County Museum.** Historical fashions and furnished rooms bring life to the 1786 home. Born in the wooden Gagetown house, Tilley attend the Charlottetown, Quebec, and London conferences. It is said he offered the suggestion for calling the newly created nation the Dominion of Canada.

Along Front Street, find a bustling pub and river views. Artisan galleries and a picturesque church build on the village's historic appeal.

The history of the Gagetown wasn't always so mild. Acadians settled here in the 1700s alongside the native Maliseet. In 1758, a British raid saw the village burned and Acadians scalped. In 1783, Loyalists founded Gagetown and laid out the village in grid-like streets.

From Gagetown, backtrack 2 kilometers (1.2 miles) to the cable ferry dock, taking the 5-minute crossing to the east bank of the Saint John River. On this lesser-populated side, abandoned houses and closed stone churches give a vacant feel. Farmlands cover the hills, and there are large meadows of Queen Anne's lace and goldenrod.

Follow Route 715 to **Jemseg,** where Route 105 heads west along the river toward Fredericton. Through the **Grand Lake Protected Natural Area,** the meadows, marsh, and riverfront grow only more beautiful. The land protects the massive **Grand Lake,** which retains so much of the summer heat that it increases the region's number of frost-free days. Watch for cows grazing on the mid-river islands—contained without a fence. The meadow between Jemseg and McGowans Corner is the province's largest wetland, so be sure to watch for wildlife amid this rich ecosystem.

Route 105 leads through the sparsely populated **McGowans Corner** and **Sheffield.** At Maugerville, about 40 kilometers (25 miles) from the Gagetown ferry, the Burton Bridge crosses the Saint John River to Oromocto.

Oromocto

For those not intrigued by one of Canada's largest military bases—which covers 1,100 square kilometers (425 square miles), or about the size of Hong Kong—continue the 20 kilometers (12.4 miles) to Fredericton along the lesser-inhabited Route 105. My preference is to explore the base's military museums.

Oromocto centers on the **Canadian Forces Base Gagetown,** named for the vastly different historic village. Follow Route 102 to the North Gate, entering the base on Ganong Road. Alternately, turn onto Tilley Road or continue to the South Gate at Cumberland.

Driving through the base you'll see troops jog past in their camouflage fatigues. Tiny churches of differing denominations and coffee shops create a feeling of the base as its own community.

Through the maze of buildings, follow the signs for MUSEUM, which will take you to **CFB Gagetown Military Museum.** WWII-era tanks, jeeps, and guns sit alongside picnic tables and a parking lot. Inside the museum, barrack and weapon displays provide insight into military routines, as well as historical figures such as General Gage who was Commander-in-Chief of America and received a grant of land on the Saint John River. The base also has the **Canadian Military Engineers Museum,** with exhibits ranging in topic from World War I trenches to the United Nations.

On the way to Fredericton, stop in at the **Oromocto Visitor Centre** at the corner of Restigouche and Wassis Roads, which can point you to the trails and the bird reserve at the large, riverside Deer Park.

Fredericton

Leaving Oromocto, the residential area of the city blends with the outskirts of **Fredericton.** Large historic homes can be ogled from Waterloo Row, which leads directly along the river to downtown. If stopping in Fredericton, head first to the visitor center at City Hall where you can obtain a free parking pass that is valid for two days.

Since parking is so convenient, walk through the **Historic Garrison District,** where family-friendly museums create a dynamic visit. The handsome stone **York Sunbury Museum** at 571 Queen St. is located in former officers' quarters and delves into the history of the capital. Nearby, the **School Days Museum** sits pupils in front of a slate to learn lessons about early science and see retro toys. Find more historical interpretation with costumed guides at the **Guard House** and the changing of the Guard in Officers' Square.

Tour the athletic galleries of the **New Brunswick Sports Hall of Fame** at 503 Queen St., or the sculptures and paintings at the **Beaverbrook Art Gallery,** 703 Queen St., which includes the dominating Salvador Dali work, *Santiago El Grande* (although the work was loaned out to an Atlanta gallery in late 2010—check ahead if you're set on seeing the work).

Across the street from the gallery, take a free tour of the **Legislative Assembly of New Brunswick** at 706 Queen St. when the legislature is not sitting.

Beyond its historic treasures, Fredericton stands out for its footpaths and bicycle trails. Rent a bicycle at the riverside **Lighthouse on the Green,** near the corner of Queen and Regent Streets. Cycle or walk across the **Bill Thorpe Walking Bridge,** or climb the hill to tour the brick buildings of the **University of New Brunswick** campus.

After exploring Fredericton, continue the scenic drive by following Regent Street onto Pointe-Sainte-Anne Boulevard. Pass the Westmorland Street Bridge and bear left on Smythe. Take a right on Woodstock to follow Route 102 west from downtown. At 51 Woodstock St. you'll pass **Government House,** the lieutenant governor's residence that dates to 1828.

Festivals and live music rate as a Fredericton highlight. In July the **New Brunswick Highland Games Festival** brings ceilidhs, pipe bands, Highland sports, and dancing to the capital. In cooler September, the **Harvest Jazz and Blues Festival** welcomes world-class musicians for free shows and other events.

Heading along a narrow stretch of the Saint John River on Route 102, you soon approach **Mactaquac Dam** to the north, about 18 kilometers (11 miles) from Fredericton. Turn right onto Mactaquac Road.

There is a parking lot where you can stop for photos before crossing the dam, which produces about one-fifth of the province's power with its six turbines.

Although, according to CBC news reports, the dam has experienced problems with concrete expansion and may be shut down in the near future.

Follow the road over a bridge back across the Mactaquac Stream Basin to **Mactaquac Provincial Park** at 1265 Rte. 105. At the park a golf course, sand beach, and campground provide a weekend escape.

Alternately, skip the Mactaquac trip to continue on Route 102 along the Saint John River to where it parallels Highway 2. At exit 253, find **Kings Landing Historical Settlement** where costumed interpreters re-create rural 19th-century life. When the Mactaquac Dam was built in the 1960s, historical buildings that had to be moved due to the rising water levels were set up to create an idyllic village here in Lower Prince William.

Farms, a church, sawmill, gristmill, door factory, and gardens spread out over the site, and interpreters revive the Loyalist history.

See outdoor sculptures at the Beaverbrook Art Gallery, Fredericton, New Brunswick.

Miramichi River

Miramichi to Boiestown

General Description: Along the banks of the Miramichi River and into the center of New Brunswick, this 137-kilometer (85-mile) drive strays from coastal scenery to experience the salmon pools and forests. The Atlantic salmon is the region's darling, having drawn royalty and celebrities to cast a line here. But explore further and find a millennia-old First Nations community, island excursions, and haunted woods.

Special Features: W. S. Loggie House & Cultural Centre, St. Michael's Museum, Beaubears Island Shipbuilding National Historic Site, Rankin House Museum, Historic Beaverbrook House, Metepenagiag Heritage Park, Doak Provincial Historic Site, Atlantic Salmon Museum and Aquarium, Central New Brunswick Woodmen's Museum, TBM Avenger Air Tanker #14, salmon fishing.

Location: From the eastern coast of New Brunswick to the geographic center of the province.

Driving Route Numbers & Names: Water Street, Wellington Street, Route 126, Sutton Road, St. Patrick's Drive, King George Highway, Highway 8, Route 425, Route 420, Route 415.

Travel Season: When the ice leaves the river, the Atlantic salmon season begins. The early catches are the salmon that have wintered in the river since the fall spawn. The first salmon run stretches from mid-June to mid-August, and a second spawning runs from mid-August to mid-October. Even if you are not fishing, it's fascinating to watch the anglers cast their fly-fishing lines in lasso-like swoops. In autumn, add the spectacular allure of the Acadian forest foliage.

Camping: Find a number of private campgrounds close to the river on the outskirts of Miramichi, offering sites for tents and RVs. For those in the area to fish, Enclosure Campground at Derby Junction offers a boat launch and the closest location to the city of Miramichi.

Services: At the start of the journey, Miramichi provides a full complement of services including gas, groceries, restaurant meals, hotel rooms, and medical care. En route, fuel up in Blackville. Find overnight accommodations by driving beyond the end of this scenic route, following Highway 8 past Boiestown to Fredericton. The provincial capital has charming historic inns and a lively university-fueled nightlife.

Nearby Points of Interest: Kouchibouguac National Park, fishing, boat tours.

Time Zone: Atlantic time zone (GMT minus 4 hours).

The Drive

Famed for its Atlantic salmon run, the "mighty" Miramichi draws anglers to its riverbanks year after year. You'll see folks out fishing from mid-May through the end of the spawning run in mid-October. The pretty river charms visitors with its ambling curves and unique attractions.

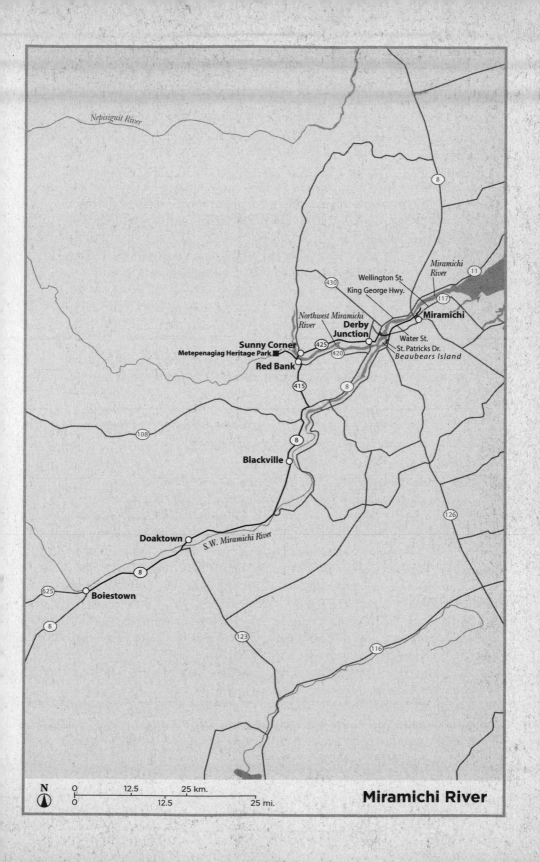

Nepisiguit River

8

Miramichi River

11

117

Miramichi

Wellington St.

King George Hwy.

430

Northwest Miramichi River

Derby Junction

Water St.

425

St. Patricks Dr.

Beaubears Island

Sunny Corner

Metepenagiag Heritage Park

420

Red Bank

415

8

108

Blackville

126

Doaktown

S.W. Miramichi River

8

625

Boiestown

8

123

116

N

0   12.5   25 km.

0   12.5   25 mi.

Miramichi River

If traveling from the north, follow Highway 8 from Bathurst or Highway 11 from Caraquet. From Moncton or Shediac, take Highway 11. This 137-kilometer (85-mile) scenic drive is an attractive alternative route to Fredericton, the provincial capital, which lies about 70 kilometers (44 miles) beyond Boiestown.

Miramichi

The city of **Miramichi** amalgamated a number of communities in 1996 that still very much retain their identities. In **Chatham** on the south riverbank, amble through the historic waterfront district of Water Street, where shipbuilders and lumber barons once attained their wealth.

The city's museums are spread out over both sides of the river. At 222 Wellington St. in Chatham, the Victorian-style **W. S. Loggie House & Cultural Centre** exhibits pieces dating from 1850 on. Uphill on Howard Street (off University Avenue), **St. Michael's Museum** houses genealogical records and antiques in the old rectory and hospital. Its neighbor is the prominent Gothic spire of **St. Michael's Basilica.**

To the west of Chatham, but still on the right-hand bank of the Miramichi, sits the **Beaubears Island Shipbuilding National Historic Site** on St. Patrick's Drive. To reach this First Nation, Acadian, and shipbuilding heritage site, follow Water Street west as it becomes Nelson Street (also posted as Route 126). Pass the hospital and drive 2 kilometers (1.2 miles) past the turn for the Miramichi Bridge. Turn right on Sutton Road and cross the railway tracks to continue down to the river. Then, make a left on St. Patrick's Drive.

The northwest and southwest branches of the Miramichi River converge around **Beaubears Island,** which was first a meeting place for the Mi'kmaq. In 1755 many Acadians fled here when faced with an English deportation order. The 1800s brought a thriving shipbuilding industry—the slips, wharves, and foundations of which are still visible. From the interpretive center, boat tours make trips to the island twice daily in summer with an evening tour that also visits Wilsons Point.

From the national historic site, backtrack along Route 126 to the **Miramichi Bridge**—the closest river crossing without detouring along the river south. Two bridges span the river: the Miramichi Bridge, completed in 1995 to replace the iron-truss Morrissey Bridge, and the **Centennial Bridge** that replaced a ferry service in 1967.

Follow the main riverside route as it passes **Yves Beach.** Along this busy road, the **Rankin House Museum** at 2224 King George Hwy. was the home of a lumber and shipping baron and dates to 1837. East along the river in Newcastle, **Historic Beaverbrook House** at 518 King George Hwy. was the childhood home of William Maxwell Aitken, who became Lord Beaverbrook—a multimillionaire, press baron, and British cabinet member.

Before Highway 8 crosses the Northwest Miramichi River, turn right and follow Route 425 toward Sunny Corner.

Miramichi hosts an abnormally large number of cultural festivals. The mostly summertime events celebrate First Nations, Acadian, Irish, and Scottish heritage.

Metepenagiag First Nation

From the junction with Highway 8, a 16-kilometer (10-mile) stretch follows the Northwest Miramichi River toward **Metepenagiag First Nation.** With the river on the left, the road climbs through forest and passes through **Eel Ground First Nation.** It's a simple country scene, and at Sunny Corner a bridge crosses the river to **Red Bank.** Small islands sit in the river flow, and tributaries feed into the watery giant as it gathers power.

Follow signs that direct right to the **Metepenagiag Heritage Park** at 2156 MicMac Rd., part of the Metepenagiag First Nation. Winding through a pine and spruce forest, you come to a new stone-and-beam heritage center. Museum exhibits provide background to the park's two national historic sites: the **Augustine Mound burial ground** and the **Oxbow Site,** which was used as a fishing site for 2,500 years before Europeans arrived. Walking trails lead through the park to explore the grounds of New Brunswick's oldest village, dating back three millennia. Inside the center, admire the crafts and gallery.

From Red Bank, two routes reconnect with Highway 8. Take the shorter Route 415 through a thick forest of maple, spruce, and silver birch. Or follow the river for 18 kilometers (11 miles) on Route 420 out to the junction with Highway 8, then take scenic Route 108 through Lower Derby, Derby, and Quarryville.

Center of New Brunswick

Highway 8 becomes monotonous as times, with one stretch of forest blending into the next. For many who travel only New Brunswick's highways, this is often their first impression of the province: trees. In **Blackville,** refresh with a quick stop at the municipal park, gardens, and picnic area. Due to its fishing pools, it's often touted as the salmon capital of the Miramichi River. Along the main street, part of Highway 8, watch for a giant fishing fly, a massive replica of those used to fly fish on the rivers here (although it is not the world's largest).

As Highway 8 journeys south, survey the scenery as you crest the area's larger hills—you'll likely glimpse the snaking river, elusive in its beauty.

Highway 8 passes directly through **Doaktown.** At the **Doak Provincial Historic Site,** 386 Main St., learn about the daily chores from pioneers, be it the spinners making thread from flax or the weavers shuttling the spun fiber through the

loom. Robert Doak, a Scot, originally settled the village in 1825 and established grist-, saw- and carding mills in the community.

Also in town, the **Atlantic Salmon Museum and Aquarium** at 263 Main St. (also called the **Miramichi Salmon Museum**) provides a great stop for families. See the flash of salmon scales in the aquarium or walk down to the riverbanks. The **Salmon and Fiddlehead Festival** celebrates two very local foods—the fish that spawn in the river and the ferns that sprout on the banks.

Continuing south on Highway 8, you'll likely see cars stopped along the shoulder in late July and August. During blueberry season, the highway slopes swell with ripe berries. Again, watch for views of the Southwest Miramichi from the hills in the 30-kilometer (19-mile) stretch from Doaktown to Boiestown—the center of New Brunswick.

Arriving in small **Boiestown,** the few attractions are conveniently clustered together on Highway 8. A giant logger and even larger log-shaped buildings give away the **Central New Brunswick Woodmen's Museum** at 6342 Hwy. 8. Venture into the grounds to see the trapper's cabin and the blacksmith's shop. As a bonus, if you're under 6 or over 96, admission is free. Across the road, admire the grounded **TBM Avenger Air Tanker #14** that serves as a memorial to lost pilots.

From Boiestown, the forested heart of New Brunswick, it's a 70-kilometer (44-mile) drive to Fredericton, which is covered fully in Drive 5. The route's scenery—you guessed it—is more river and forest.

The Miramichi River is famous for its salmon runs. Learn about the Atlantic salmon at the Miramichi Salmon Museum in Doaktown, New Brunswick.

Acadian Peninsula

Grande-Anse to Caraquet to Miscou Island

General Description: From painted lobster traps to deck furniture, you'll lose count of the times you see the Acadian flag—the blue, white, and red flag with the gold star—as you travel this 117-kilometer (73-mile) scenic drive along Chaleur Bay. A historic Acadian Village, Popes' Museum, and large churches show the region's ties to the Roman Catholic faith, while an aquarium, ecological park, and peat bogs ground it to the natural environment.

Special Features: Chaleur Bay, Popes' Museum, Village Historique Acadien, Éco-musée de l'Huître (Oyster Museum), Musée Acadien de Caraquet (Acadian Museum), Inkerman National Migratory Bird Sanctuary, New Brunswick Aquarium and Marine Center, Ecological Park of the Acadian Peninsula, Sainte-Cécile Church, Miscou Island Lighthouse.

Location: Northeastern New Brunswick, on the Acadian Peninsula between Chaleur Bay and the Gulf of St. Lawrence.

Driving Route Numbers & Names: Highway 11, Route 145, Route 335, Route 345, Route 113, Route 313.

Travel Season: During the first two weeks of August, celebrate Acadian pride with the Festival Acadien de Caraquet. Most houses don colorful strings of flags, and the ever-present Acadian pride intensifies. The weeks lead up to the Acadian National Holiday on August 15 with the noisy Tintamarre—a parade of thousands in costumes with noisemakers. June through October offers pleasant weather, but fog can roll in even in the height of summer.

Camping: Although there are no provincial park campgrounds in the area, Caraquet, Shippagan, and Miscou Island all have private campgrounds with full camping and RV services.

Services: Caraquet has all the essentials including medical care, gas stations, and grocery stores. For heritage bed-and-breakfasts, inns, and chain motels, the large town also has ample options. In Shippagan, you'll easily find gas stations, accommodations, and restaurants.

Nearby Points of Interest: Bathurst Heritage Museum, Tracadie Historical Museum.

Time Zone: Atlantic time zone (GMT minus 4 hours).

The Drive

French greetings, Acadian flags, and cultural festivals delight on this 117-kilometer (73-mile) scenic drive to the Acadian Peninsula. Ocean-side churches, old convents, and the continent's only papal museum show the force of Roman Catholicism here. But there are also marshland trails, a monstrous lighthouse, and an aquarium to create a lovely balance of attractions.

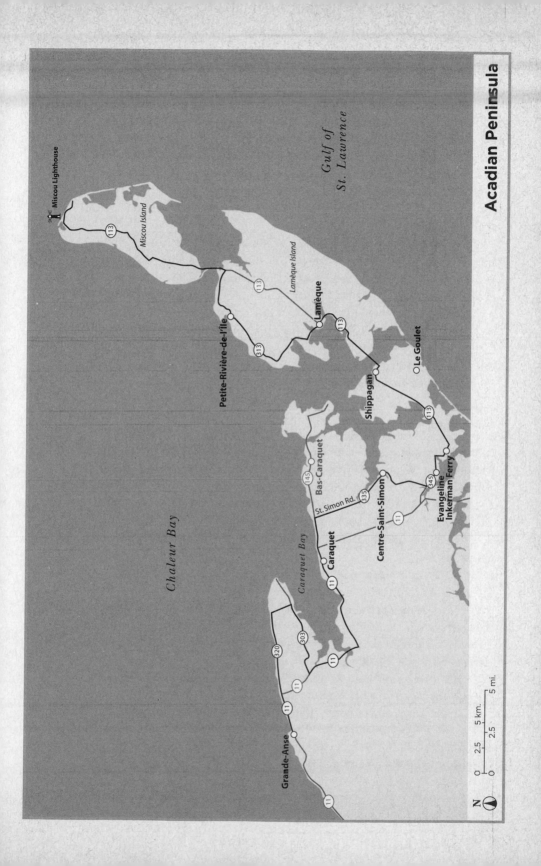

Acadian Peninsula

North from Miramichi or east from Bathurst, Highway 11 is the main artery to the peninsula. Heed the moose warning signs on the mostly two-lane highway.

At the shoreline of Chaleur Bay, follow Highway 11 to **Grande-Anse.** (If you are arriving from Miramichi, this drive does require a short backtrack through Caraquet.) In the town of fishing boats and beaches, the **Popes' Museum** at 184 Acadie St. stands on the main route and is the only one in North America. A scale model of St. Peter's Basilica, replica of the original spire at the Grande-Anse church, and many pieces of religious art display the foundation of the Roman Catholic faith here.

Fog can roll in quickly and thickly in **Chaleur Bay,** but good visibility allows views out to the Quebec shore. The tourist information lighthouse is decorated with an eye-catching Acadian-flag paint job. The salty smell of the ocean—*anse* means "cove" in French—enhances the appeal of stopping at the picnic area.

Continuing east on Highway 11 back toward Caraquet, a fishing boat marks the road to Anse-Bleue. While the main route bears right, continue straight on Route 320 to follow the Chaleur coast. Following the point of land out, round the other side along **Caraquet Bay** on Route 303.

Caraquet

Back on Highway 11, drive through forest and marshlands to visit the **Village Historique Acadien** in **Rivière-du-Nord.** Just west of Caraquet, the historical re-creation is a full-day affair. Bake bread, hook rugs, eat a typical Acadian meal, and watch dinner theater. Those lacking French can enjoy the music, costumed actors, and historically restored buildings.

Passing through the **Bertrand Marshes,** cross the **Caraquet River** and keep left on Highway 11 at the junction with Route 325. West of town, **Éco-musée de l'Huître (Oyster Museum)** at 675 West St-Pierre Blvd. digs into all-things oysters. The mollusks are raised at aquaculture sites in the bay.

Known as the **capital of L'Acadie,** busy **Caraquet** shadows the road, making the local services all easy to find. A visitor information center is well appointed at 39 West St-Pierre Blvd. Inside, find binoculars for viewing seabirds and whales in Caraquet Bay as well as the standard brochures.

Near the main town junction, Highway 11 heads south to Miramichi. Continue straight along the bay on Route 145 toward Bas-Caraquet. The waterfront complex on Caraquet Harbour—**Carrefours de la Mer**—features a minigolf course and accommodations. The French-only exhibits at the nearby **Acadian Museum,** 15 East St-Pierre Blvd., tell important histories of local Acadian families through original documents and photos.

About 3 kilometers (2 miles) past the visitor center, turn right at St. Simon Road (Route 335) to follow the route inland. The treed thruway catches occasional water views as it passes North Saint-Simon Bay. Turn left onto Route 345 to drive through **Evangeline,** then a second left onto Route 113 at **Inkerman Ferry.** On nearby **Pokemouche Bay,** the **Inkerman National Migratory Bird Sanctuary** is part of the Pointe aux Rats Musques heronry—home to the largest colony of black-crowned night herons in the Maritimes.

Route 113 cuts an economical distance inland from a meandering coastline, bypassing the South Saint-Simon and Petit-Pokemouche Bays. At Pokemouche Road, find a detour down to **Le Goulet,** where there is a beach with washrooms, showers, and a picnic area.

Shippagan

Shippagan, about 35 kilometers (22 miles) from Caraquet, is an industrial area and a hub port for fishing boats. The Shippagan campus of the **Université de Moncton** features the **New Brunswick Aquarium and Marine Centre.** Bright blue signs painted on the pavement direct you to the aquarium at 100 Aquarium St., where you can meet a fishing-boat captain, touch oysters and sea cucumbers, or watch the harbor seals as they eat herring for dinner.

On J. D. Gauthier Boulevard, part of Route 113, the small **St. John's United Church** represents the region's small Anglophone community. It holds service just once a year in August.

Commercial fishing boats line up at the town wharves. Stop at the waterfront park near the bridge to **Lamèque Island** to watch for boat traffic.

Shippagan is connected to Savoy Landing on Lamèque Island via a causeway and lift bridge. Cross the narrow passage to the island. Follow Route 113—which draws a line through the center of the island—before turning left on Route 313 as it branches left into **Lamèque.**

More road paint, this time in green, leads to another excellent attraction: the **Ecological Park of the Acadian Peninsula** at 65 Du Ruisseau St. A boardwalk leads out across the marshes from the visitor center to explore the park's ecosystems: forest, river estuary, beach, wetland, and peat bog.

The peat industry, along with fishing, is a significant business on the island and is celebrated with the annual **Lamèque Provincial Peat Moss Festival** in July. Peat is amazing stuff, its uses ranging from absorbing oil spills to adding a smoky hint to whiskey.

Ask directions to **Petite-Rivière-de-l'Île,** also on Route 313, where the vibrantly painted **Sainte-Cécile Church** is home to the midsummer **Lamèque International Baroque Music Festival.** The church's dizzying pastel paint job weaves a motif of swirls, stars, bells, music notes, and crosses.

The lighthouse on Miscou Island sits on the tip of the Acadian Peninsula, New Brunswick.

Miscou Island

Follow Route 313 until it rejoins the main road at a T-junction. Turn left to continue north to **Miscou Island.**

The smell of low tide may welcome you to the island, where fishing for herring and lobster is still the main industry. The Miscou Island Bridge crosses the Miscou Channel. It replaced a ferry that ran here until 1996.

A visitor information center can point directions, but with just one long main road that again slices through the center of the island, it is difficult to get lost. Follow Route 113 north as it passes through marshes and the **Miscou plains.** While not achingly scenic at first, consider the bird and bug life that these wetlands sustain. Walking trails do explore this precious ecosystem, like the **bird observation trail** over the **St. Pierre peat bog.**

At the end of Route 113, **Miscou Island Lighthouse** is close to being the northernmost point in New Brunswick (a point near Dalhousie edges it out). Climb to the top of this 1856 lighthouse that was once powered by seal oil. The wooden lighthouse has one of the stoutest profiles of any Maritime navigational beacon.

Along the shores of Miscou Island find a sheltered beach with soft sand, snack canteen, and picnic tables—all engaging a longer visit to this tip of the Acadian Peninsula.

Acadian Shore

Shediac to Bouctouche to Kouchibouguac National Park

General Description: A 140-kilometer (87-mile) coastal trip through fishing villages out to a Dark Sky Preserve, this drive is about discovery. En route visit a bison farm, a 12-kilometer (7.5-mile) sand dune, and a village pulled from the Acadian fiction of Antonine Maillet. Go bird watching for migratory shorebirds, see seafood aquaculture sites, or watch for twinkling stars and lighthouses on the Acadian coast.

Special Features: Parlee Beach Provincial Park, Pascal-Poirier Historic House, world's largest lobster, Musée des Pionniers de Grande-Digue (Pioneer Museum), Bouctouche Dune, Le Pays de la Sagouine, Irving Arboretum, Kent Museum, Seawind Buffalo Ranch, Irving Eco Nature Park, Olivier Soapery, Hudson Oddities, Bonar Law Historic Site, Richibucto River Museum, Kouchibouguac National Park (Dark Sky Preserve), swimming, walking, beaches, camping.

Location: Southeastern coast of New Brunswick along the Northumberland Strait.

Driving Route Numbers & Names: Route 133, Route 134, Route 530, Route 535, Route 475, Route 505.

Travel Season: Time a spring or fall visit to catch the migratory birds, including plovers and sandpipers, that feed along the shoreline. In summer, the swimming at Kouchibouguac National Park is some of the best in Atlantic Canada, with water temperatures reaching an average of 19.1 degrees Centigrade (66 degrees Fahrenheit) during July.

Camping: Parlee Beach Provincial Park and a host of private campgrounds offer full services near Shediac. Kouchibouguac National Park, at the northern end of this drive, provides the greatest number of camping options with more than 200 sites for tents and RVs.

Services: Fuel up in Shediac or Bouctouche, or in Saint-Louis-de-Kent outside the national park. This scenic drive is close to Moncton at its southern start and Miramichi to the north. Both cities have hospitals.

Nearby Points of Interest: Magnetic Hill, heritage museums, local galleries, and shopping, all in Moncton.

Time Zone: Atlantic time zone (GMT minus 4 hours).

The Drive

Drive this 140-kilometer (87-mile) coastal amble, which is part of the provincially marked **Acadian Coastal Drive** (look for the starfish highway signs throughout). Following the coast along the Northumberland Strait, various rural roads link fishing wharves, bird-watching beaches, and lighthouses. The scenery is quiet but ever moving, as the tides sweep in or out, birds flock and fly south, and fishing boats pull into the harbor.

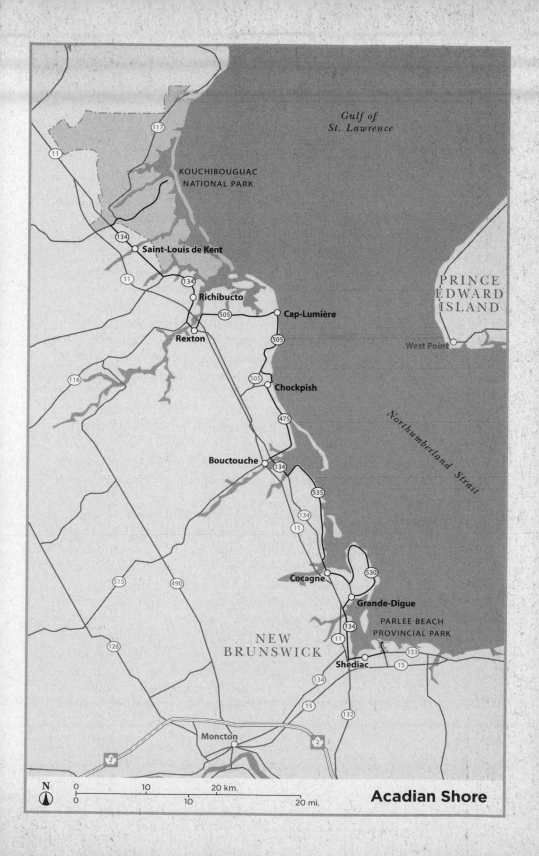

Gulf of
St. Lawrence

117

11

KOUCHIBOUGUAC
NATIONAL PARK

134

Saint-Louis de Kent

11

134

PRINCE
EDWARD
ISLAND

Richibucto

505   Cap-Lumière

West Point

Rexton

505

116

505   Chockpish

475

Northumberland Strait

Bouctouche   134

535

134

11

515   490

Cocagne   530

Grande-Digue

126

PARLEE BEACH
PROVINCIAL PARK

NEW
BRUNSWICK

134

11   133

Shediac   15

134

15   132

Moncton   2

2

N

0   10   20 km.

0   10   20 mi.

Acadian Shore

From Moncton, take Highway 15 to Shediac (about 25 kilometers [15.5 miles] from downtown to downtown). If traveling from Nova Scotia, follow the Trans-Canada or Highway 2 from the provincial border and then take exit 467B to connect with Highway 15.

Shediac

Shediac is a bustle of cars and people. Along the main street, businesses pack in closely to offer dining and shopping. At the south end of town, find **Parlee Beach Provincial Park,** 45 Parlee Beach Rd., which has a campground and beach on **Shediac Bay.** Warm swimming waters, summer festivities, and sunshine draw large crowds to the park, which charges a day-use fee.

Pascal Poirier Historic House at 399 Main St. traces the history of Pascal Poirier, who became the first Acadian senator in 1885. But the town's biggest attraction, literally, is the world's largest lobster at the head of Shediac Harbour. You'll not miss the speckled mass of legs, giant claws, and protruding antennae as crowds climb up for a photo next to the giant crustacean. Neighboring visitor services answer questions and provide brochures. Shediac hosts an annual Lobster Festival, complete with lobster-eating contests and entertainment.

Follow Route 133 out of Shediac, and it quickly becomes Route 134 along the coast. On your right, look out to Shediac Island and the much smaller Skull Island.

At Shediac Bridge, a one-lane bridge signals the backroad nature of the route. Leaving Westmorland County and entering Kent County, turn right on Route 530 to **Grande-Digue**.

In Grande-Digue the Musée des Pionniers (Pioneer Museum), at 468 B Rte. 530, shows the coast's pioneer life with wooden buildings that include a barn, chapel, school, lighthouse, and the Gagnon family house. From the museum follow the roundabout Route 530 as it traces the coast around Caissie Cape and Renards Point. Amid hay fields and marshlands, an odd rusty tractor signals the area's mostly bygone farming industry, although a few organic and small-scale farms remain. At De La Côte Road, bear right toward **Cocagne.**

Coming into wide Cocagne Harbour, turn right onto Route 134. You'll cross the Cocagne River on a newly constructed bridge. Large tidal beaches draw seabirds to the plentiful feeding grounds, but the shoreline also shows erosion. On the water's edge, some cabins appear to have the earth washed out from underneath. The fairly flat landscape has sparse, immature forest. Look for the five-point stars on homes and the bright Acadian flags flying from poles.

The giant speckled lobster in Shediac is the world's largest.

Turn right on Route 535 as it trims the coast inside Cocagne Island. Although the attractions are minimal from here to Bouctouche, shorebird sightings and views of Prince Edward Island in the distance will fill in the scenery until the stunning Bouctouche Dune.

Bouctouche

At **Saint-Thomas-de-Kent,** 14 kilometers (8.7 miles) past Cocagne, look right to see the tip of the 12-kilometer (7.5-mile) **Bouctouche Dune** with a lighthouse on the very end. Rows of aquaculture buoys sit in the well-protected **Buctouche Bay**. Although the dune sits no more than 4 kilometers (2.5 miles) offshore at the farthest, its lone connection to the land is a 20-kilometer (12.4-mile) drive north near Saint-Édouard-de-Kent.

Crossing the Buctouche River on Acadie Street, look left to see the tiny fictional Acadian village of **Le Pays de la Sagouine** on a river island. Walk the boardwalk to **l'Île-aux-Puces** where the village throbs with costumed actors, kitchen musicians, and the daily gossip. Pulled from the imagination of Bouctouche writer **Antonine Maillet,** the village recreates Acadian life with a bootlegger, traditional cuisine, and the house of **La Sagouine**—a washerwoman and Maillet's best-known character.

Acadie Street leads across the Buctouche River to a T-intersection with Route 475. Take Irving Boulevard east through Bouctouche toward the dune. The large **Irving Arboretum** lies hidden behind a stone wall on Irving Boulevard. The garden is poorly marked, but the thousands of trees are worth finding. At Convent Lane, you'll pass the 1880 white **Convent of the Immaculate Conception,** which now houses the **Kent Museum.**

Perry Road and then Route 134 lead inland on a detour to the **Seawind Buffalo Ranch** on St-Pierre Road. A tractor tour of the farm takes visitors for a drive through buffalo pasture. The bulky beasts patiently flick away the flies as they graze. The farm raises the buffalo, also called bison, for meat—which is lauded for its minimal fat content and low cholesterol.

Back on the coast, the Bouctouche Dune tapers in to the mainland at the **Irving Eco Nature Park,** 1932 Rte. 475. Climb the observation tower, visit the nature interpretive center, and then walk along the snaking 2-kilometer (1.2-mile) boardwalk (designed with its pleasing curves to withstand tidal surges and ice). Watch for birds in the dune grasses and along the shoreline. It's possible to enjoy a beach walk along the 12-kilometer (7.5-mile) dune out to the lighthouse, but this fragile habitat is best left alone.

From Bouctouche the road heads north to Kouchibouguac National Park along a scenic coastline with limited attractions. At low tide you may see clammers digging for the bivalve mollusks in the tidal flats.

The boardwalk at the Bouctouche dune snakes out over the saltmarsh and beach.

At **Chockpish** you can choose between two routes. Either turn left on Route 475 then turn right on Route 505 to visit the **Olivier Soapery**—an economuseum that demonstrates the craft of natural soap making and gives tours. Alternately, follow the starfish scenic drive signs right on Ste-Anne Road and continue through to the junction with Route 505. Here, opt to follow the coast with a right turn. The northward drive heads over a one-lane bridge and past a seafood packaging plant, before cutting the point short at **Cap-Lumière**.

Kouchibouguac National Park

Following Route 505 from Cap-Lumière, the scenery fills with forest as it nears the national park. Follow the rural route through Rexton, Richibucto, and Saint-Louis-de-Kent. You'll pass a few historical museums and attractions on the way to the national park. The beach glass workshop at **Hudson Oddities** at 338 Bas De L'Allée Rd. in **Richibucto-Village** operates from a lighthouse, crafting items from sea-tumbled glass, also called mermaid tears.

The **Richibucto River Museum,** which gives guided tours by appointment, shares a location with the birthplace of British prime minister Andrew Bonar Law at the **Bonar Law Historic Site** at 31 Bonar Law Ave. in **Rexton.**

(For the navigator, the route follows Route 505 to Rexton, then heads north on Route 134. Highway 11 is the faster option and no less scenic, but it skips the museums.)

Just up the Richibucto River, the **Elsipogtog First Nation** holds an annual Powwow on Labour Day weekend with drumming, dancing, and food. In Richibucto, indulge your love of seafood at the **July Scallop Festival.**

A number of roads thread into **Kouchibouguac National Park.** An extension of the Acadian Coastal Drive, Route 117 pulls clear through to the Pointe-Sapin. Follow this main road to signs for the national park and Kelly Beach.

A treed 11-kilometer (6.8-mile) road leads into the national park and to the beaches, salt marshes, and largest campgrounds. Long barrier dunes protect warm swimming lagoons along the **Gulf of St. Lawrence** exposure.

Created in 1969, Kouchibouguac protects this environment of Acadian forest, peat bogs, lagoons, salt marshes, and barrier islands. Its name means "river of the long tides" in the Mi'kmaq language. Some of the estuary channels in the park even dip meters below sea level.

Walk out over the salt marsh boardwalk to bird watch for migratory species along the shore. If camping for the night, you'll trace the constellations in the national park, which is a designated Dark Sky Preserve.

Side Trip: Moncton

Close to the starting point for this drive lies the **city of Moncton.** One of the fastest growing areas of the province, Moncton is also the most metropolitan, with shopping, spas, amusement parks, and golf courses to add to the attractions list.

Inland from the Bay of Fundy, although it still experiences the tidal action along the Petitcodiac River, the Moncton scenery takes second seat to urban entertainment. Theaters and galleries complement the historical homes and museums.

Magnetic Hill is the city's most trumpeted attraction—a phenomenon that will see your car, when put in neutral gear, seemingly travel uphill on Mountain Road.

NOVA SCOTIA

Fossil Coast

Truro to Parrsboro to Cape Chignecto

General Description: This is a 165-kilometer (103-mile) shoreline scenic drive where the Fundy tides sweep in and out of Cobequid Bay and the Minas Basin. But it's also a land of dinosaur fossils, the summer home of a former prime minister, and a World War II observation point. Sample locally made pie, practice your shipbuilding skills, and catch a live theater show as you journey out to the protected end of the peninsula, Cape Chignecto.

Special Features: Truro Tidal Bore, Bass River Heritage Museum, That Dutchman's Farm, Thomas' Cove Coastal Reserve, Cobequid Interpretation Centre, Five Islands Provincial Park, Fundy Geological Museum, Ottawa House, Ship's Company Theatre, Age of Sail Heritage Centre, Cape d'Or Lighthouse, Cape Chignecto Provincial Park, hiking, camping, clam digging, tidal zones.

Location: Northern Nova Scotia, south of the Cobequid Mountains.

Driving Route Numbers & Names: Route 2, Route 209.

Travel Season: Summer beaches bring clammers and campers to Five Islands

Provincial Park. Many of the attractions on this drive can also be explored in the shoulder season during the months of May, June, September, and October.

Camping: Five Islands Provincial Park makes a lovely family camping destination with its beach and full facilities. At Cape Chignecto Provincial Park—a wilderness park with a coastal hiking trail—there are no drive-in campsites, but the New Yarmouth campground can be found just off Eatonville Road. For avid backpackers, secluded campsites are spaced out around the peninsula.

Services: Get any essentials in Truro before setting out. For heritage accommodations, theater, and seafood, stop in Parrsboro. You can fuel up along the scenic drive route in Economy or Parrsboro.

Nearby Points of Interest: Colchester Historical Society Museum, Little White Schoolhouse Museum, Nova Scotia Provincial Exhibition Harness Racing, Debert Military Museum, Joggins Fossil Cliffs, Anne Murray Centre, Springhill Miners' Museum.

Time Zone: Atlantic time zone (GMT minus 4 hours).

The Drive

As Highways 102 and 104 meet in Truro, it's a relief to escape the tangle of exits and take a quiet country drive. Take exit 14A off Highway 104 and follow posted signs for Highway 2, west to Parrsboro. If you happen to be passing through at the rising tide, however, first visit the **Tidal Bore Observation Deck** on Tidal Bore Road off exit 14. Try the **Palliser Motel**—which offers accommodations, dining, and a gift shop at the site—for exact times to watch for the rush of saltwater up the Salmon River.

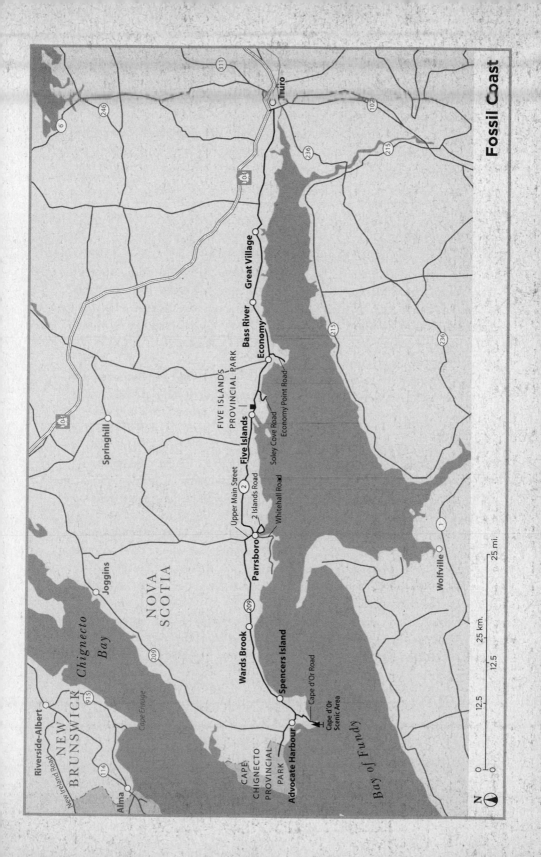

Fossil Coast

Highway 2 heads west from exit 14A, through the residential areas of Central Onslow and Masstown. Set in from the shore, the road provides occasional glimpses out to the purple-red tidal flats of Cobequid Bay. Crossing the Debert River, see how the arable land yields thick crop fields.

At Great Village, about 24 kilometers (15 miles) from the highway exit, turn left to continue on Highway 2. (A right turn would reconnect with Highway 104.) West of Great Village the road draws closer to the shoreline, giving views of the mud flats (or watery bay at high tide) to the south, and coniferous forests and marshlands to the north.

Economy Shore

Through small towns, the road winds along the coast of the **Economy Shore.** In **Bass River,** a relocated church on Highway 2 houses the **Bass River Heritage Museum.** The museum explores local genealogy and history, including that of the **Dominion Chair Company,** whose factories once shipped Bass River furniture worldwide. Although a 1989 fire ceased production, the company still operates a general store with a furniture gallery in town.

Continuing west on Highway 2, stop for a snack at **That Dutchman's Farm,** at 112 Brown Rd. in Upper Economy. A regular vendor at the Halifax Farmers' Market, the farm declares itself to be "always open." Farm animals and a petting area are great for kids, while grownups will appreciate the walking trails and subtleties of the Dragon's Breath blue cheese.

At **Economy Point,** turn left on Economy Point Road and then make a right turn to **Thomas' Cove Coastal Reserve.** Two 4-kilometer (2.5-mile) loop hiking trails provide coastal views from Economy Point. Close to the greatest height of the Fundy tides, the tidal range here is 16 meters (53 feet).

In nearby Economy, you'll easily find the **Cobequid Interpretive Centre** on the highway with its World War II observation tower. Climb the three steep sets of stairs to the tar-paper roof, stopping to admire newspapers and the historical artifacts on the levels in between. Ask at the information center about walking trails along the Economy River.

Across the street from the World War II observation tower, buy a few souvenirs at the **Glooscap Country Bazaar.** The local cooperative sells homemade pies, garden vegetables, mustard pickles, handmade baby items, and jewelry. Prices are very reasonable, and the quality is excellent.

From Economy, views to the left at high tide are impressive but more dramatic when the bay is drained. For a quick detour, turn left on Soley Cove Road in **Lower Economy.** The **flowerpot rock** here is lesser known, and less enchanting, than its Fundy cousins at Hopewell Rocks, New Brunswick. Still, the curious tidal-carved pillar crowded with trees makes for lovely photos of the bay.

Just 3 kilometers (2 miles) past Lower Economy, turn onto Bentley Branch Road toward **Five Islands Provincial Park.** The park offers hiking trails and a clam-digger's delight. At low tide one can just about walk out to the dumpling islands that give park its name.

First Nation legends tell of a beaver that flooded the garden of the Mi'kmaq god Glooscap. Unhappy with the animal, Glooscap threw clumps of earth at the beaver. The mud pats landed on the Bay of Fundy, creating the Five Islands. In destroying the beaver's dam, Glooscap also created the tides.

And the tides do move with the quickness of a flood—more quickly in parts than some can run. Know the tide table and do not venture too far out. Walk on the bottom of the bay, get muddy, and find some beach treasures. Then, as the tide rises, return to walk the park trails, lookout from the viewpoints, and barbecue in the campground.

The **Not Since Moses Race** provides unique 5- and 10-kilometer (3- and 6.2-mile) courses over the drained basin. Happening in August, the running course crosses the tidal zone. A good incentive to run faster!

Parrsboro

Heading west from Five Islands, the road twists and turns, losing the shore to venture between forested hills. At **Parrsboro,** Highway 2 cuts sharply north on Upper Main Street.

Instead, turn left on Main Street and cross **Parrsboro Harbour** on Two Islands Road. The road leads to a wharf with a beach, small canteen, and lighthouse. Nearby, visit the **Fundy Geological Museum** at 162 Two Islands Rd., where dinosaur exhibits easily engage kids with the fossils. Dinosaur footprints were discovered in the area in 1984, leading to the discovery of thousands more fossils. The museum also hosts the August **Nova Scotia Gem and Mineral Show,** known as the "Rockhound Roundup."

On the harbor waterfront, the MV *Kipawo* is firmly beached as **Ship's Company Theatre.** A summer season delights with plays and camps. A storied history docks with the *Kipawo.* Launched in 1924, it was originally a passenger ferry shuttling between Kingsport, Parrsboro, and Wolfville in the Minas Basin (the name is derived from the first letters of each town). In the 1940s, the *Kipawo* tended anti-submarine nets in Conception Bay and went on to become a Bell Island Ferry (see Drive 28). Before returning to its first homeport, the steel ship also provided tours in Newfoundland's Terra Nova National Park.

For a different historical bent, visit **Ottawa House** at 1155 Whitehall Rd. The house, built in 1775, was a summer home to Sir Charles Tupper, Canada's sixth and shortest-serving prime minister. Tupper held the position for barely two months (May 1 to July 8, 1896) before Wilfred Laurier, the longest-serving prime

minister, came to power. Historical furnishings fill the 21-room mansion, while hiking trails explore nearby Partridge Island, a stop on Samuel de Champlain's 1607 voyage.

Backtrack through Parrsboro to where Highway 2 intersects Route 209 to Cape Chignecto. Western Avenue also connects with Route 209.

About 15 kilometers (9 miles) from Parrsboro along Route 209, the road draws close to the shoreline again at Fox River and explores the treed hilly area of Greville Bay. At Port Greville, turn left on Cochrane Road and drive down to the beach for views of Nova Scotia's **Cape Split**—a hook-shaped land spit where a hiking trail leads out to the cragged cliffs. For more in that area, see Drive 10 covering the Annapolis Valley.

In Wards Brook the surprising **Age of Sail Heritage Centre** provides a lovely stop with a cafe and hands-on activities. Kids can use a wood plane to smooth out a plank for the ship works or hear a mother's story about her lost son. A lighthouse and boathouse add to the heritage appeal of the converted 1854 church.

Cape Chignecto

Take a quick detour on Spencers Island Road for lunch or beach views in **Spencers Island**—a favorite spot for camping and kayaking.

Continuing west on Route 209, follow well-posted signs that direct you down a 6-kilometer (3.7-mile) gravel road near East Advocate to **Cape d'Or Scenic Area.** The restaurant, accommodations, and red-and-white lighthouse sit on a rocky point overlooking Cape Split and Cape Chignecto.

Continue through fishing villages toward the large wilderness area of **Cape Chignecto Provincial Park.** Ask at the interpretive center about hikes to the abandoned village of Eatonville or Red Rocks Beach—both of which are much shorter options than the full 51-kilometer (32-mile) wilderness hike around Cape Chignecto.

Side Trip: Joggins Fossil Cliffs

From the Cape Chignecto area, Route 209 cuts north across the peninsula toward **Joggins.** From Cape Chignecto, drive 57 kilometers (35 miles) to the **Joggins Fossil Cliffs,** a UNESCO World Heritage Site on Chignecto Bay.

A large interpretive center and guided hikes will help you identify the fossils that dot the shoreline and are continually being discovered. The drive is less scenic than the route along Cobequid Bay, but finding your own piece of ancient history is a weighty enough draw.

The Age of Sail Heritage Centre in Wards Brook, Nova Scotia, displays exhibits that are hands-on and historic.

Annapolis Valley to Fundy Tides

Windsor to Grand Pré to Wolfville to Halls Harbour

General Description: This 80-kilometer (50-mile) route wends through Annapolis Valley farmlands to Nova Scotia's Bay of Fundy coast. Starting in Windsor—with its hockey museum, oldest Canadian block-house, and giant pumpkins—the journey ventures across rivers, dike lands, and heritage districts. Be lured by freshly roasted coffee, touched by the deportation of the Acadians in the mid-1700s, and arrested with the views from the Lookoff. Finally, savor a sunset and a lobster supper on the wharf at Halls Harbour, while you view Nova Scotia's version of the world's highest tides.

Special Features: West Hants Historical Society Museum, Fort Edward Blockhouse National Historic Site, Windsor Hockey Heritage Centre, Haliburton House, Shand House Museum, Howard Dill Enterprises, Grand Pré National Historic Site, Evangeline Beach, Randall House Museum, Acadia University, Robie Tufts Nature Centre, Fox Hill Farm, the Lookoff, Halls Harbour Lobster Pound, the Red Fishhouse Museum, the Old Schoolhouse, eagle watching, tidal zone, lobster suppers, beach walks, beachcombing.

Location: Western Nova Scotia.

Driving Route Numbers & Names: Highway 1 (Evangeline Trail), Highway 101, Route 358, Gospel Road, Route 359.

Travel Season: From the spring apple blossoms to the fall harvest and winter eagle watching, this is close to an all-season drive. Private gardens are at their peak in June and July while the monster pumpkins fatten up for the autumn harvest. Just west of Canning, in Sheffield Mills, January and early February bring the best bald-eagle watching. Although July and August are most popular with visitors, avoiding these months can be recommended, as the Annapolis Valley records some of the hottest temperatures in the province. Summer days often top 30 degrees Centigrade (86 degrees Fahrenheit) plus humidity.

Camping: Walk-in and drive-in campsites are available in Blomidon Provincial Park, just above Canning. Near Windsor, Smileys Provincial Park has a dump station, toilets, and water. Reservations are taken for both sites at (888) 544-3434 or http://parks.gov.ns.ca. Find additional private campgrounds near Grand Pré and Wolfville.

Services: This drive passes through a number of small towns, all with gas stations, restaurants, and accommodations. Most of the places to stay in the area are heritage-home bed-and-breakfasts or inns. Medical care is available in Windsor and Kentville.

Nearby Points of Interest: Blomidon Provincial Park, Cape Split, hiking.

Time Zone: Atlantic time zone (GMT minus 4 hours).

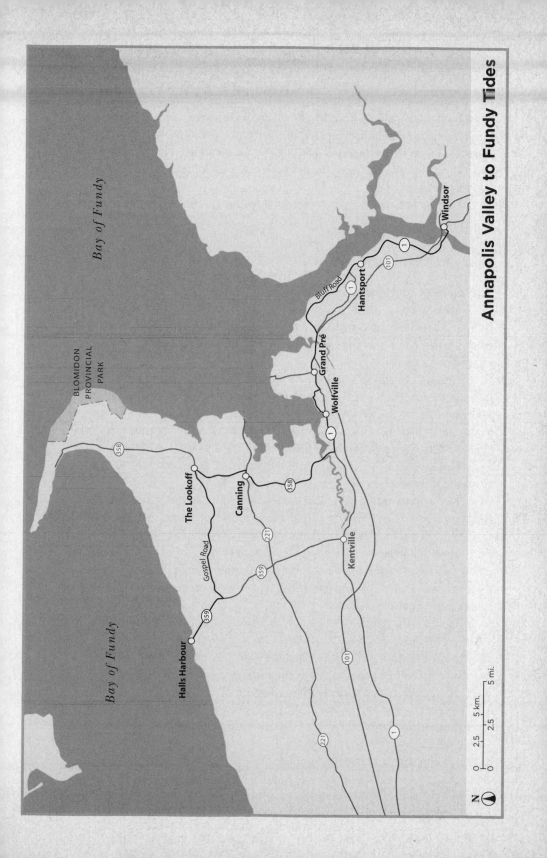

Annapolis Valley to Fundy Tides

The Drive

This 80-kilometer (50-mile) drive connects a string of historic and scenic towns in Nova Scotia's agricultural heartland, the Annapolis Valley. From the once-grand Windsor, follow the Evangeline Trail through the university town of Wolfville and make a side trip for an eagle-watching session or stunning lookouts—often called look offs in Nova Scotia. Wrap the day on the Bay of Fundy, dining at the lobster pound in Halls Harbour.

About 65 kilometers (40 miles) from downtown Halifax, Highway 101 is the main artery to Windsor.

Heritage Windsor

Start the drive in **Windsor,** where it's easy and delightful to lose the main route when arriving in town. The town's one-time opulence still shows in the gabled roofs and ornate wooden trim. Depending on your interests chose a route through the town that stops in at the varied selection of museums, covering bicycles to pumpkins to hockey.

Cutting through town on King Street, visit the impressive community museum run by the **West Hants Historical Society** at 281 King St. Wedding dresses, photographs, and Windsor furniture pieces crowd the by-donation museum. On Fort Edward Street off King, **Fort Edward Blockhouse National Historic Site** sits on a prominent hill overlooking the junction of the St. Croix and Avon Rivers. Both rivers flow into the Bay of Fundy, famous for its tides that rise and fall as much as 16 meters (53 feet) twice daily.

The first settlers, the Mi'kmaq, named the place Pesaquid, meaning "junction of waters." The French later settled the area in 1685, followed by the British in 1749. And it is the British that have left the most indelible mark on the town. Fort Edward Blockhouse, the oldest blockhouse in Canada, was built as part of an elaborate English defense system. With another blockhouse on the opposite hill, the garrison could survey the rivers. Today, climb to the second-level of the blockhouse to peer out the cannon loopholes.

Visiting town you'll notice a public-relations plug for Windsor as **"the Birthplace of Hockey."** Thomas Chandler Haliburton—whom I'll get to next—wrote about students at King's College, Canada's oldest independent school, playing "hurley" on Long Pond. In the shopping district, review the case for the disputed claim in the **Windsor Hockey Heritage Centre** at 128 Gerrish St.

West of the downtown, follow Albert Street and then Clifton Avenue to stop in at **Haliburton House,** the estate of Judge Thomas Chandler Haliburton. Apple orchards, lush lawns, and a sprawling white house named Clifton feature in the estate. Haliburton is known for penning the humor tales of Sam Slick. Today we know less his name and more his turns of phrase turned clichés, which include "It's raining cats and dogs."

Make a loop up past King's-Edgehill School and stop in at its odd neighbor: **Howard Dill Enterprises** at 400 College Rd. There, farmer Howard Dill grew world-record-size pumpkins fit for a Cinderella coach. The Dill family continues the tradition, and at the farm you can buy seeds to start your own pumpkin patch.

The heritage-home-lined streets tend to slope down toward Water Street. The **Shand House Museum** at 389 Avon St. delves into a bygone era of penny-farthing bicycles and the rich families of Windsor.

Off Water Street avoid the controlled-access Highway 101 as a bridge spans a narrow tentacle of the Avon River. Opt instead for the meander of Highway 1 toward Hantsport.

After 12 kilometers (7.5 miles), Highway 1 follows Hantsport's Main Street. Pass through town and turn right on Bluff Road to catch views of **Blomidon Provincial Park** and its 180-meter (591-feet) cliffs on the horizon.

The two-lane road with a narrow shoulder sneaks lovely river views in with the roadside wildflowers like goldenrod and Queen Anne's lace. Hay fields in various stages of cutting, drying, and baling abut apple orchards and animal-feed cornfields. Roads are sliced with railroad tracks that lead to the Hantsport gypsum plant.

Bluff Road meets Highway 1 and Highway 101 after 8 kilometers (5 miles) in order to cross the Gaspereau River. To reach Grand Pré, hop on Highway 101 for one exit (from 9 to 10).

Grand Pré Acadians

Take exit 10 and your nose will lead you to **Just Us! Coffee Roasters,** at 11865 Hwy. 1. Not a planned stop for most, the invading smell of freshly roasted coffee seems to turn the signal indicator light on all by itself. Pull in for fair-traded, organic coffee. While you wait for your brew, look through the varied displays in the fair trade museum.

Continue on Highway 1 toward Grand Pré, making a right turn at Grand Pré Road to follow signs for the **Grand Pré National Historic Site.** The admission building looks like a train station (the land was once owned by Dominion Atlantic Railway), but venture through to discover postcard-worthy scenery: the iconic memorial church, statue of Evangeline—poet Henry Wadsworth Longfellow's fictional Acadian heroine, and pretty grounds filled with flowering arbors, rambunctious ducks, and even an archaeological dig.

In the interpretive center view the film, excavated artifacts, and scale models that help piece together the Acadian story. As they settled in the Maritimes, Acadians reclaimed marshes from the sea. When they refused to pledge allegiance to the

English, who had most recently gained control of the territory, the Acadians were deported starting in 1755. About 9,000 were uprooted in the Great Upheaval, and many died en route to exile in France and the United States.

End the visit with a drive farther along Grand Pré Road (about 3 kilometers [2 miles] each way) as it cuts across the dike lands. This particular agricultural area covers 3,013 acres (1,219 hectares) that are below sea level. On my most recent visit, I spotted three bald eagles perched on utility poles above the flats.

The road climbs back above sea level and ends above **Evangeline Beach,** with views of the Minas Basin and Blomidon Ridge. On the red-sand shore, flocks of endangered semipalmated sandpipers roost and feed on the rich tidal flats, fattening up for their 20,000-kilometer (12,427-mile) migration route. For those whose lunch doesn't include invertebrates from the mud flats, there is a small canteen at the beach.

Wolfville's Lovely Main Street

Return on Grand Pré Road to Highway 1 and continue west 5 kilometers (3 miles) to **Wolfville.** You'll pass the lovely **Grand Pré Winery** at 11611 Hwy. 1, which welcomes guests for wine tasting, a walk through the grapevines and simple museum, or a fine dinner under the patio arbor.

Wolfville's Main Street, which is also Highway 1, confirms the town's place as one of most desirable and artistic communities in the province. Wolfville hosts the **Canadian Deep Roots Music Festival** each September.

Wrought-iron-style lampposts, flower boxes, and pub patios, create a historical but lived-in feel. The town revolves around **Acadia University**—the students of which double the town population during the school year. Established in 1838, the Acadia University buildings sit west of downtown and feature ornate clock towers and smooth columns.

In Wolfville, which was originally named Mud Creek, stop in at the Dijon-colored **Randall House Museum,** 259 Main St., and the lovely gardens at **Blomidon Inn,** 195 Main St. Historic inns and heritage homes offer lots of accommodation choices in the town.

If it's near dusk, wait around at the **Robie Tufts Nature Centre** (Front Street and Elm Avenue) for the chimney swifts that reportedly swoop into the chimney as the sun sets.

If not, depart from Wolfville along Highway 1 (which leads west to traffic-clogged Kentville) and cut toward the Bay of Fundy through cow pastures and cornfields.

A statue of Evangeline stands in front of the Memorial Church at Grand Pré National Historic Site, Nova Scotia.

Route 358 leads across the Cornwallis River toward Canning and the coast. After about 4.5 kilometers (2.8 miles) Church Street intersects the route for an easterly detour to **Fox Hill Farm** at 1678 Church St. Taste aged cheddars and smoked Goudas at the cheese farm and store, which raises the cattle on-site. The shop area includes a glassed-in production facility with a few interpretive displays.

Returning on Church Street to Route 358, the road continues north to **Canning.** The tiny town features a rather unique memorial—a monument honoring Harold Borden, who died in the Boer War. Harold Borden was the son of Sir Frederic Borden, a government minister. Another relation Robert Borden, who was born in nearby Grand Pré, served as prime minister during the First World War.

Sheffield Mills, west of Canning, lures in the Audubon crowd with its winter **Eagle Watch Festival.** Eagles are fed most mornings in January and early February, and the birds of prey flock by the dozens to the local fields for the snack.

Although Route 358 continues to Scots Bay and a wonderful hike along **Cape Split** (about 12 kilometers [7.5 miles] over easy-to-moderate terrain) as well as **Blomidon Provincial Park,** this drive turns around after a steep climb to the Lookoff.

Known as **the Lookoff,** a parking area along the right side of the road places you in perfect position to enjoy stunning views from more than 300 meters (984 feet) up. The hill plummets down to near sea level before flattening out into grassy fields, straight hedgerows, white farmhouses, domed pigsties, and red barns. The scene ripples out to the Bay of Fundy coast.

Farms in the area produce rich fruit and vegetable harvests, from strawberries to cucumbers and broccoli. Try to identify the crops as you drive past the many local farms. Agricultural festivals abound here, from the spring **Apple Blossom Festival** in Wolfville to the autumn **Valley Pumpkin Fest.**

Tidal Zone in Halls Harbour

From the Lookoff, take a local-worthy shortcut through Arlington and Glenmont (it's the right turn at the sharp bend when returning from the Lookoff). Not so much a scenic route as a means to reach a scenic destination, the 18-kilometer (11-mile) route along Gospel Road climbs and descends the terrain of **North Mountain.** At the peaks, catch brief views of the **Parrsboro Shore** and **Five Islands Provincial Park.**

The Lookoff near Canning, Nova Scotia, lives up to its name with views of farms, fields, and the Minas Basin.

The road connects with Route 359, which cuts a more direct route to **Halls Harbour** from Kentville. After a couple of tight turns, you're on West Halls Harbour Road—the only road through town. Park near the town wharf, where fishing boats sit at the mercy of the tides, or near the beach and **Halls Harbour Lobster Pound.** The restaurant serves lobster suppers on a wharf patio, sometimes with blueberry shortcake for dessert.

The town has two community museums, **the Red Fishhouse Museum** run by the Halls Harbour Historical Society, and **the Old Schoolhouse,** which was the last one-room school in Kings County when it closed in 1970.

Before or after a meal, wander down to the beach for views across the Bay of Fundy to Cape Chignecto. Facing west, you're in the perfect location to catch the sunset.

Brier Island

Annapolis Royal to Digby to Brier Island

General Description: Over a favorite, 135-kilometer (84-mile) scenic drive, follow the ferries and views out to Nova Scotia's most westerly point. Lush gardens and Acadian history define Annapolis Royal, while scallops and sea captains are at home on the wharf in Digby. Follow the Digby Neck and Islands Scenic Drive west: Hike to the precarious-looking Balancing Rock, watch sea birds, and learn about the first solo round-the-world sailor, Joshua Slocum.

Special Features: Annapolis Royal Historic Gardens, Fort Anne National Historic Site, O'Dell House Museum, Sinclair Inn Museum, Annapolis Tidal Generating Station, Melanson Settlement National Historic Site, Port Royal National Historic Site, Upper Clements Parks, Annapolis Basin Look-off Provincial Park, Digby scallops, Admiral Digby Museum, Balancing Rock, Joshua Slocum Monument, Northern Point Lighthouse, Brier Island whale watching.

Location: Western Nova Scotia, along the Bay of Fundy coast.

Driving Route Numbers & Names: Highway 1, Highway 101, Route 303, Route 217.

Travel Season: Whales feed in these waters starting in the spring, although late summer and fall are the best times for viewing humpbacks, dolphins, porpoises, minkes, finbacks, and the endangered right whales.

Camping: Private campgrounds in Digby and Annapolis Royal offer complete facilities for tents and RVs. Inland, about 50 kilometers (31 miles) from Annapolis Royal along Highway 8, Kejimkujik National Park has forested campsites close to canoeing lakes, swimming beaches, boat rentals, and hiking trails.

Services: As Nova Scotia's dock for the Saint John–Digby ferry, the scallop-famous town of Digby offers many basic accommodations. For heritage charm, book a stay at one of the many large Victorian homes-turned-B&Bs in Annapolis Royal. Both Annapolis Royal and Digby offer medical services as well as gas stations and supplies.

Nearby Points of Interest: Yarmouth-area Acadian shore, Bear River Heritage Museum, Bear River First Nation Heritage and Cultural Centre.

Time Zone: Atlantic time zone (GMT minus 4 hours).

The Drive

Starting at a military stronghold that flipped from French to British control and then traveling out to the westernmost tip of the province, this 135-kilometer (84-mile) scenic drive packs in some of Nova Scotia's best attractions. Whale watch or hike; take tea in the garden or eat a scallop dinner; learn about Acadian settlers or ride a roller coaster.

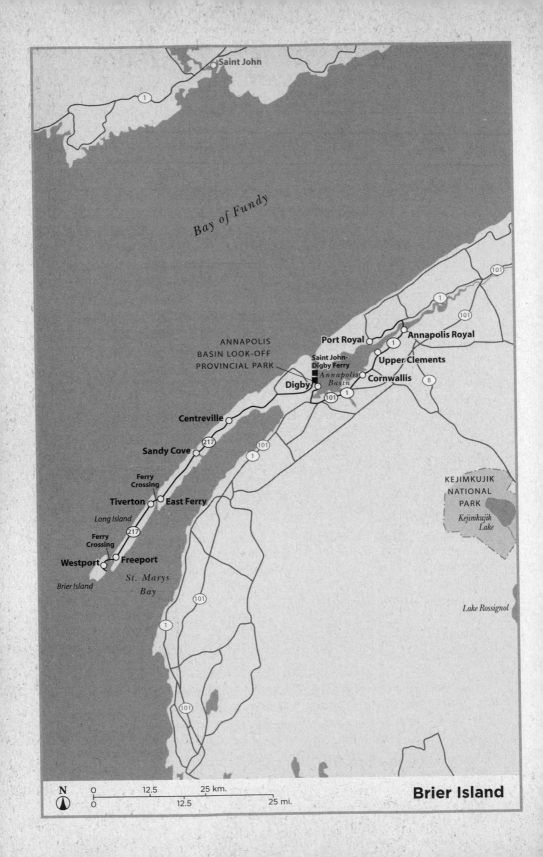

Saint John

1

Bay of Fundy

ANNAPOLIS
BASIN LOOK-OFF
PROVINCIAL PARK

Port Royal   **Annapolis Royal**

Saint John-
Digby Ferry   1

Upper Clements

*Annapolis
Basin*   **Cornwallis**

Digby

101   1   8

101

Centreville

217

101

Sandy Cove   1

Ferry
Crossing

Tiverton   **East Ferry**

Long Island   217

Ferry
Crossing

Westport   **Freeport**

Brier Island   *St. Marys
Bay*

101

1

101

101

101

1

KEJIMKUJIK
NATIONAL
PARK

*Kejimkujik
Lake*

Lake Rossignol

N

0   12.5   25 km.

0   12.5   25 mi.

Brier Island

Drive Highway 101 to exit 22, taking Highway 8 into Annapolis Royal. Alternately, arrive on Highway 8 via Kejimkujik National Park (see the side trip at the end of this drive), cutting through the center of the province.

Annapolis Royal

Tucked between the wide Annapolis River and the small Allains River, **Annapolis Royal** boasts a compact heritage district filled with Victorian homes and museums. Highway 8 intersects the Evangeline Trail (Highway 1) in town. From there, quickly access the town's delightful historic attractions.

At 441 St. George St. (Highway 8), the **Annapolis Royal Historic Gardens** offer lush summer blooms over 6 hectares (17 acres). Lovely features include a rose garden, aquatic plants, and Acadian dike land. A thatched Acadian cottage is a special treat as it shows life before the 1755 deportation. The garden is open May to Oct, with spring blossoms and fall foliage in the shoulder seasons.

Fort Anne National Historic Site, also on St. George Street, sits on watch over the river. Three blocky white chimneys and steep grassy slopes give away its position. Fort Anne was Canada's first national historic site and the scene of much upheaval as groups struggled for control of the region. For more historic exploration, stop in at the **O'Dell House Museum,** 136 St. George St., and the **Sinclair Inn Museum,** 230 St. George St.

Before traveling west on the scenic drive along the Annapolis Basin, take a detour to the river causeway—a bridge to the North Mountain side. On the causeway, the Annapolis Tidal Generating Station turns the energy of the Fundy tides into electricity. Turn left on Granville Road to visit **Melanson Settlement National Historic Site,** the location of an Acadian settlement prior to deportation. Only a few mounds and depressions remain in sight to show where Charles Melanson dit La Ramée settled in 1664.

Continue along the coast to **Port Royal National Historic Site.** The site reconstructs Samuel de Champlain's original 1605 fur-trading post, and costumed actors bring the historical figures to life. The site also revives Canada's first social club—the Society of Good Cheer.

Cross the Annapolis River causeway back to Annapolis Royal, following Highway 1 west along the coast. Amid rolling forested hills, find **Upper Clements Parks**—one of the few places to ride a roller coaster or zipline in the province.

Although HMCS/CFB Cornwallis closed in 1994, Cornwallis Park still has the look of a military base with barracks-style housing. The **Cornwallis Military Museum** at 726 Broadway recalls that this was the British Commonwealth's largest naval training base when it opened in 1942 during World War II.

About 4 kilometers (2.5 miles) after Cornwallis Park, join Highway 101 as it bridges Bear River, then follow signs to Digby at exit 26.

Digby

Route 303 connects the controlled-access highway to the **Digby** town center. Scallop dinners and wharf cats define the waterfront district of this slightly rough-edged community. Walk down to the fishing wharf where the scallop boats are moored. The **Admiral Digby Museum** at 95 Montague St. focuses on the region's fishing history as well as the Loyalists.

Digby Scallop Days celebrates the famous local seafood in August, while thousands of motorcycles gather for the Wharf Rat Rally over Labour Day weekend.

The **MV Princess of Acadia** departs Digby making one or two trips daily to Saint John, New Brunswick. Before continuing on the drive, head north of town past **Digby Pines Resort** to admire the view from **Annapolis Basin Look-off Provincial Park** on Shore Road.

Over a 70-kilometer (44-mile) stretch of the Digby Neck and Islands Scenic Drive, follow Route 217 west across islands connected by ferries. Mostly forested but with the feel of the sea close by, the drive arrives in ever-smaller communities. Pass through Seabrook, then Centreville. At **Sandy Cove** see what the ocean has washed ashore on the sheltered beach. Near **Little River,** a wind turbine rises above the forest landscape.

About 45 kilometers (28 miles) from Digby, the road switchbacks down to wharves and a ferry dock. Gulls circle above the shore. Cross Petite Passage by ferry from East Ferry to Tiverton. Ferries generally depart on the half hour, and at press time the fare was $5 per crossing, with no return fee collected.

The 5-minute ferry ride provides a quick opportunity to take in the coastal scenery. At **Tiverton,** disembark and drive 6 kilometers (3.7 miles) to **Central Grove. Central Grove Provincial Park** provides a basic picnic spot, but the highlight of Long Island is the **Balancing Rock** on the opposite side of the road. A 1.5-kilometer (0.9-mile) hike through marshland and forest leads to a staircase and viewing platform. Admire the basalt-rock coastline and the seemingly set-in-place Balancing Rock.

Drive along Route 217 to Freeport, where the second ferry runs on the hour to Westport on Brier Island.

Brier Island

A second ferry connects Long Island to **Brier Island.** The fare is again $5, and the journey takes about 10 minutes.

Basalt rock, seabirds, and a lighthouse form a picturesque complement off Brier Island, Nova Scotia.

Sign the guestbook at Grand Passage Lighthouse on Brier Island, Nova Scotia.

Turn left off the ferry to follow Water Street around to **South Point.** A small park pays tribute to **Joshua Slocum,** who lived on Brier Island as a boy and was the first man to solo circumnavigate the world in his boat the *Spray.* Slocum wrote *Sailing Alone Around the World* about the experience. Today, the **Joshua Slocum Monument** stands next to a small park area. Hike over a rocky, fireweed-covered bluff to view the basalt coastline. Binoculars are handy to observe the birds out on Peter Island in Grand Passage.

Whale-watching cruises leave from Brier Island to observe the huge marine mammals that feed offshore. Local species that visit the Bay of Fundy during summer include minkes, finbacks, humpbacks, and endangered right whales. The latter also mate in the Bay of Fundy.

Drive north on Water Street from the Slocum Monument, passing the ferry dock. Follow the gravel road to its end at **Grand Passage Lighthouse.** A guest book there makes a fun place to record your observations—be it about seabirds, whales, or fishing boats.

The Grand Passage Lighthouse is also the island's newest, having been built in 1901. The light on Lighthouse Road was built in 1809, and the Peter Island light in Grand Passage was constructed in 1850.

Side Trip: Kejimkujik National Park

A starkly different ecosystem inland near Maitland Bridge, **Kejimkujik National Park** protects a forest and network of lakes in the heart of Nova Scotia. The park is a cultural site for the Mi'kmaq people with petroglyphs and traditional camps that pay testament to their long history in the area.

Hike forest trails, swim off the beaches, and watch for loons and other bird life. The park rents canoes and kayaks at **Jakes Landing.** More than 300 campsites are located at **Jeremys Bay campground,** but those paddling a canoe can access many more backcountry sites, including some situated on lake islands and riverbanks.

12

LaHave River

Lunenburg to LaHave to Rissers Beach

General Description: Along the banks of the LaHave River and out to Nova Scotia's loveliest beaches, this 70-kilometer (44-mile) scenic route combines history with a river crossing and coastal scenery. Travel on a cable ferry before eating lunch at a local bakery. Visit Mi'kmaq wigwams, a mission cemetery, and lighthouse at Fort Point Museum, or walk beaches and a boardwalk at Rissers Beach Provincial Park.

Special Features: Halifax & Southwestern Railway Museum, Masons Beach, the Ovens Natural Park, Hirtles Beach, LaHave River cable ferry, Fort Point Museum, Crescent Beach, LaHave Islands Marine Museum, Bush Island, Rissers Beach Provincial Park, Green Bay.

Location: Southwestern Nova Scotia, Lunenburg County.

Driving Route Numbers & Names: Highway 3, Route 332, LaHave River cable ferry, Route 331, Crescent Beach Road.

Travel Season: In the summer, hit the beaches—Hirtles, Crescent, and Rissers on this route—to enjoy the warmest swimming. The shoulder seasons, June and September, are particularly lovely on Nova Scotia's South Shore.

Camping: Camp at Rissers Beach Provincial Park, where 90 sites offer options for RVs and tents. Showers, washrooms, a canteen, and a playground add comfort to the camping experience.

Services: Lunenburg, at the start of this drive, and Bridgewater, which lies inland along the LaHave River, both offer a good selection of services. Groceries, gas, and medical attention are available in both towns. Lunenburg offers superb heritage bed-and-breakfasts amongst the hilly streets, but on busy festival weekends, motels and inns in Bridgewater will likely have greater availability.

Nearby Points of Interest: DesBrisay Museum, Wile Carding Mill Museum, Miller Point Peace Park, Petite Riviere Vineyards.

Time Zone: Atlantic time zone (GMT minus 4 hours).

The Drive

Over 70 kilometers (44 miles), this coastal and riverbank drive visits some of the province's loveliest beaches. Find perfect crescents of sand near coastal hikes, island museums, and provincial campgrounds.

Begin the drive in **Lunenburg,** where diverse museums and heritage accommodations (covered in Drive 13 on the Lighthouse Route) line the hilly streets. West of downtown Lunenburg, drive along Falkland Street and then Victoria Street as Highway 3 leads inland toward Bridgewater.

You'll pass the **Halifax & Southwestern Railway Museum** on Victoria Street (Highway 3), which recalls the long-past days of steam engines in the area. An

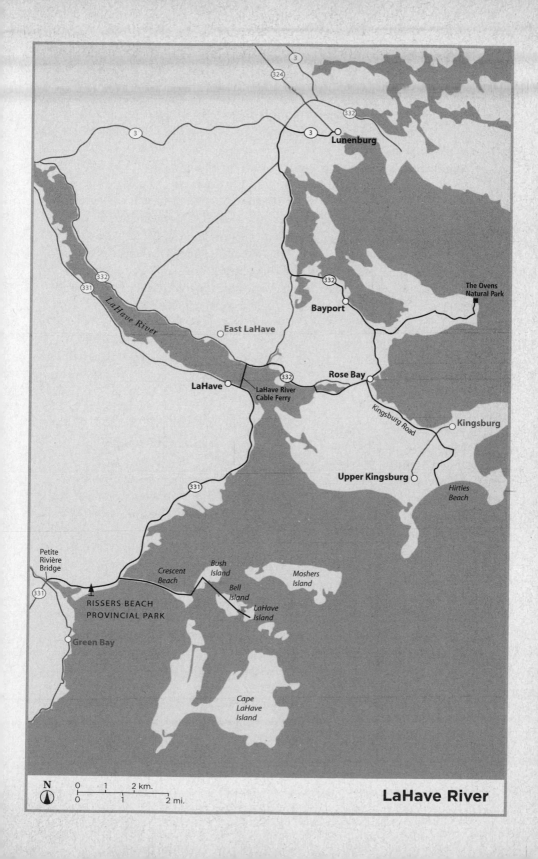

3

324

3

332

Lunenburg

3

331

332

LaHave River

East LaHave

332

Bayport

The Ovens
Natural Park

LaHave

LaHave River
Cable Ferry

332

Rose Bay

Kingsburg Road

Kingsburg

Upper Kingsburg

Hirtles
Beach

331

Petite
Rivière
Bridge

Crescent
Beach

Bush
Island

Moshers
Island

331

Bell
Island

LaHave
Island

RISSERS BEACH
PROVINCIAL PARK

Green Bay

Cape
LaHave
Island

N

0   1   2 km.

0   1   2 mi.

LaHave River

intensely detailed scale model shows the route of the train, with buildings recreating the Lunenburg waterfront and Bridgewater rail yard. The tracks torn up, railway beds around the province have now been converted to a trail system.

At the junction with Route 332, turn left toward Bayport.

Route 332 follows the water through First South, where a left turn leads to the sheltered **Masons Beach.**

Pass through Bayport on the shore of Lower South Cove. About 12 kilometers (7.5 miles) from Lunenburg, turn left to follow Feltzen South Road out onto the hooked peninsula. Take a right on Ovens Road to find the 77-hectare (190-acre) **Ovens National Park** where gold panners once swirled the sand looking for flakes and nuggets. The Nova Scotia gold rush started in 1861, and the frenzy grew enough to sustain a local community of more than 1,000 miners. You can still pan for gold on Cunards Beach and hike coastal trails. The park's namesakes, the Ovens sea caves, are perhaps the most dramatic attraction: Descend a boardwalk to hear the waves boom in Cannon Cave. Boat tours are another way to view the sea caves at the park, which also boasts a campground and cabins.

Over a 2-kilometer (1.2-mile) less-coastal stretch on Route 332, the road heads toward Rose Bay, where it branches left to Upper Kingsburg and right to East LaHave.

Rose Bay

Turn left toward Kingsburg and follow the road down to **Hirtles Beach.** With about 3 kilometers (2 miles) of tide-washed sand on Hartling Bay, the beach is popular for dog walking, surfing, picnicking, and beachcombing. Out to the west (right when looking offshore), the protected Gaff Point offers an excellent 6.5-kilometer (4-mile) hike to hidden coves. View the remote and wave-washed **West Ironbound Island** that sits off the point.

Follow Kingsburg Road back to Route 332 where the lesser-known **Sand Dollar Beach** on Rose Bay is far more sheltered. Exposed only at low tide, the sandbar offers the delight of collecting sand dollars. Live sand dollars are brown, while the dead ones (and the ones okay to collect) are white.

Head west on Route 332 toward the LaHave cable ferry. The ferry crosses the mouth of the LaHave River, connecting East LaHave and Riverport with LaHave on the far shore. The 10–15 minute crossing costs $5, or less if purchasing tickets by the book. Fishing boats, wharves, and heritage commercial buildings edge the river.

To bypass the ferry, or if it's not running, follow Route 332 for 18 kilometers (11 miles) up the river to the bridge crossings in Bridgewater. You'll pass the

Walkers stroll through the tidal zone on Hirtles Beach, Nova Scotia.

wooded trails and a geocaching treasure hunt at **Miller Point Peace Park** on the way.

LaHave

Docking in **LaHave,** stop in at the **LaHave Bakery** in the heritage LaHave Outfitters building. Treats and breads stock the shelves, while a small cafe serves simple lunch fare. My favorite? The fresh herb-and-cheese rolls.

Less than a kilometer past the ferry dock, watch for Fort Point Road on the left. Make the left turn, and continue out on the point to visit **Fort Point Museum and Lighthouse,** the place Lieutenant General Isaac de Razilly settled as the first capital of New France in 1632. The fort was abandoned in 1636 when de Razilly died, but the story survives through the lighthouse and museum. To protect itself, the fort had 25 cannons. Capuchin monks established a chapel and mission here. Outside, a cemetery and garden offer more to explore.

Above all, look out to the river from the museum. Since the 1600s this point has eroded, and the original location of Fort Sainte Marie de Grace is out in the low-tide zone.

Long before de Razilly's arrival, however, the Mi'kmaq people lived along the LaHave, Nova Scotia's largest river. Festivities bring Mi'kmaq culture back to this place, and in summer there are canvas Mi'kmaq wigwams erected in the park.

Called Pijenooiskak by the Mi'kmaq, meaning "having long joints," the **LaHave River** was first mapped by Samuel de Champlain in 1604. Champlain moved on to establish a colony first on St. Croix Island (see side trip for Drive 2) and later at Port Royal (see Drive 11). De Razilly's New France settlers started the local lumber industry, clearing land for agriculture near Petite Riviere. As British and other Europeans settled the area in the 1700s, the forests of mature lumber begat sawmills and shipyards.

Today, the LaHave's salmon runs draw anglers to the riverbanks, and many use the river for recreational boating.

Crescent Beach & Bush Island

Follow Route 331 past Bull Cove toward Dublin Shore. You're passing islands and coves tucked in behind the shelter of the LaHave Islands. In fact the spot is so protected it is even called **Snug Harbour.** At Crescent Beach Road, turn left to explore a beach that is also the road to Bush, Bell, and LaHave Islands.

The 2-kilometer (1.2-mile) sand bar of Crescent Beach was once the only route to Bush Island. Now a road connects to the mainland, but cars are still permitted to drive along the compact sand area of the beach. There are access points at both ends of the beach. If you choose that route, drive slowly and watch for pedestrians. My preference, however, is to keep to the road as families picnic on the beach.

Continue over a one-lane bridge to Bush Island, where the **LaHave Islands Marine Museum** at 100 LaHave Islands Rd. shows exhibits in a heritage United Church. Outside, the double-ender *Vera Mae* is a preserved Bush Island boat that was built on adjacent Bell Island.

Rissers Beach

Back on Route 331 from Crescent Beach Road, you'll soon enter **Rissers Beach Provincial Park.** One of the few provincial campgrounds in the area, it quickly fills up in summer with beachgoers. Walk the boardwalk over the marshlands, relax on the sands, and learn about the local wildlife species.

To the west, look out along the Lunenburg County coast to Green Bay. To the east lies the wide, H-shaped Cape LaHave Island with its tiny Green Point.

Inland from Petite Riviere Bridge, Crousetown Road tours past **Petite Riviere Vineyards.** The winery uses local grapes and features an art gallery, reviving a wine-making tradition that the French started with their settlement in the 1600s.

13

Lighthouse Route

Peggy's Cove to Chester to Mahone Bay to Lunenburg

General Description: This is an iconic 195-kilometer (121-mile) coastal drive featuring shipwrecks, lighthouses, and buried treasure. At its full length the Lighthouse Route continues south to Yarmouth. But this first stretch from Halifax to Lunenburg holds the weightiest treasures. Watch the ocean spray at Peggy's Cove, take the ferry to Tancook Island, reach into a touch tank at the Lunenburg Fishermen's Museum, or sail on the *Bluenose II*.

Special Features: SS *Atlantic* Memorial, Peggy's Cove Lighthouse, William E. deGarthe Memorial, Swissair Memorial, Bayswater Beach, Graves Island Provincial Park, Chester Playhouse, Oak Island, Mahone Bay Settlers Museum, Amos Pewter, Second Peninsula Provincial Park, Lunenburg Academy, *Bluenose II*, Fisheries Museum of the Atlantic, Knaut-Rhuland House Museum, St. John's Church.

Location: Southwest Nova Scotia, from the Halifax Regional Municipality to Lunenburg County.

Driving Route Numbers & Names: Route 333, Terence Bay Road, Highway 3, Route 329.

Travel Season: Summer festivals draw many to Mahone Bay and Lunenburg, and the sunny weather attracts all to the beaches and coast. But this drive can be completed close to year-round, save in bad winter conditions. September is a particularly lovely month to visit the South Shore, when the attractions and restaurants are still open but crowds have lessened.

Camping: Graves Island Provincial Park, mid route near Chester, offers waterside camping with full services for tents and RVs. Private campgrounds in Lunenburg and Martins River offer additional options. Rissers Beach Provincial Park is featured in Drive 12 and lies about 24 kilometers (15 miles) from Lunenburg via the LaHave River cable ferry.

Services: Halifax, near the start of the drive, offers the greatest array of services (including medical). Find a hospital in Lunenburg. You'll locate gas stations along the route in Chester, Mahone Bay, and Lunenburg, towns that also tempt with heritage inns and homey bed-and-breakfasts. Call a few and book based on the friendliness of the host.

Nearby Points of Interest: Tancook Island, Ross Farm Museum, as well as attractions on Drive 12 along the LaHave River.

Time Zone: Atlantic time zone (GMT minus 4 hours).

The Drive

Trace the Nova Scotia coastline with a drive to shipwrecks, lighthouses, and islands. The road meanders around hidden coves, past fishing wharves, and into friendly small towns.

Begin this 195-kilometer (121-mile) scenic drive at exit 2 on Highway 103. Or, follow Highway 3 west from Halifax and head toward the coast on Route 333.

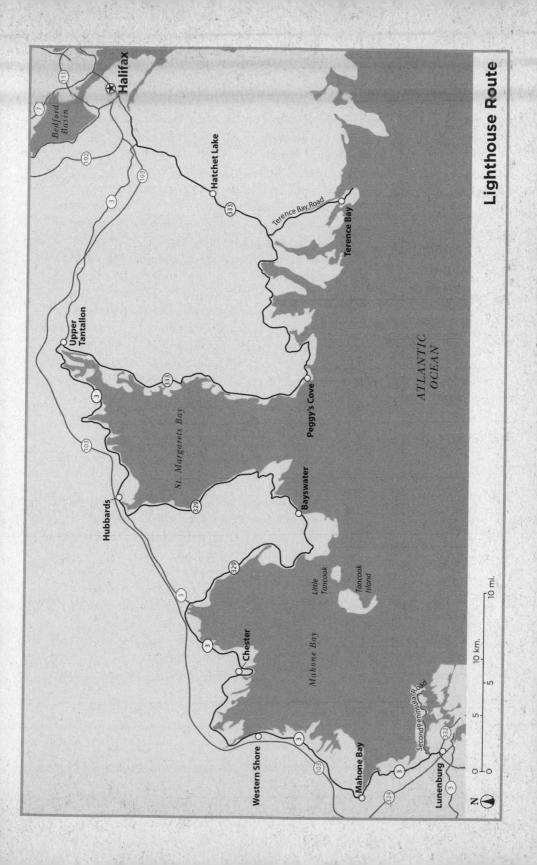

Lighthouse Route

The first stretch of the drive passes through unscenic commercial and residential buildings. But think instead about the area's fishing schooners, shipwrecks, and seafaring history—about the perseverance needed to live on the coast.

At Terence Bay Road in **Whites Lake,** turn left and follow the route for about 8 kilometers (5 miles). Turn left to Sandy Bay (right goes to Lower Prospect) and follow signs for the **SS _Atlantic_ Memorial** at 180 Sandy Cove Rd. Instead of sandy beaches, this coastline is edged with granite shores. The fairly flat but uneven landscape is pitted with boulders left by the last ice age. Lobster traps, fishing wharves, and docked boats show the local heritage.

On April 1, 1873, a storm battered the SS _Atlantic,_ a White Star Line ship, as it headed to Halifax to refuel for its crossing from New York to Liverpool. The ship, carrying 954 people, smashed against Mars Rock. In the largest shipwreck before the _Titanic,_ 562 people died. Of those, 277 are buried at the memorial site.

Walk the pretty trail down to the shoreline memorial. A seawall protects a mass grave from the ocean's force, while a boardwalk leads to the community cemetery. An interpretive site records the details of the shipwreck, including a report from the captain, James A. Williams. Nearby, the old foundation of St. Paul's Church, which was struck by lightning and burnt down in 1942, lies near the new church.

This reflective note of the day will continue, as Route 333 heads toward an airplane crash memorial and a fishermen's memorial.

Peggy's Cove

Past Blind Bay, the landscape empties. **Peggy's Cove Preservation Area** treasures both the icons and the environment of the Chebucto Peninsula. Scant trees are rooted in this boulder-dotted landscape. The verdant green contrasts the fog-gray granite with its vitality.

Make a left turn at Peggy's Point Road and drive through the active fishing village, clustered with shingled buildings and wharves. Red-and-white **Peggy's Cove Lighthouse** sits at the far end of the road, cemented firmly to its granite bluff. Park at the interpretive center and then explore the village on foot.

Cafes and restaurants will be busy with tourists, perhaps escaping the chill of the Atlantic fog.

The **William E. deGarthe Memorial Monument** on Peggy's Point Road is a 30-meter (19-mile) granite sculpture and fishermen's monument. Chiseled into the outcropping behind the artist's house, the granite features 32 fishermen, their families, and Saint Elmo, the patron saint of sailors.

The trip out to Peggy's Cove is a popular route for tour buses—try not to get stuck behind one when leaving.

Return to Route 333 and follow the road to the quiet vantage of the **Swissair Memorial Site** at Whalesback. On September 2, 1998, local fishermen and emergency workers helped with rescue and then recovery efforts after Swissair Flight 111 crashed off the Nova Scotia coast. There were no survivors; 229 people died.

Driving toward the head of **St. Margarets Bay,** for which Peggy's Cove Lighthouse marks the entrance, look out for sail boats in the Atlantic waters and craft galleries along the shore. The homes along this stretch show more heritage style than previous sections of Route 333. Islands parallel the coast as the route passes timber fishing wharves and leaning boatsheds to reconnect with Highway 3 in Upper Tantallon. Here, turn left on Highway 3 to travel west toward Hubbards and Chester.

Through to Hubbards the coastline is defined by almost-white-sand beaches—first **Black Point Beach,** then **Cleveland Beach** and **Queensland Beach.** With such sparkling sand, all are summer favorites. In the pretty village of **Hubbards,** find the **Shore Club,** which is renowned for its lobster dinners.

Just past the village, turn left on Route 329 out to Fox Point and the **Aspotogan Peninsula.** The rocky point separates St. Margarets and Mahone Bays.

While this 40-kilometer (25-mile) coastal detour lacks definitive attractions, the docked boats and fishing nets drying alongside the road create an authentic scene. Watch for hand-painted signs advertising smoked mackerel or Solomon Gundy—a local specialty of pickled herring and onion—which might be available for sale at local homes.

Near the tip of the peninsula, you'll find **Bayswater Beach Provincial Park** at 404 Rte. 329 to be emptier than most along the South Shore. But as the internment site of the Swissair disaster victims, the park also strikes a somber note.

From Bayswater, the road cuts along more sheltered waters for 4 kilometers (2.5 miles) to Blandford. In the core of the peninsula, the **Blandford Nature Reserve** was set aside by millionaire Cyrus Eaton to foster the birding area around Hollahan Lake. Formerly a game sanctuary, it is now fully protected.

Chester

At East River, the drive rejoins Highway 3 to pass the large family campground at **Graves Island Provincial Park.**

Make a left turn on Duke Street to visit the **village of Chester.** At the Front Harbour, turn onto Water Street and drive into the heart of the New England–style village. The Cape Cod feel comes from the Massachusetts settlers who arrived in this area during the 1750s.

Today, yacht races and seafood restaurants have turned the charming village into a refined destination. Bakeries and coffee shops complement the pretty waterfront. The **Chester Playhouse** hosts a lively summer season of theater. **Chester**

Race Week runs the third week of August, filling Mahone Bay with spinnakers and sails.

For a day trip, drive past the yacht club to the end of Peninsula Road, taking the daily Tancook Island ferry out to the year-round island community. Summer savory crops and the herring fishery provide a livelihood. Just off the coast of Tancook is **East Ironbound,** the island that inspired the 1928 Frank Parker Day novel *Rockbound.*

Lookout to the islands as the route follows the coast of Mahone Bay through Western Shore. In the small fishing community, **Wild Rose Park** provides bathrooms and a convenient picnic area. You'll also pass **Oak Island,** where tales of treasure abound.

Since 1795, excavations to recover the **Oak Island treasure** have occupied many a mind and led to the death of six men. It began when three teenage boys discovered a depression in the ground beneath a tree. Curious, they dug into the earth and hit flagstones and layers of logs. But no treasure. A second excavation of the present "Money Pit" uncovered layers of coconut fibers as well as charcoal and putty. Subsequent digs were hampered by the accidental deaths of six men, pit flooding, and dwindling funds. Franklin Roosevelt was even involved in a 1909 excavation.

Theories on the island's treasure range from the works of Shakespeare to the crown jewels of France, and of course pirate booty. Whatever it is—or isn't—Oak Island makes for a great tale.

Although the island is currently privately owned, the Friends of Oak Island Society have organized walking tours around the treasure island in recent years.

Mahone Bay & Lunenburg

Look out to the ocean where dozens of islands create a picturesque scene as you drive along Highway 3 toward Mahone Bay.

Views of the **Three Churches** greet you in **Mahone Bay.** Take photos across from the **Inlet Café** or venture down Oakland Road for water-framed views. For local information, stop in at the visitor center on the main road at 165 Edgewater St.

Come to a full stop at the three-way intersection that is a bit of a nightmare for unfamiliar drivers (tip: go slowly; generally the alternating rule applies when crossing the other lane of traffic), and turn left toward Lunenburg.

Mahone Bay's Main Street is lined with vividly painted shops and galleries, the brightest of which is **Amos Pewter** at 880 Main St. The nearby **Mahone Bay Settlers Museum,** at 578 Main St., tells of the area's European settlement in 1754, although the Mi'kmaq fished and summered on the coast here long before.

Once known for its wooden boat festival (a version of which, the Classic Boat Festival, still runs in summer), it's now the autumn **Scarecrow Festival** that

The famous three churches of Mahone Bay, Nova Scotia, edge the town's waterfront.

draws the largest crows to see carved pumpkins and scarecrows decorating the town. Mahone Bay also hosts the winter Father Christmas Festival.

At Maders Cove, Highway 3 cuts inland toward UNESCO World Heritage Site Lunenburg. Along the way, detour to the delightfully serene **Second Peninsula Provincial Park** along Second Peninsula Road. Trails and picnic tables trim a sheltered day-park.

About 9 kilometers (5.6 miles) from Mahone Bay on Highway 3, signs at a T-junction direct you left toward **Lunenburg.**

Make the turn, then either turn immediately right onto Maple Avenue, which becomes Dufferin Street and heads directly into downtown, or continue straight to see the best views of **Lunenburg Academy** at 97 Kaulback St, If choosing the latter route, you'll arrive in Lunenburg via the back harbor—taking Kissing Bridge Road then Cornwallis Street down to the central Pelham Street.

On a well-scheduled or lucky visit, Bluenose Drive will deliver its namesake, the **Bluenose II.** A replica of the famed fishing schooner sailed by Captain Angus Walters, the *Bluenose II* gives harbor tours when it is in its home berth, **although the ship is scheduled to be off the water for a refit until 2012.** The original sailing schooner plied the waters from 1921 to 1946 and is now featured on the Canadian dime (10 cent coin).

Also on the waterfront, the **Fisheries Museum of the Atlantic** at 68 Bluenose Dr. engages with a touch tank, moored vessels, and other activities.

Stroll the Lunenburg waterfront, past the bright red Adams & Knickle Building and dory-building shops to see men packing trucks with ice or a boat securing its mooring. The colorful heritage buildings lie in theater-like rows up from the waterfront. Walk uphill to discover seafood restaurants and historic properties including the **Knaut-Rhuland House Museum** at 125 Pelham St. and **St. John's Church** at 81 Cumberland St. The church is Canada's second oldest Anglican church and has been mostly rebuilt following a destructive 2001 fire. Volunteers are often on hand in summer to give tours.

The **Lunenburg Folk Harbour Festival** is a favorite for its musical entertainment and dozens of performers. Another delightful event with a strong following is the **Nova Scotia Folk Art Festival,** where vibrant folk art by local artists is on display and for sale.

Check in to a heritage inn or comfortable bed-and-breakfast before sampling best-in-the-province fare at the buttercup-yellow **Fleur de Sel** at 53 Montague St. Or choose a lobster from one of the many live tanks at the local seafood restaurants.

When in her homeport of Lunenburg, Nova Scotia, the Bluenose II *takes visitors on tours of the harbor.*

14

Day Trip Beaches from Halifax

Dartmouth to Lawrencetown Beach to Martinique Beach

General Description: From views of downtown Halifax to a panorama of vast sandy beaches, this 96-kilometer (60-mile) scenic drive makes an outdoorsy day-trip escape from the Nova Scotia capital. Marshland boardwalks, surfable waves, and bike trails let you engage with the environment. Acadians, train conductors, Quakers, and fishermen all give a different perspective of the local history.

Special Features: Evergreen House and Quaker House, both run by Dartmouth Heritage Museum; McNabs and Lawlor Islands Provincial Park; Shearwater Aviation Museum; Fisherman's Cove; Rainbow Haven Beach Provincial Park; Shearwater Flyer, Salt Marsh, and Atlantic View trails; Cole Harbour Heritage Farm Museum; Cole Harbour-Lawrencetown Coastal Heritage Park System; Lawrencetown Beach Provincial Park; Porters Lake Provincial Park; Acadian House Museum; Musquodoboit Railway Museum; Martinique Beach Provincial Park.

Location: North of Halifax, along the eastern shore.

Driving Route Numbers & Names: Route 7, Alderney Drive, Route 322, Cow Bay Road, Bissett Road, Route 207, Highway 7, East Petpeswick Road.

Travel Season: These beaches are sensational year-round. In winter, you'll have the place to yourself to beachcomb, but most museums will be closed. Easily enjoy the trails from May through October, but the best beach weather is in July and August. The fall and winter swells bring surfers to these shores—you'll need a wetsuit to spend time in the saltwater.

Camping: Camp at Porters Lake Provincial Park, about 7 kilometers (4.4 miles) from Lawrencetown Beach along Crowell Road. The park has 80 campsites for tents and RVs, some lakeside. The picnic area and boat launches are also popular as a day trip.

Services: Halifax and Dartmouth, separate communities but both within the Halifax Regional Municipality, have a full complement of services. From shopping to gas stations to hospitals, the cities lack no comforts. Halifax and Dartmouth also offer dozens of accommodation options in heritage properties, motels, and full-service hotels. Heading along the drive, you'll find bed-and-breakfasts tucked in the sheltered harbors of fishing communities.

Nearby Points of Interest: Old Hall Wilderness Heritage Centre, Hope for Wildlife, Fisherman's Life Museum, J. Willy Krauch & Sons Smoked Salmon; in Halifax: Maritime Museum of the Atlantic, Pier 21 Museum, Art Gallery of Nova Scotia, Halifax Public Gardens, Point Pleasant Park, Halifax Citadel National Historic Site, Alexander Keith's Brewery.

Time Zone: Atlantic time zone (GMT minus 4 hours).

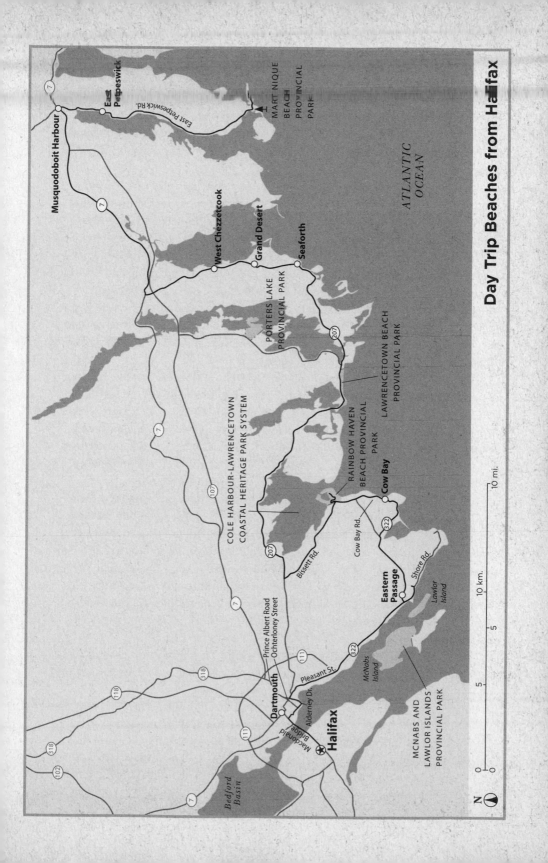

Day Trip Beaches from Halifax

N

ATLANTIC OCEAN

7 · Musquodoboit Harbour

East Petpeswick

East Petpeswick Rd.

MART NIQUE BEACH PROVINCIAL PARK

7

West Chezzetcook

Grand Desert

Seaforth

PORTERS LAKE PROVINCIAL PARK

207

107

COLE HARBOUR-LAWRENCETOWN COASTAL HERITAGE PARK SYSTEM

LAWRENCETOWN BEACH PROVINCIAL PARK

RAINBOW HAVEN BEACH PROVINCIAL PARK

Cow Bay

Cow Bay Rd.

322

Bissett Rd.

207

Eastern Passage

Shore Rd.

Lawlor Island

Prince Albert Road
Ochterloney Street

111

Pleasant St.

Alderney Dr.

322

McNabs Island

MCNABS AND LAWLOR ISLANDS PROVINCIAL PARK

318

118

Dartmouth

Macdonald Bridge

111

Halifax

Bedford Basin

7

102

318

0   5   10 km.

0   5   10 mi.

The Drive

This 96-kilometer (60-mile) coastal scenic drive escapes the city to enjoy Nova Scotia's longest beach, surfing breaks, and salt-marsh trails. **Dartmouth**—for years overlooked by tourists—offers history and worthwhile vantages of the Halifax skyline and island parks. Three world-class beaches put a little sand in your driving shoes.

Cross to Dartmouth from Halifax on the Macdonald Bridge (toll 75 cents). Make an immediate right onto Wyse Road and drive to a T-junction with Windmill Road. Turn left at the lights. Just down the hill Windmill Road becomes Alderney Drive, or Highway 7.

Heritage homes in this across-the-harbor city sit in the sling of Alderney Drive. **Alderney Landing** is the city hub, with a waterfront boardwalk and panoramic view of the Halifax skyline. It's also where the Dartmouth–Halifax ferry docks. Branching inland, Ochterloney Street is the main route up from the waterfront, passing the **Quaker House Museum,** a 1785 home originally belonging to Quaker whalers from Nantucket. Farther north on Prince Albert Street lies **Lake Banook,** ever busy with canoeists and kayakers.

Backtrack down Ochterloney to Alderney Drive and continue along the waterfront to Pleasant Street. Make a right on Pleasant to follow Route 322 east.

While still close to downtown, turn right at Albert Street and venture a block closer to the waterfront to learn more about the city's history at the **Evergreen House Museum,** 26 Newcastle St. The blue house was home to Helen Creighton, the celebrated folklorist who recorded many of the province's traditional songs and tales, including the sad and rousing "Farewell to Nova Scotia."

Follow Pleasant Street, Route 322, as it heads southeast through the industrial side of town. At the junction with Highway 111 continue straight toward the community of Eastern Passage. The hospital, Canadian Forces Base Shearwater, and refinery towers have caused some folks to conjure unflattering impressions of this side of the harbor. **Shearwater Aviation Museum** at 34 Bonaventure St. displays aircraft and flight exhibits at its airbase location. The Nova Scotia International Air Show is a grand annual event in the province and is intermittently held at Shearwater. Flybys of heritage aircraft and fighter jets draw large crowds.

From Route 322 look right to **Georges Island,** best known for views of its lighthouse (visible from the Halifax side). On the small bare island, **Fort Charlotte** was a prison for expelled Acadians and a strategic World War II position. A national historic site is slowly being developed to open to the public.

Other islands in the harbor include the large, treed **McNabs Island** with its Mi'kmaq shell middens, **Fort McNab,** abandoned summer homes, a lighthouse, and 22 kilometers (14 miles) of hiking trails. The smaller **Lawlor Island** sits closer to the shore. Both islands are part of the **McNabs and Lawlor Islands Provincial**

Park and can be visited on a day trip from Halifax or Eastern Passage. Check in with Friends of McNabs Island (www.mcnabsisland.ca) for recommendations on local boat operators.

As Route 322 bears inland to the left, continue along the waterfront on Shore Road. **Fisherman's Cove,** 30 Government Wharf Rd., in Eastern Passage maintains its bustle as a working waterfront. Boats tied up to the government wharf and ocean-inspired galleries provide a prettified feel of the Atlantic.

To continue the scenic drive, backtrack to Route 322 and turn right to continue east (the route is also labeled as Marine Drive and Cow Bay Road).

Rainbow Haven Beach

Marine Drive leads through an unremarkable residential neighborhood for about 5 kilometers (3 miles). As Route 322 and now Dyke Road continue straight, turn right onto Cow Bay Road. The road follows the coast out to Osborne Head and then curves around into the shelter of **Cole Harbour.**

Stop in at the drive's first beach—**Rainbow Haven Beach Provincial Park,** at 2248 Cow Bay Rd. The sheltered beach sits at the narrow mouth of a large protected area. Rainbow Haven has sandy shores, a canteen, and family activities. Lifeguards supervise a swimming area during summer.

The park exit takes you across a causeway surrounded by saltwater marsh. Watch for herons fishing in the sheltered water on both sides of the causeway.

As you rejoin the pavement, turn right onto Bissett Road to continue on Marine Drive.

On the main route, about 2.5 kilometers (1.5 miles) from Rainbow Haven, you'll pass the trailhead for the **Shearwater Flyer Trail.** Cutting inland from the Canadian Forces Base Shearwater, the gravel pathway connects with the Salt Marsh Trail to cross the cragged bay of the **Cole Harbour–Lawrencetown Coastal Heritage Park System** by islands and trails.

After the provincial railway lines were abandoned in the 1980s, local groups throughout Nova Scotia began transforming the beds into recreational corridors available to walkers, runners, and cyclists. The Shearwater Flyer, Salt Marsh, and Atlantic View trails along this drive all form part of that network.

Lawrencetown Beach

Bissett Road ends at Route 207 in Cole Harbour. Here, turn right on Route 207 to drive along the head of the coastal park toward **Lawrencetown.**

For a family-friendly detour, however, turn left on Route 207 to visit the farm animals and tearoom at **Cole Harbour Heritage Farm Museum.** The demonstration farm is located at 471 Poplar St., off Otago Drive.

Toward Lawrencetown, the road follows a network of sheltered coves and marshy islands where birds feed and take refuge. On West Lawrencetown Road, the Salt Marsh Trail connects with the Atlantic View Trail and leads to **Lawrencetown Beach Provincial Park.**

A sure sign of the beach is the mansard-roofed, hilltop tearoom; there is also a surf shop. Coming down the hill to the beach you'll see the full expanse of sand, although as you descend to sea level the storm walls hide the views. Park and walk over the rock wall to the beach. Here you look out at the Atlantic Ocean. Lawrencetown, like the other main beaches featured in this drive, has bathrooms, changing rooms, and canteens.

In all seasons, surfers ride the waves along the Nova Scotia coast. Particularly as the hurricane and winter swells reach the shores, you'll see surfers out in their neoprene wetsuits, waiting for waves at Cow Bay, Lawrencetown, and Martinique.

To continue the scenic drive after tea or a surf lesson at Lawrencetown Beach, drive east on Route 207. The turnoff at Crowell Road leads to **Porters Lake Provincial Park**—a lakeside park with picnic areas, a boat launch, and campsites.

Pass through Three Fathom Harbour and Seaforth before stopping in the Acadian-heritage village of **Grand Desert,** named for the starkness of the landscape. You'll see Acadian flags posted on driveways and wharf poles.

Although Chezzetcook is a Mi'kmaq name meaning "water flowing rapidly in many channels," West Chezzetcook also has Acadian history. Visit the **Acadian House Museum** at 71 Hill Rd. to learn about the French-speaking history on the shore. The small, shingled house is a museum with hands-on exhibits (more like chores!). A garden, restaurant, and barn fill the small grounds.

Before the Acadian deportation, starting in 1755, the area was sparsely settled. When the Acadians were released from imprisonment on Devils Island, they resettled this area, and locals spoke French here until the 1960s.

Martinique Beach

At the head of island-studded **Chezzetcook Inlet,** 17 kilometers (10.6 miles) from Lawrencetown Beach, Route 207 ends at Highway 7.

Make a right turn on this busy route to Musquodoboit Harbour. Another 9 kilometers (5.6 miles) along Highway 7 and the route becomes Marine Drive through Musquodoboit Harbour.

The big rust-colored **Musquodoboit Railway Museum** stands out on Highway 7. The 1916 station is a well-preserved remnant on the now-decommissioned rail line. Historic cars, a visitor center, and nearby trails all augment the stop.

The Acadian House Museum in West Chezzetcook sees guides completing daily chores in the wooden house, barn, and small garden.

From Musquodoboit Harbour, follow signs for Martinique Beach. Turn right on East Petpeswick Road.

Over 12 kilometers (7.5 miles), the road along **Petpeswick Inlet** passes a yacht club and fishing wharves before arriving at the provincial park.

Known for its clean, near-white sands, **Martinique Beach Provincial Park** is often less crowded than more-accessible Lawrencetown. Measuring 5 kilometers (3 miles) from end-to-end Martinique is the longest beach in the province—a sure guarantee there'll be room for your beach blanket. Trails, a canteen, and washrooms provide the necessities for a day trip. For camping, head inland from Musquodoboit Harbour to off-the-main-trail **Dollar Lake Provincial Park.**

Side Trip: Halifax

Nova Scotia's largest city makes a top destination for shopping, dining, theater, music, and galleries. Located at the start of this drive over the Macdonald and MacKay Bridges, **Halifax** has a dense downtown, making it easy to walk the historic streets on foot.

Along the waterfront, docked ships are open as exhibits. The **Maritime Museum of the Atlantic** on Lower Water Street gives perspectives on the *Titanic* sinking in 1912 and the catastrophic Halifax Explosion, which killed 2,000 in 1917. Shipbuilding, fishing, and other local sea industries are explored. At **Pier 21 Museum,** in the newly developed Halifax Seaport district, the concrete architecture of the historic location adds a starkness to the poignant stories of immigrants arriving in Canada and young men going off to war.

The **Art Gallery of Nova Scotia** at 1741 Hollis St. features a permanent exhibit of work by Nova Scotia folk artist Maud Lewis, and even has her colorfully painted, garden-shed-size house on display.

The **Halifax Public Gardens** and **Point Pleasant Park** are two outstanding green spaces. The first is a manicured park of duck ponds and flower borders; the latter, a walking trail maze to gun batteries, historic towers, and ocean views.

Above the city, you'll often catch glimpses (and sounds) of the **Halifax Citadel National Historic Site,** with its protective stone walls, town clock, and cannons readying to fire a salute. Costumed interpretive guides tamp the gunpowder, play the bagpipes, and revive fort life.

Dining and accommodation options in Halifax are the most varied in the province. Dine on sushi and stay in a hostel, feast on seafood and bunk at a bed-and-breakfast, or pair local wine with a steak and stay in a waterfront hotel. On weekend evenings live music and locally brewed beers—including India Pale Ale from **Alexander Keith's Brewery**—flow freely.

15

Cape George–
The Little Cabot Trail

Antigonish to Cape George to Sutherlands River

General Description: The shoreline drive around Cape George is a 115-kilometer (71.5-mile) scenic route that's excellent in either direction. Take a rural detour when traveling to or from Cape Breton to visit lighthouses, geologically rich parks, and a tuna-fishing community. Hiking trails and quiet beaches are perfect for independent travelers.

Special Features: Antigonish Heritage Museum, Mahoneys Beach, Cape George Heritage School Museum, hiking trails, Ballantynes Cove Bluefin Tuna Interpretive Centre, Cape George Point Lighthouse, Arisaig Provincial Park, Big Island Beach.

Location: Northern mainland Nova Scotia, on the Northumberland Strait.

Driving Route Numbers & Names: Highway 4, Route 337, Route 245.

Travel Season: Clear weather will mean the best views out to Cape Breton and Prince Edward Island from along the coast and at Cape George Point. Most attractions—the parks, trails, and lighthouses—are outside, making a further case for fine weather. In the Maritimes, June through September offers the best chances of a sunny day.

Museums on the route are open during the summer season.

Camping: Although no provincial camping parks lie directly on the scenic drive, Caribou-Munroes Island Provincial Park lies west of New Glasgow and close to the Prince Edward Island ferry. Private campgrounds in Antigonish provide options for tents and RVs.

Services: Two major centers—New Glasgow and Antigonish—bookend this drive. New Glasgow features more commercial options such as chain hotels, while Antigonish retains a little more of its heritage charm with downtown bed-and-breakfasts and budget accommodations at Governors Hall on the St. Francis Xavier Campus (summer only).

Nearby Points of Interest: Nova Scotia Museum of Industry, Pictou County Sports Heritage Hall of Fame, Carmichael-Stewart House Museum in New Glasgow; Grohmann Knives Factory Tours, Hector Heritage Quay, McCulloch House Museum, Prince Edward Island ferry, Northumberland Fisheries Museum in Pictou.

Time Zone: Atlantic time zone (GMT minus 4 hours).

The Drive

Enjoy a relaxed pace and take the long, coastal route around Cape George Point between Antigonish and New Glasgow. This 115-kilometer (71.5-mile) scenic drive is perfect to tag onto a return trip from Cape Breton, or enjoy it as a summer day trip. Driven in either direction, the itinerary takes about an afternoon to a full day, dependent entirely on the length of stops.

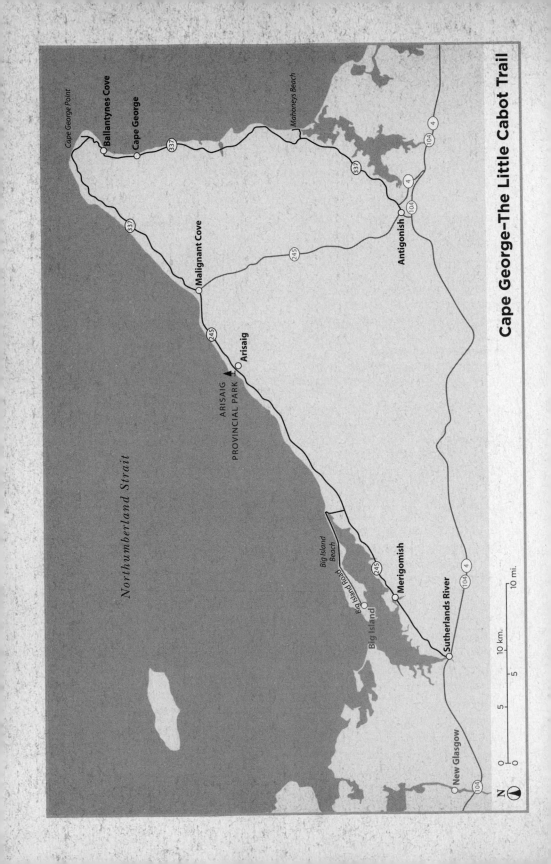

Cape George—The Little Cabot Trail

Cape George Point

Ballantynes Cove

Cape George

337

Mahoneys Beach

4

104

337

337

104

Malignant Cove

Antigonish

245

245

Arisaig

ARISAIG
PROVINCIAL PARK

Northumberland Strait

Big Island Beach

Big Island Road

Merigomish

104

4

Big Island

Sutherlands River

104

New Glasgow

104

N

0   5   10 km.

0   5   10 mi.

With lighthouses, parks, and fishing interpretive centers, there is plenty to explore with the views of Cape Breton and Prince Edward Island on the horizon.

Antigonish

From exit 32 on Highway 104, turn onto West Street toward downtown **Antigonish.** To the right of the street, the campus of **St. Francis Xavier University** features multistory brick buildings on a compact campus. West Street becomes St. Ninian then Main Street, bearing east as part of Highway 4.

At 20 East Main St., the **Antigonish Heritage Museum** displays local history exhibits in a preserved 1908 railway station. Following Main Street east across Rights River, the road becomes Route 337, which takes the coastal path out to Cape George Point.

Beyond Antigonish Route 337 passes through Lanark and Harbour Centre. Side roads lead down to residences on **Antigonish Harbour.** Farmlands of corn and hay show the region's arable land and agricultural history.

At Mahoney Beach Road turn right and follow the road to the shoreline at **Mahoneys Beach.** A broad beach with views of St. Georges Bay contrasts the sheltered Antigonish Harbour, which is nearly cut-off from the ocean by the beach. Look east to Cape Breton's Inverness County. This route out to Cape George is sometimes called the Little Cabot Trail for its coast-and-hills scenery that is similar to the Cabot Trail on Cape Breton Island. Geologically, the regions share the same beginnings.

Cape George Point

Cliffs, coves, farms, and beaches trim the road over the 16 kilometers (10 miles) from Mahoneys Beach to the community of **Cape George.** The **Cape George Heritage School Museum** is a one-room school turned museum. The little white school opened in 1925, and one teacher taught as many as 50 local children here. The museum, with artifacts and information on the local heritage, opens in summer only. The rest of the year, use the school as a base to explore the **Cape George Hiking Trails,** maps of which were available at the community notice board in the parking lot when I visited.

At Ballantynes Cove Wharf Road turn right down to the docked fishing boats and stacked lobster traps. The waterfront **Ballantynes Cove Bluefin Tuna Interpretive Centre** gives a quick perspective on the local fishing industry. From the weathered tuna-fishing "fighting chair" to the dish-bucket retrieved from a tuna's stomach, the center provides an important and concerned perspective about these massive fish. Atlantic bluefin tuna can live to be 20 or more years old and weigh more than 450 kilograms (1,000 pounds). The largest bluefin tuna was caught in

1979 in nearby Aulds Cove, on the Strait of Canso. The giant fished weighed in at 678.5 kilograms (1,496 pounds).

Eroding red cliffs hem in the marina, wharf, and seafood canteen. Above the cove a little roadside lookout savors views of sailboats in St. Georges Bay.

Driving up a hill that may remind you of the Cabot Trail inclines, watch for Lighthouse Road on the right. Make the turn and follow the half-kilometer road to **Cape George Point Lighthouse** at 152 Lighthouse Rd. A parking area and picnic tables are ideal for a lunch stop.

The present towering white lighthouse was built in 1968, the third on this point. The original lighthouse was established in 1861 but was destroyed by fire.

Arisaig Provincial Park

From the lighthouse, follow Route 337 as it rounds Cape George Point and follows the Northumberland Strait coast. At Malignant Cove, where there is a small beach, Route 337 ends and meets Route 245. One branch heads inland through Maryvale and returns to Antigonish, but continue straight on the coastal Route 245.

Just before the provincial park, Arisaig Point Road leads off right to a wharf with a small lighthouse. The lighthouse is a replica of the original, which burned down in the 1930s, and is now the site of a visitor information center.

Arisaig Provincial Park sits on the Northumberland Strait, with faint views of Cape Bear at the eastern end of Prince Edward Island. Interpretive signs provide clues to the ancient geology of the area. Search the shoreline for fossils, which can include snails, trilobites, and clams in the Silurian rock. While much of Cape George dates to the Precambrian (1,400 to 540 million years ago) and Devonian to Early Carboniferous periods (374 to 320 million years ago), a fault separates Arisaig. The park features the red sandstone, similar to that in Chéticamp on the Cabot Trail, which dates to the more recent Late Carboniferous period (320 to 286 million years ago).

Any fossils found are the property of the province, and it is illegal to remove fossils from the beach.

West from Arisaig, land cleared for hay fields, grazing pastures, and summer homes allows great views out to the ocean. Crossing into Pictou County, make a right on Big Island Road.

At a sharp bend left, the rural road parallels perhaps one of Nova Scotia's most gorgeous beaches. Drive over the causeway, and then park at the roadside stopping areas to walk through to enjoy the sands at **Big Island Beach.** The sheltered, lagoon-like **Merigomish Harbour** is a rewarding spot for bird watching. Farms and summer homes lie farther down the road.

Ballantynes Cove, Nova Scotia, is a port for fishermen and has a bluefin tuna interpretive center.

From the junction with Big Island Road, Route 245 continues southwest through Merigomish Harbour and Back Harbour. The route ends at the Trans-Canada at Sutherlands River. Highways 4 and 104 make a short dash to **New Glasgow.** Plan to visit during the summer festivals, such as the **New Glasgow Riverfront Jubilee** or the **Festival of Tartans,** featuring the local Scottish heritage—ranging from kilted golf to caber tossing.

Antigonish, also accessible by the Trans-Canada, celebrates its Celtic heritage with **Antigonish Highland Games,** the oldest event of its kind outside Scotland.

16

The Cabot Trail

Ingonish Beach to Meat Cove to Chéticamp

General Description: The 115-kilometer (71.5-mile) section of the Cabot Trail that climbs and descends through the Cape Breton Highlands National Park is truly dramatic. Cliff-side roads, windswept plateaus, vibrant villages, and moose sightings form the main appeal of this well-traveled route. While many tour the Cabot Trail in a clockwise direction, owing to the larger visitor center at the beginning, and perhaps a nervousness about traveling beside the water, this version puts a counter spin on the trail. You'll see the same stunning views (saving the best for last) and likely enjoy less traffic. Add a 58-kilometer (36-mile) tangent out to isolated Meat Cove to see more incomparable coast.

Special Features: Giant MacAskill Museum, Cape Smokey Provincial Park, Cape Breton Highlands National Park, North Highlands Community Museum, Cabot Landing Provincial Park, Whale Interpretive Centre, Les Trois Pignons: Museum of Hooked Rug and Home Life, Acadian Museum and Restaurant Acadien, hiking, camping, wildlife watching, swimming, beaches.

Location: Northern Cape Breton Island in northern Nova Scotia.

Driving Route Numbers & Names: Cabot Trail, New Haven Road, Bay St. Lawrence Road, Meat Cove Road.

Travel Season: The fall colors of the old-growth sugar maples and other hardwoods make autumn in the Cape Breton Highlands vibrant and spectacular. In summer, camp at various locations throughout the park and enjoy the beaches, swimming, and hiking. The road is twisty, and winter weather can be treacherous. Sections of the Cabot Trail close in the worst weather, particularly the steep climbs at French and Mackenzie Mountains. But winter also brings an opportunity to ski at Cape Smokey or on cross-country trails.

Camping: Throughout Cape Breton Highlands National Park you'll find well-equipped and central campgrounds with hiking trails nearby. Six park campgrounds are spaced along the drive at Ingonish, Broad Cove, Big Intervale, MacIntosh Brook, Corney Brook, and Chéticamp.

Services: As most of this roadway is inside the boundaries of Cape Breton Highlands National Park, take opportunities to fuel up and stock up when possible. Ingonish, Cape North, and Chéticamp all have gas stations. For accommodations, you'll find the iconic Keltic Lodge in Ingonish Beach at the start of the drive. Motels, inns, and a hostel can be found in Pleasant Bay and Chéticamp.

Nearby Points of Interest: Great Hall of the Clans, Joe's Scarecrow Village, Margaree Salmon Museum, Margaree Fish Hatchery, Alexander Graham Bell National Historic Site, Bras d'Or Lakes Interpretive Centre.

Time Zone: Atlantic time zone (GMT minus 4 hours).

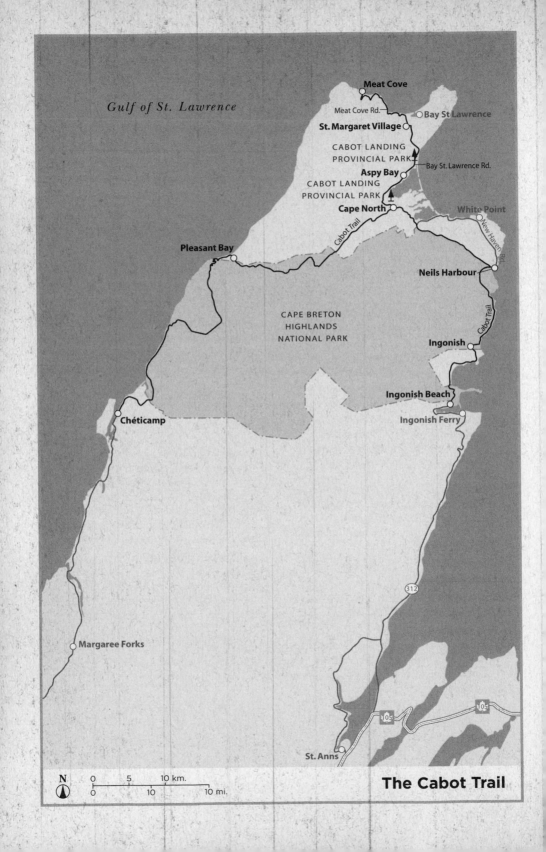

Gulf of St. Lawrence

Meat Cove

Meat Cove Rd.

Bay St Lawrence

St. Margaret Village

CABOT LANDING
PROVINCIAL PARK

Aspy Bay

Bay St. Lawrence Rd.

CABOT LANDING
PROVINCIAL PARK

Cape North

White Point

New Haven Rd.

Cabot Trail

Pleasant Bay

Neils Harbour

CAPE BRETON
HIGHLANDS
NATIONAL PARK

Cabot Trail

Ingonish

Ingonish Beach

Chéticamp

Ingonish Ferry

312

Margaree Forks

105

St. Anns

105

N

0   5   10 km.
0   10   10 mi.

The Cabot Trail

The Drive

At Baddeck the **Cabot Trail** officially begins on Highway 105, along the shores of the Bras d'Or Lakes. Then at South Haven it branches west, along St. Anns Harbour and toward the renowned scenic vistas.

If traveling from Sydney, you'll cross Boularderie Island and Great Bras d'Or on Highway 105, then climb Kellys Mountain where there are two lookouts—the first over the lakes and the second out to St. Anns Harbour.

To start the Cabot Trail, either continue south on Highway 105 to travel through St. Anns, or follow Route 312 and cross the harbor on the Englishtown ferry. If taking the latter route, just before the ferry dock you'll pass the **Giant MacAskill Museum,** dedicated to Angus MacAskill, who measured 2.36 meters (7 feet 9 inches) tall.

The ferry makes a smooth trip across St. Anns Bay to dock at the sand spit of St. Anns Beach, where anglers often stand casting their lines. The long sandy finger nearly pinches St. Anns Harbour closed.

The two routes—via St. Anns or via the Englishtown ferry—meet on the north side of Murray Mountain. Ahead, the mountains build to the left while the water is ever near on the right.

After 30 kilometers (18.6 miles) through forest and rural houses, the road approaches **Smokey Mountain.** Go slowly around the tight turns that elevate you to greater heights. A lookout to the right of the Cabot Trail and **Cape Smokey Provincial Park** thereafter are the first opportunities for real highland views. Although the roadside lookout is convenient, pull in to the provincial park and explore the short rocky trails that descend to the fenced-off cliffs. Take your camera. A longer trail, 11 kilometers (6.8 miles) return, takes advantage of the elevated coastline and snakes out to Cape Smokey's Stanley Point.

Ingonish Beach

The Cabot Trail cuts inland at Cape Smokey and descends to near sea level at Ingonish Ferry. Crossing the Ingonish River, follow the road around South Bay Ingonish, and pass through **Ingonish Beach.** Here you enter the eastern side of **Cape Breton Highlands National Park** and the true start of this scenic drive.

A small visitor center off the main route sells park passes (mandatory for stopping at lookouts, beaches, or trails) and provides details on guided hikes, facilities, and safety. Fuel up here so you can explore side roads without being concerned with running out of gas. Accommodations are nearby, including a national park campground and (tipping the other end of the scale) the golf course, spa, and luxury accommodations at **Keltic Lodge.**

From Ingonish Beach, the Cabot Trail winds 115 kilometers (71.5 miles) through to **Chéticamp** on the western side of the park. It sounds a short distance,

The Cabot Trail winds along the coast of Cape Breton, Nova Scotia.

but consider this: Over those kilometers you'll round hairpin turns, climb and descend hills, picnic on beaches, hike to lookouts, and spot wildlife. Allow one day at a minimum, two or more if you plan on activities such as hiking, whale watching, or swimming. The park boundaries end at residential areas, which they do here as you pass through Ingonish.

Reentering the park, the Cabot Trail quickly unveils its stunning views. The road sits on the edge of the park, looking out over the Atlantic Ocean.

Broad Cove, where there is a park campground, is the first of many inlets, points, and beaches along the shore. The lookouts also begin here, such as the **Little Cape Smokey Lookoff.** Driving counterclockwise around the Cabot Trail makes it easier to pull over and enjoy the mountains-meet-ocean views. Bluffs and coves add beautiful curves to the coast and make for a fun drive.

The **Cape Breton Highlands** formed millions of years ago. The eastern Ingonish side is largely granite, an intrusive igneous rock. But faults through the center of the national park have also created a geological mix dating to the Precambrian, Ordovician to Devonian, and Devonian to Early Carboniferous periods. Only Chéticamp shows the red sandstone of the late Carboniferous period, and is some of the youngest rock at 320 to 286 million years old. The late Carboniferous period also produced the province's major coal deposits in Glace Bay, Stellarton, and Springhill.

It's possible to stop every kilometer or so to admire the scenery from a new vantage. But before spontaneously pulling over, watch for cyclists who are bravely pedaling up the hills.

Moose warning signs persist throughout the park. Although moose were wiped out in Cape Breton by 1924, Parks Canada reintroduced them with 18 animals from Alberta in the late 1940s. The moose refound their footing, and in the 1990s the population in northern Cape Breton reached about 5 animals per square kilometer (about 13 per square mile). Because the moose in Cape Breton descended from the Alberta animals, they are different subspecies from Nova Scotia's mainland moose, which is listed as endangered.

The pretty **Black Brook Beach** makes a good stop for a swim or hike. A coastal trail traces the shore from the beach to **Neils Harbour.** A branch trail circles **Jigging Cove Lake.**

The park boundaries break at **Neils Harbour,** where there are a hospital, gas station, and other services. The next stretch of driving cuts inland before an intense stretch of inclines and declines.

Meat Cove

From Neils Harbour the Cabot Trail crosses fairly flat terrain for 13 kilometers (8 miles) toward South Mountain. To take a coastal detour, follow New Haven Road from Neils Harbour on to White Point. A hiking trail leads out to White Point and around Burnt Head. After 18 kilometers (11 miles) from Neils Harbour, White Point Road reconnects with the Cabot Trail, tracing the coast of Aspy Bay and South Harbour.

At Cape North, take a break at the **North Highlands Community Museum.** Displaying artifacts from the days of the early Highland settlers, the museum tells the story of an independent people. Watch the bellows blast in the forge and walk through the settlers' gardens. Next door the **North Highlands Cultural Centre** occasionally features music, ceilidhs, and lecture-style presentations.

For those looking to explore the side roads, drive approximately 29 kilometers (18 miles) one way out to **Meat Cove on Bay St. Lawrence Road.** Along the route, protected North Harbour sits inside sand bars, islands dot the panorama, and North Mountain looms to the west, like a person sleeping under a sheet.

Along the coast of Aspy Bay, **Cabot Landing Provincial Park** features a quiet beach, picnic sites, and historical markers, including a **bust of John Cabot.** A

Venetian sailor, Cabot crossed the Atlantic in the *Matthew* and landed somewhere on the east coast of Canada on June 24, 1497. He was searching for a route to Asia but instead rooted Britain's claim on North America. The park also commemorates the **Atlantic Cable**—the line that connected Aspy Bay to Port-aux-Basques, Newfoundland, and was part of the first telegraph link with Europe.

At St. Margaret Village the road splits right to Bay St. Lawrence, a departure point for whale-watching tours, and left to Meat Cove. A 13-kilometer (8-mile) dirt road winds up, down, and around to Meat Cove. There, great slabs of rock seem suspended in a slide into (or out of) the ocean. A canteen and campground at Meat Cove has the best location, and the most scenic spots along the cliff are part of the property.

Watch for kayakers below the cliffs or enquire about the hiking trail out around Cape St. Lawrence. Then backtrack on the dirt and paved roads to the main Cabot Trail at **Cape North.**

West on the Cabot Trail from Cape North, the route traverses different scenery blending forest, valleys, and rivers. **Big Intervale campground** is a home base for exploring the Cape Breton Highlands plateau. It's also a good halfway point for campers completing the route over two days.

Big turns and steep inclines cross the south and north branches of the Aspy River. The tributaries sit in the valley between South and North Mountains, which are also divided by fault lines. North of the Cabot Trail lies the **Polletts Cove-Aspy Fault Wilderness Area**—an unmarred area that is popular for moose hunting and wilderness-only travel.

Lookouts on both sides of the river valley show the expanse of trees and vibrant life. The forests are a mix of deciduous and coniferous trees, making a lovely autumn scene when the leaves turn.

Atop North Mountain, which pans out at more than 400 meters (1,300 feet) elevation, the alpine plateau creates a stark contrast to the lush river valleys below. Windswept balsam fir and black spruce show signs of a harsh life: their stunted trunks and twisted branches battered by winter winds and snows.

Approaching the Gulf of St. Lawrence coast, watch for the hobbit-like cabin of Lone Shieling. In the Grande Anse Valley, the stone structure with a thatched roof pays tribute to the Scottish heritage in Pleasant Bay. It sits amid trails through a forest of 350-year-old sugar maples.

Pleasant Bay

The Cabot Trail exits the park boundary as it approaches **Pleasant Bay.** Drive down to the town wharf to visit the **Whale Interpretive Centre** on Harbour Road. Exhibits on 16 species provide an introduction to the largest ocean mammals. Apply the new-found knowledge with a whale-watching tour or use binoculars to look for pods of pilot whales off the coast. Like Ingonish and Chéticamp, Pleasant Bay is another good spot to secure accommodations or a meal with an ocean view.

From Pleasant Bay, the road slowly climbs up **MacKenzie Mountain** to cross another alpine plateau at 335 meters (1,100 feet). The plateau is part of the Appalachian Mountains chain that runs from Newfoundland down to Georgia.

Benjies Lake Trail provides access to the stark landscape, although the **Skyline Trail** with its headland coastal views is the national park's best-known hike. In recent years coyotes have been a problem in the area. In 2009 a lone female hiker was attacked and killed by coyotes while hiking the trail, and in 2010 a girl was attacked while camping in the park. Hike in groups (even if it means waiting at the trailhead for a hiking buddy) or join a guided sunset hike.

French Mountain, near the Skyline Trail, is one of the highest points in the park at 455 meters (1,493 feet). Descend from these heights via the tight turns of the Cabot Trail toward Chéticamp. This is the most-photographed section of the trail, where the road snakes between deep green highlands, red cliffs, and blue ocean. You'll easily be able to pull off the road to look both up and down the route. Many of the park's two dozen lookouts also have interpretive signs.

At **Cap Rouge,** hike a trail to learn about the one-time Acadian community near the red, wedge-shape landmark. Nearby, find **Corney Brook campground** and more options for walking. This is another great area to rest awhile and take in the monument-like surroundings.

Chéticamp

Past Pillar Rock you'll start to see **Chéticamp,** now just 12 kilometers (7.5 miles) off. The **spire of St. Peter's Church**—or St-Pierre in French—is unmistakable and was long a landmark to Chéticamp fishermen and sailors. For scenery, the mountains are still present to the left while the gulf lies to the right.

Before entering the town, stop in first at the larger national park visitor center. A campground provides longer-stay facilities. The relief map showing the valleys, slopes, and plateaus of the highlands, and the interpretive exhibits detail the park geology and wildlife.

In Chéticamp, the Stella Maris, or gold star, of the Acadian flag shines brightly. Museums and restaurants invite visitors into the culture—you'll eat, sleep, and even hook rugs with the locals. The first stop in town is **Les Trois Pignons**—a cultural center and hooked-rug museum at 15584 Cabot Trail. The museum centers on the work of **Elizabeth LeFort,** a legendary rug maker from the Chéticamp area. If you're rusty on your rug hooking know-how, take a look at the detail in LeFort's work. Biblical stories, fishing scenes, and portraits of politicians create a diverse body of work.

Continue a cultural immersion with a visit to the **Acadian Museum** at 15967 Cabot Trail. A museum downstairs and craft cooperative upstairs give a full perspective on the local way of life. The craft gallery staff may also demonstrate the rug hooking technique—using a flattened nail to pull a continuous piece of wool through burlap. If you're enamored with the art, take-home kits are for sale in the shop.

In the other half of the building, dine at the **Restaurant Acadien.** You're likely to be served in French, which is still the community's predominant language. Fish cakes, meat pie, and potato pancakes are all on the Acadian-style menu. For dessert, raisin and blueberry puddings are thickly drizzled with a brown-sugar sauce.

On the west side of Chéticamp Harbour, take a short scenic amble around **Chéticamp Island,** which is capped with **Enragee Point Lighthouse.**

Side Trip: Baddeck & the Bras d'Or Lakes

From Chéticamp the Cabot Trail heads south along the coast and follows the Margaree River inland. Passing through the **Margaree Valley,** the dramatic, towering views notch down to a lush river valley.

Margaree Forks marks the division of the road and the river. At the confluence of the Southwest and Northeast Margaree Rivers, the Cabot Trail meets Highway 19, or the **Ceilidh Trail.**

The **Margaree Salmon Museum** at 60 East Big Intervale Rd. is worth a stop for its collection of fishing flies and tales of the "big one."

Continue east to **Baddeck,** a central location where there's a ceilidh—Gaelic for "visit"—every night of the week. On the shores of the Bras d'Or Lakes watch sail boats in front of **Kidston Island Lighthouse.** From the **Alexander Graham Bell National Historic Site** on Chebucto Street you can see the inventor's old home at **Beinn Bhreagh.** Exhibits at the historic site engage visitors with Bell's inventions—a short list of which includes the telephone, the metal detector, and the Silver Dart airplane.

Walk along the well-kept main street, and then stop in at the stone **Bras d'Or Lakes Interpretive Centre** to learn more about the lakes that the French christened "arms of gold."

PRINCE
EDWARD
ISLAND

17

The Confederation Bridge

Cape Jourimain to Victoria to Rocky Point

General Description: When arriving on the island via the Confederation Bridge, most head straight for Charlottetown, Summerside, or Cavendish. Instead, drive this 75-kilometer (47-mile) scenic route along the south coast—it yields a string of interesting harbors, historical sites, and farmland views. From the route where iceboats once transported the mail to the first European settlement on the island, this scenic drive makes a perfect summer detour.

Special Features: Cape Jourimain Nature Centre, Confederation Bridge, Gateway Village, Borden-Carleton Lighthouse, Cape Traverse Wooden Iceboat Display, Victoria Seaport Lighthouse Museum, Argyle Shore Provincial Park, Port-la-Joye-Fort Amherst National Historic Site, Blockhouse Point Lighthouse, views to the Charlottetown waterfront, beaches, swimming.

Location: Across the Confederation Bridge and along the Northumberland Strait, through southeastern Prince County and southwestern Queens County.

Driving Route Numbers & Names: Confederation Bridge, Highway 1, Route 10, Route 116, Route 19.

Travel Season: Waterfront towns are most fun to explore in the summer, when you can walk along the beach at low tide in bare feet. The summer music-and-fireworks Festival of Lights in Charlottetown can be seen from the end point of this drive, Rocky Point. In autumn, the red leaves add another hue to the red farm soil, red tractors, and red sands that give this drive its rosy reputation.

Camping: No provincial parks have campgrounds on this stretch of coast, but find a private campground in Borden-Carleton or head north to the hundreds of sites at Prince Edward Island National Park.

Services: Arriving on island, Gateway Village covers the basics—from gas to wine to ice cream. Medical services are available in Summerside, about 25 kilometers (15.5 miles) from the bridge, as well as in Charlottetown, less than 25 kilometers (15.5 miles) from Rocky Point.

Nearby Points of Interest: Car Life Museum; in Charlottetown: Founders' Hall, Province House National Historic Site, Beaconsfield Historic House, Ardgowan National Historic Site of Canada, Confederation Centre of the Arts, St. Dunstan's Basilica, heritage walking tours, dining, live music.

Time Zone: Atlantic time zone (GMT minus 4 hours).

The Drive

A coastal drive, this 75-kilometer (47-mile) route includes the requisite lighthouse and beaches. But it also traverses the link to the island, the Confederation Bridge, and overlooked heritage sites. To cap the drive, you'll look out over the busy Charlottetown waterfront to see the skyline of the city where Canada was born.

This drive is ordered for those arriving on the island via the Confederation Bridge, but it can easily be flipped to become a day trip from Charlottetown.

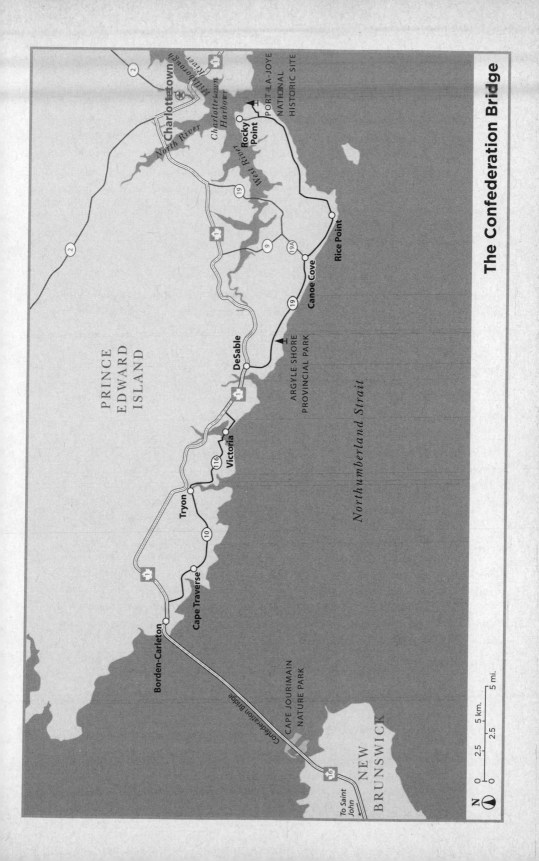

The Confederation Bridge

PRINCE EDWARD ISLAND

Charlottetown

Hillsborough River

Charlottetown Harbour

North River

West River

Rocky Point

PORT-LA-JOYE NATIONAL HISTORIC SITE

Rice Point

Canoe Cove

DeSable

ARGYLE SHORE PROVINCIAL PARK

Victoria

Tryon

Cape Traverse

Borden-Carleton

Northumberland Strait

Confederation Bridge

CAPE JOURIMAIN NATURE PARK

NEW BRUNSWICK

To Saint John

N

0   2.5   5 km.
0   2.5   5 mi.

The Confederation Bridge links Borden-Carleton, Prince Edward Island, to Cape Jourimain, New Brunswick. Just inside the New Brunswick side of the province's border with Nova Scotia, Highway 16 heads east toward the bridge. Begin with a stop in **Bayfield** at the **Cape Jourimain Nature Centre,** part of a 675-hectare (1,668-acre) wildlife reserve that encompasses **Cape Jourimain** and **Jourimain Island.** Seabirds flock to the salt marshes as part of their migration routes, and ospreys fish off the coast. Hiking trails and beaches allow you to trek out to the **Cape Jourimain Lighthouse,** which is home to a cliff swallow colony. Facilities include washrooms and a restaurant, making it a well-planned stop for those who are mid road trip.

Confederation Bridge

From New Brunswick's Highway 16, the **Confederation Bridge** first gently climbs and then descends to the red shores of Prince Edward Island. The bridge is the final piece in fulfilling an 1873 promise by the federal government—to provide a continuous link to the island from the mainland. Although the idea of Canada was seeded at the Charlottetown Conference in 1864 and the Dominion of Canada was formed in 1867, Prince Edward Island did not join until 1873. This link to the mainland and absorbing the island's railway construction debt were the main draws for the farmland island.

Prior to the completion of the billion-dollar bridge, ferries provided transport to Prince Edward Island; from May to December, the Wood Islands ferry still provides daily service from Caribou, Nova Scotia. The bridge, completed in May 1997, was the final delivery on the Confederation promise.

The bridge spans almost 13 kilometers (8 miles); you'll avoid the toll on the island-bound journey and instead pay a roundtrip toll on the way off ($43.25 for two-axle vehicles in 2011). Pedestrians and cyclists cross the bridge by shuttle. On the Prince Edward Island side, the bridge connects with Highway 1 (Trans-Canada Highway)—the main route to Charlottetown. Before turning right on Route 10 to follow the Red Sands Drive, grab supplies (or just ice cream) at the shops and services at **Gateway Village.** From the Borden-Carleton waterfront, see great views of the bridge from the **Borden-Carleton Lighthouse.** The lighthouse was decommissioned when the bridge replaced the ferry.

Throughout PEI, blue-and-white signs along the highway will direct you to restaurants, craft galleries, and accommodations.

About 2 kilometers (1.2 miles) past the tollbooths, turn right off Highway 1 to follow Route 10. The rural road passes **Amherst Cove** before reaching the **Cape Traverse iceboat display,** where a roadside park displays an historic iceboat. The

The Confederation Bridge links Prince Edward Island to New Brunswick.

iceboats once scuttled mailbags and passengers across the ice-clogged Northumberland Strait to Cape Tormentine. The tin panels on the boat helped protect the hull from the ice, and runners allowed it to glide over the surface. The service started December 19, 1927—perhaps too late to post that year's Christmas cards.

Hedges of mountain ash edge fields of baled hay, potato plants, and feed corn. These are the initial scenes of the province's great tracts of farmland. Look for the red earth between the rows of potatoes—a soil that made PEI and its spuds famous.

Across the fields and the Northumberland Strait, you can see Cumberland County in Nova Scotia when there is good visibility.

Cross the Tryon River to Tryon and, before reaching the Trans-Canada, turn right off Route 10 onto Route 116—the slow road (40 kilometers or 25 miles per hour) to the seaside town of Victoria.

Victoria

A picturesque setting, **Victoria** sits at the harbor edge where sand flats, a lighthouse, and fishing boats converge at the shoreline. A public wharf is the center of activity amid red cliffs and tidal flats. The **Victoria Seaport Lighthouse Museum** on Water Street maintains the local history along with the red-capped lighthouse, which is the island's second-oldest lighthouse. The narrow boat channel—look for it marked by red and green navigation buoys—shows the shallowness of the harbor.

The **Victoria Playhouse** produces theater shows, music performances, and historic-pageant events during summer at the historic venue. Walk the waterfront, visiting tiny canteens (perhaps the cutest spot to order a takeout). The delectable treats at **Island Chocolates** on Main Street are also the centerpiece for the **Island Chocolate Company Chocolate Festival** in September.

Causeway Road leads east from town along Route 116, passing a picnic park outside of the main village. Route 116 ends at Highway 1, where you make a right turn on the main route to DeSable.

About 4 kilometers (2.5 miles) along the Trans-Canada, turn right on Route 19 in **DeSable.** Less than 300 meters (0.2 miles) after the intersection, Monument Road leads to the **Franklin Knight Lane Monument.** Born in DeSable, Lane excelled in US politics, serving as interstate commerce commissioner and secretary of the interior under Woodrow Wilson. A large grassy area and heritage sign commemorate his birthplace.

Through farm fields, Route 19 follows the coastline to **Argyle Shore Provincial Park,** a day-use park with a popular family beach. The access road for the park runs parallel to a private driveway, which leads to private cabins. A small sign points the way, but mind to take the left road to reach the park.

Small canteens in Victoria, Prince Edward Island, are a favorite summer lunch stop.

The Argyle Shore refers to the area's Scottish heritage. While walking the beach you'll see the red cliffs that give this drive its official name: the Red Sands Shore.

Note the distinct angle of the Prince Edward Island roads. Many follow county lines or run parallel to the original land lot divisions. In the 1760s Samuel Holland, a Dutch engineer and surveyor, was tasked with mapping the island—then called St. Johns Island. Over two years Holland divided the island into 67 lots and 3 royalties. Most lots had access to the waterfront and were fairly rectangular tracts given the variance of the coastline. Prior to the arrival of the English settlers, the Mi'kmaq lived, fished, and hunted throughout the island.

As you drive up and down over rolling farmlands, try to identify the harvests. PEI is famous for its potatoes, but the island farmers also grow corn, strawberries, oats, and brussels sprouts, to name only a few crops.

Rounding Rice Point, crossing Nine Mile Creek, and then coming through Cumberland, follow the brown-and-white signs for the national historic site near Rocky Point.

Port-la-Joye

Port-la-Joye–Fort Amherst National Historic Site tells a tumultuous tale. Walk through the grassed-over fort walls, find the Gallant memorial, and look out on the Charlottetown waterfront. In 1720, 300 settlers arrived from France to establish a colony. Acadians from other parts of the Maritimes joined the settlement, which benefited from a good natural harbor and PEI's rich soil.

French and British struggled over control of Atlantic Canadian regions, leading to much upheaval and the expulsion of the Acadians from Nova Scotia and New Brunswick regions starting in 1755.

In August 1758 a British force came to seize possession of the fort, which had been given up with the surrender of Louisbourg in July 1758. About two-thirds of the 4,600 colonists were deported that same year, mostly to France. About half died during the journey.

On the site of Port-la-Joye, the British built **Fort Amherst**—the grassy humps of which remain at the site today.

A metal cross sits at the best viewpoint on the site. It commemorates the Great Upheaval of the Acadians, when 10,000 were deported from around the Maritimes to France, England, and the United States, including Louisiana where the Cajun culture took root.

Watch boats sailing in the harbor, which is the Fleur-de-lis-like confluence of three rivers: the Hillsborough, the North, and the West. Smokestacks and church spires, including those of **St. Dunstan's Basilica,** rise above the city skyline. It's a concrete contrast to the meadows and trees sloping down from Port-la-Joye.

At the end of Blockhouse Road lies the **Blockhouse Point Lighthouse,** a square-set station that dates to 1876.

The national historic site is a perfect location to admire the fireworks displays in the **Charlottetown Harbour.** The site is also less than 25 kilometers (15.5 miles) from the capital city, where varied dining options, heritage inns, live music venues, shops, and galleries line the historic streets.

Worthwhile attractions include **Province House National Historic Site,** which offers self-guided tours through the halls of Confederation, and the Victorian elegance of the furnishings and chinaware at **Beaconsfield House.** For a more thorough introduction to Charlottetown stop in at **Founders' Hall** on the waterfront, where costumed guides lead walking tours around the city in French and English.

Acadians, First Nations & Oysters

Summerside to Malpeque Bay via the Acadian Coast and Lennox Island

---

General Description: This 160-kilometer (99-mile) scenic loop explores Celtic, Acadian, and Mi'kmaq heritage. The thrumming College of Piping in Summerside, a towering brick Catholic Church at Mont-Carmel, the serene water of Malpeque Bay, and the Mi'kmaq heritage center on Lennox Island each add a new cultural curve to the route. Attractions include museums about Lucy Maud Montgomery, foxes, and shellfish, plus parks and trails.

Special Features: College of Piping, Eptek Art & Culture Centre, PEI Sports Hall of Fame, International Fox Museum, Wyatt House Museum, Linkletter Provincial Park, Acadian Museum, Union Corner Provincial Park and Schoolhouse Museum, Mont-Carmel Museum of Religious Art, the Bottle Houses, Lennox Island Mi'kmaq Cultural Centre, Indian Art & Crafts of North America, Malpeque Bay, Bideford Parsonage Museum, PEI Shellfish Museum, Green Park Provincial Park and Shipbuilding Museum, Yeo House.

Location: From Summerside in Prince County, along the coast of the Northumberland Strait to Malpeque Bay.

Driving Route Numbers & Names: Route 11, Route 133, Route 12, Route 163, Route 166.

Travel Season: At its loveliest in summer, PEI is best visited between June and September. But the spring freshness and fall colors are also inviting, particularly in the bay-side Green Park Provincial Park. Book accommodations ahead if visiting in July and August, although campgrounds generally have availability outside of holiday weekends.

Camping: Both Linkletter Provincial Park (close to Summerside) and Green Park Provincial Park at the end of the drive have campgrounds. Showers and washrooms cover the basics, while playgrounds, kitchen shelters, and firewood make the stay more fun.

Services: Summerside, PEI's second largest city after Charlottetown, has all the needed services. Gas stations, medical care, and waterfront restaurants are all readily available in the Prince County center.

Nearby Points of Interest: L. M. Montgomery Lower Bedeque Schoolhouse Museum, Confederation Trail.

Time Zone: Atlantic time zone (GMT minus 4 hours).

The Drive

Begin this scenic loop on Summerside's Water Street, part of Route 11. On the shore of Bedeque Bay, **Summerside** is a busy city with fishing wharves, shopping districts, and local colleges. The **College of Piping** produces a summer

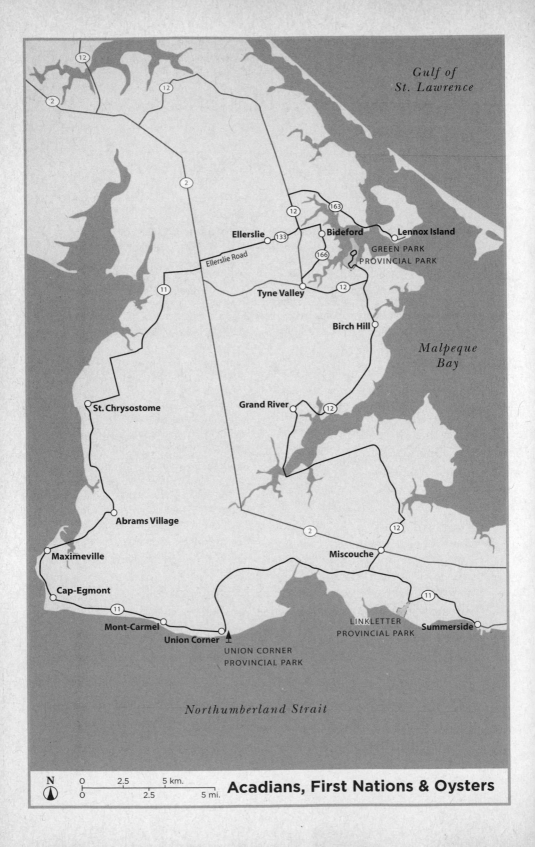

Gulf of
St. Lawrence

12

12

2

12

12

163

2

Ellerslie   133   Bideford   Lennox Island

166   GREEN PARK
PROVINCIAL PARK

Ellerslie Road

11

Tyne Valley   12

Birch Hill

Malpeque
Bay

St. Chrysostome

Grand River   12

Abrams Village

2   12

Maximeville

Miscouche

Cap-Egmont

11

LINKLETTER
PROVINCIAL PARK

Summerside

Mont-Carmel

Union Corner

UNION CORNER
PROVINCIAL PARK

Northumberland Strait

N   0   2.5   5 km.

0   2.5   5 mi.

Acadians, First Nations & Oysters

performance to showcase bagpipes and Highland dancing. Inspired? Then take a tour or a class at the school.

Follow the waterfront along Harbour Drive. The cute shops and ice cream at **Spinnakers Landing** draw you in, as does a quick stop at the wharf-side visitor information center. Theaters, galleries, and music shows make Summerside a center for the arts. Regularly changing exhibits at the **Eptek Art & Culture Centre** range from needlecrafts to carvings. Next door, the **Prince Edward Island Sports Hall of Fame** records the successes of the province's athletes.

For a historical look at the city, take a walking tour led by the folks at Wyatt Heritage Properties. The historic properties encompass five locations open to the public, including the **International Fox Museum** at 33 Summer St. and **Wyatt Historic House** at 85 Spring St.

For those who fall for the Prince County city and its many attractions, Summerside boasts an inviting mix of top seafood restaurants and comfortable accommodations. In July, bibbed diners gather for the **Lobster Carnival.**

Back on Water Street, Route 11 continues west out of the urban center. After 5 kilometers (3 miles) a left-hand turn to **Linkletter Provincial Park** leads to a beachfront campground. As the road bends sharply right here, there is a roadside map and information board about the North Cape Coastal Drive.

Acadian Shore

As the suburban-style properties become farms, you pass Lady Slipper Drive—an inland route to **Miscouche.** Either turn right to visit the **Acadian Museum** in Miscouche now, or include it at the end of the drive to discover PEI's Acadian heritage. It's a 3-kilometer (2-mile) detour return.

To continue the drive, follow Lower Miscouche Road (still part of Route 11) toward Union Corner. A half-dozen gravel roads branch off from the main road before the route emerges on the shore of the Northumberland Strait.

The **Union Corner Schoolhouse Museum** is situated at the top of Union Corner Road and above **Union Corner Provincial Park.** Drive down to the waterfront to look out from the red cliffs and see the Confederation Bridge to the east. Although the park has picnic tables, fire pits, washrooms, and change rooms, camping is not permitted.

Follow the shoreline for about 3.5 kilometers (2.2 miles) from Union Corner to **Mont-Carmel.** Above the tiny community—I strain to think how it supports such a large church—rise the twin spires of Our Lady of Mont-Carmel Church. The **Mont-Carmel Museum of Religious Art** lies across the street at Le Club d'age d'or.

Route 11 traces the coastline to a tangent of attractions in the **Cap-Egmont** area. **The Bottle Houses,** at 6891 Rte. 11, present the work of a quirky island

artist and builder. Édouard Arsenault constructed three, life-size buildings entirely from recycled bottles—about 25,000 of them in all. A house, chapel, and tavern welcome sunlight through the transparency of the glass. Nearby, drive along Phare du Cap Egmont Road out to the **Cap-Egmont Lighthouse,** which went into operation in 1864. Road names in the area show the blend of heritages: you'll see Scottish, French, and English surnames attached to roads, as well as those named for the ocean. A September festival—**L'Exposition Agricole et le Festival Acadien de la Region Evangeline**—celebrates the region's agricultural history and Acadian culture.

Past Cap-Egmont Lighthouse, Route 11 comes to the large **Egmont Bay.** Fishing communities like **Abrams Village** (notable for the large Acadian Fishermen's Co-op on the wharf) sit in the region known as the Evangeline coast. Abrams Village also hosts the July **Evangeline Bluegrass and Traditional Music Festival,** which features three days of music for a well-priced admission.

At the wetlands and forest of the **St.-Chrysostome Wildlife Management Area,** the road makes a series of sharp right-angle bends. Follow Route 11, keeping left at the intersections with Routes 128 and 130.

In **Mount Pleasant,** Route 11 ends at a T-junction with Highway 2. Turn left and follow the main highway north for 500 meters (0.3 miles), then turn right onto Route 133 (Ellerslie Road).

After 6.5 kilometers (4 miles) on Route 133 through Ellerslie, turn left at the T-junction with Route 12. Drive 2 kilometers (1.2 miles) and then make a right on Route 163, or East Bideford Road, to Lennox Island.

Lennox Island

The one-way-in road follows a twisting arm of Malpeque Bay before connecting to the island causeway. **Lennox Island** is a First Nations community, its history stretching back thousands of years. At the **Lennox Island Mi'kmaq Cultural Centre** on Sweetgrass Trail, learn about the use of traditional plants in medicine, the songs in the Mi'kmaq culture, and the development of a written language.

Across from the center is the small white **St. Anne's Church.** When Grand Chief Membertou was baptized in 1610 by French missionaries, Saint Ann was adopted as the Mi'kmaq patron saint.

On the village waterfront, a large new ecotourism complex provides clear views of the bay, including oyster aquaculture sites. Next door on Eagle Feather Trail, **Indian Art & Crafts of North America** displays finely crafted wares, from baskets to dream catchers to pottery. In the western half of the island, find walking trails that loop through the community, past the shoreline, and into forest.

Spinnaker's Landing in Summerside, Prince Edward Island, offers ice cream, souvenirs, and visitor information.

At the Bideford Parsonage, Lucy Maud Montgomery boarded while she worked at her first teaching position.

Malpeque Bay

Return across the Lennox Island causeway and back to Route 12. Follow the main route south toward **Bideford** through the countryside scenery of goldenrod meadows and hay bales. Turn left onto Route 166 to visit the **Bideford Parsonage Museum** at 784 Bideford Rd. As a 19 year old, *Anne of Green Gables* author Lucy Maud Montgomery boarded at this Methodist parsonage during her first teaching post at Bideford No. 6 School. Built in 1878, the cute yellow home with white gingerbread trim is restored to that time, displaying a series of exhibits on the author as well as local shipbuilding—a strong industry on the island until the advent of steel-hulled liners. On Wednesday nights during summer, the parsonage museum hosts readings from Montgomery's works.

On the Malpeque Bay shore, the wharf-side **PEI Shellfish Museum** explains the life cycle of spats, or baby oysters, as they grow into a table delicacy. The admission fee even includes a sample! The museum also covers lobsters, clams, and other shellfish.

Follow Route 12 through sweet **Tyne Valley,** which hosts an oyster festival in early August, and toward **Green Park Provincial Park** in Port Hill. An oasis of beautiful tree stands, camping, and history on Trout River, the park is a lively spot during its mid-August blueberry social.

Penniless Englishman James Yeo arrived in Tyne Valley in 1819. He worked for a local businessman, opened a store, and then started building boats. More than 350 ships later, Yeo was considered the richest man on the island. The impressive **Shipbuilding Museum** in the park tells more about Yeo and this significant island industry. The gorgeous Victorian gables invoke a time of hard-earned luxury. **Yeo House** is now restored with historical furniture.

From Port Hill, Route 12 wends its way southeast toward Miscouche. You'll pass two pairs of facing churches in Birch Hill and a lovely wide estuary in Grand River. Aquaculture buoys bob, and bird life feeds along the shoreline.

As Route 12 meets Highway 2 in Miscouche, stop in now to the Acadian Museum or continue along the highway for dinner and a performance in Summerside.

19

Wind Turbines & Stompin' Tom

West Point to Miminegash to Skinners Pond to North Cape

General Description: A 95-kilometer (59-mile) coastal drive along PEI's windy shore, this route passes electricity-generating turbines and the home of "Bud the Spud" singer Stompin' Tom Connors. Unique rock formations, sandy beaches, fishing wharves, and shoreline hikes provide lots to do. Nearby find museums that explore Acadian history and a cafe that serves a true local delicacy: seaweed pie.

Special Features: West Point Lighthouse Museum, Cedar Dunes Provincial Park, Giant's Armchair, Irish Moss Interpretive Centre, seaweed pie, Stompin' Tom's Skinners Pond Schoolhouse, Elephant Rock, Atlantic Wind Test Site, North Cape Interpretive Centre, North Point Lighthouse.

Location: Prince County in western Prince Edward Island, northwestern tip of the island.

Driving Route Numbers & Names: Route 14, Norway Road (Route 182), Route 12.

Travel Season: Boasting a long travel season, PEI has lovely temperatures from May through October. The wind turbines are fun to watch in any season, provided a breeze is blowing, but most museums keep seasonal hours, usually June through September.

Camping: Cedar Dunes Provincial Park, Mill River Provincial Park, and Jacques Cartier Provincial Park all offer camping facilities in close proximity to this drive. Expect washrooms, showers, kitchen shelters, and playgrounds at the provincial parks, which accommodate both tent and RV campers.

Services: O'Leary and Tignish provide the best options for services such as banks, gas stations, restaurants, and medical care (O'Leary only). Ocean-side cottages are dotted along the drive, making it a fun beach getaway.

Nearby Points of Interest: Tignish Cultural Centre, Kildare Capes Red Sandstone Cliffs, Jacques Cartier Provincial Park, Alberton Museum, O'Leary Museum, PEI Potato Museum, Mill River Provincial Park, Mill River Fun Park, Confederation Trail.

Time Zone: Atlantic time zone (GMT minus 4 hours).

The Drive

From Stompin' Tom to seaweed pie, this 95-kilometer (59-mile) drive is a delight for the senses. Towering white wind turbines, quiet sandy beaches, and marshland trails give this more remote part of the island ample appeal. There are fantastic beaches along the entire length of this drive, including at West Point, Campbellton, Miminegash, and Skinners Pond.

From Summerside or Charlottetown, take Highway 2 west toward Tignish and the island's North Cape. Turn left onto Route 14 at Carleton, about 50

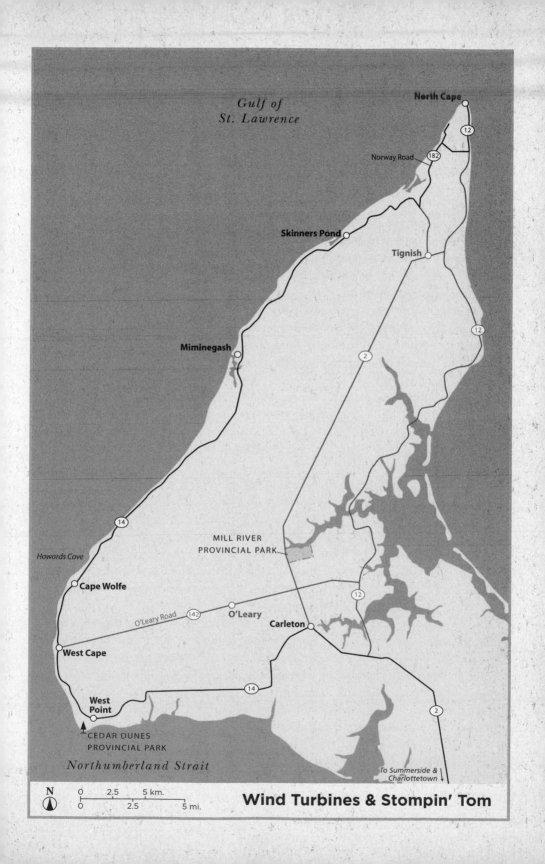

Gulf of
St. Lawrence

North Cape

12

Norway Road   182

Skinners Pond

Tignish

12

Miminegash

2

14

Howards Cove

MILL RIVER
PROVINCIAL PARK

Cape Wolfe

12

O'Leary Road   142   O'Leary

Carleton

West Cape

14

West
Point

CEDAR DUNES
PROVINCIAL PARK

2

To Summerside &
Charlottetown

Northumberland Strait

N

0   2.5   5 km.

0   2.5   5 mi.

Wind Turbines & Stompin' Tom

kilometers (31 miles) west of Summerside. (Here, don't confuse Carleton with Borden-Carleton—the community near the Confederation Bridge.)

Route 14 cuts west just south of O'Leary, through grain, clover, and potato fields. Turn left at a yield sign and then bear right toward Milo. After traveling 21 kilometers (13 miles) in from Highway 2, make the first stop on the coast at West Point.

West Point & Cedar Dunes

The provincial park and lighthouse sit on the outer reaches of Egmont Bay, part of the Northumberland Strait. The picnic park, beach, and camping facilities at **Cedar Dunes Provincial Park** make an early stopping spot. Visit the **West Point Lighthouse Museum** to discover the history of the 1875 light station. Bold signature black-and-white bands define the island's tallest lighthouse. Boardwalks, comfortable accommodations, and a restaurant add to the destination appeal.

Leaving the provincial park you'll spot the first of dozens of wind turbines on this scenic drive. **West Cape Wind Farm** stretches from West Point to West Cape, farther along Route 14. Towering above the farmland hay fields, tractors, and cows, the churning wind turbines have the same shiny white sheen as *Star Wars* stormtroopers' armor.

Follow Route 14 along a smooth coastline around Carey Point and Cape Wolfe. In Howards Cove turn left on the wharf road to sit in the **"Giant's Armchair"** and survey the large fishing wharf. A seat-like stone, the chair can fill with rain, so it's only a good photo stop on a clear day. Nearby is the squat **Howards Cove Lighthouse.**

From Howards Cove continue on Route 14, following signs for Roseville and Miminegash. The coast occasionally treats with sights of red cliffs.

Seaweed Pie & Skinners Pond

After Burton and a beach in Campbellton (which is a duplicate town name on the island, with another near New London), Route 14 curves slightly inland. As the ocean reappears, you arrive in **Miminegash.**

The **Irish Moss Interpretive Centre,** famed for its **Seaweed Pie Cafe,** sits on the right-hand side and the main Harbour Road to the left. The interpretive center covers the journey of Irish moss, from its cultivation on the ocean bed and coastal rocks to the seaweed harvest on the beach. It is a source for carrageenan, an Irish moss extract that is added as a thickener to ice cream and toothpaste. Seaweed pie, made with carrageenan, shows more quirky island spirit. The cafe serves the pie by the slice, and it's neither green nor slimy.

West Point Lighthouse, near Cedar Dunes Provincial Park, offers accommodation at the distinctly striped tower.

If that's not enough to convince you how much these folks love the local seaweed, the **Irish Moss Festival** is an annual June event in nearby **Tignish,** coinciding with the beach harvest.

As Route 14 follows the coast, PEI farmlands become less prevalent, and the fleets of fishing boats grow larger. Acadian flags and five-point stars on houses show the region's French-speaking heritage.

About 14 kilometers (8.7 miles) past Miminegash, you'll arrive in the unexpectedly famous **Skinners Pond**—the home of **Stompin' Tom Connors.** A folk singer and songwriter, Stompin' Tom is best known for "The Hockey Song" and "Bud the Spud"—true Canadian anthems.

Born in Saint John, New Brunswick, Stompin' Tom was adopted by a family in Skinners Pond; years later he hitchhiked around the country working odd jobs. His ensuing music career has spanned six decades.

At the intersection of Route 14 and Knox Lane sits a historic schoolhouse. Originally built in the early 1800s and thought to be the oldest on the island, Skinners Pond School was preserved at the behest of Stompin' Tom, who attended the one-room schoolhouse.

Skinners Pond is also a fishing community, and the location of a lovely, smooth-sand beach. Across from the schoolhouse Harbour Road heads down to the wharf and beach. From here you can spy the wind farm at North Cape.

Continue northeast along the coast and after Nail Pond, take Norway Road (Route 182) until it takes a doglegged turn east. Keep to the coast and detour on the dirt-surfaced Waterview Road down to Elephant Rock and more views of the **wind turbine farm.**

Elephant Rock is a sea stack and home to seabirds. Similar to the Hopewell Rocks in New Brunswick, the pillar is dark orange, the color of PEI mud. Green meadows, sharp drop offs, ochre-red cliffs, and white wind turbines create a vibrant contrast. From this point the **Black Marsh Trail** connects to North Cape over a 3-kilometer (2-mile) route of boardwalk and trails.

North Cape

Follow the dirt road back to Route 182 and make a left, taking the paved Nelligan Road to the T-junction with Route 12. Make another left toward Seacow Pond and North Cape. After a short distance, Route 12 ends at the parking lot of the **Atlantic Wind Test Site** and **North Cape Interpretive Centre.**

The wind test site features two types of towering wind turbines: the V47s that stand 73 meters (240 feet) and the V90s that stand 125 meters (410 feet) in total height. Three slim blades per turbine churn with the power of the wind. Only until you walk through the exhibits (inside and out) and see the blades up close does their size—similar to that of an airplane wing—make an impact.

Windmills and hay fields are common sights near North Cape, Prince Edward Island.

Ask about getting your Tip-to-Tip recognition here. For visiting both East Point and North Cape, the tourism bureaus offer ribbons and certificates—a way of encouraging visitors to visit the whole island. You'll reach the other tip along Drive 22.

Walk out to **North Point Lighthouse** to see the northernmost tip of Prince Edward Island. Local residents placed an impromptu light here before the lighthouse was completed in 1867.

Green Gables & Red Sands

New London to Cavendish to Dalvay-by-the-Sea

General Description: This 84-kilometer (52-mile) scenic drive encompasses PEI's most famous icons: *Anne of Green Gables* and Cavendish Beach. Over farmlands and rivers, the route journeys to the shoreline where lighthouses, fishing boats, and red sandstone cliffs await in the island's only national park. Offbeat attractions include a farmer-started bank, a display of mounted birds, and a mansion-sized summerhouse. Of course, the drive couldn't miss a stop at Cavendish, Brackley Beach, or the near-countless Green Gables attractions.

Special Features: Lucy Maud Montgomery Birthplace, Stanley Bridge Marine Aquarium, Prince Edward Island National Park, Cavendish Beach, Green Gables House, Site of Lucy Maud Montgomery's Cavendish Home, North Rustico Harbour Lighthouse, Rustico Harbour Fisheries Museum, Farmers' Bank Museum, Doucet House, Brackley Beach, the Dunes Studio Gallery and Café, Covehead Lighthouse, Dalvay-by-the-Sea National Historic Site, hiking, cycling, beaches.

Location: Central PEI, on the northern shore of Queens County.

Driving Route Numbers & Names: Route 6 (Cavendish Road), Grahams Lane (New Park Road), Gulf Shore Parkway, Cawnpore Lane (Route 13), Harbour View Drive, Church Road, Route 15.

Travel Season: In summer the national park swells with beachgoers. But with about 40 kilometers (25 miles) of shoreline, it's still possible to find a mostly secluded spot in the park, even in the height of the season. Attractions, in general, are open from June through September.

Camping: Stay in Prince Edward Island National Park, with campgrounds at Cavendish, Brackley, and Stanhope. Campgrounds are equipped with the basic facilities such as water, washrooms, showers, and play areas. There are also a number of private campgrounds in the area.

Services: This drive starts near Kensington and ends about 20 kilometers (12.4 miles) from Charlottetown. Gas stations, groceries, and supplies are available in both. For medical services, head to Charlottetown or Summerside. Along the entire stretch of the drive, cabins, cottages, bed-and-breakfasts, and motels will mark the meters. But book ahead in summer as even with the density of accommodations, favorite spots do put up No VACANCY signs.

Nearby Points of Interest: Kensington Railyards, Kensington Towers & Water Gardens, Woodleigh Replicas, Old Millman Heritage Road, Anne of Green Gables Museum, L. M. Montgomery Heritage Museum.

Time Zone: Atlantic time zone (GMT minus 4 hours).

The Drive

Travel to New London along Route 6 from Kensington, or Route 8 from Summerfield (on Highway 2). From Kensington, the rolling hills of farmland undulate down to the Southwest River. Smaller waterways join the larger, and the road crosses Tunlin Creek, Harding Creek, and Durant Creek.

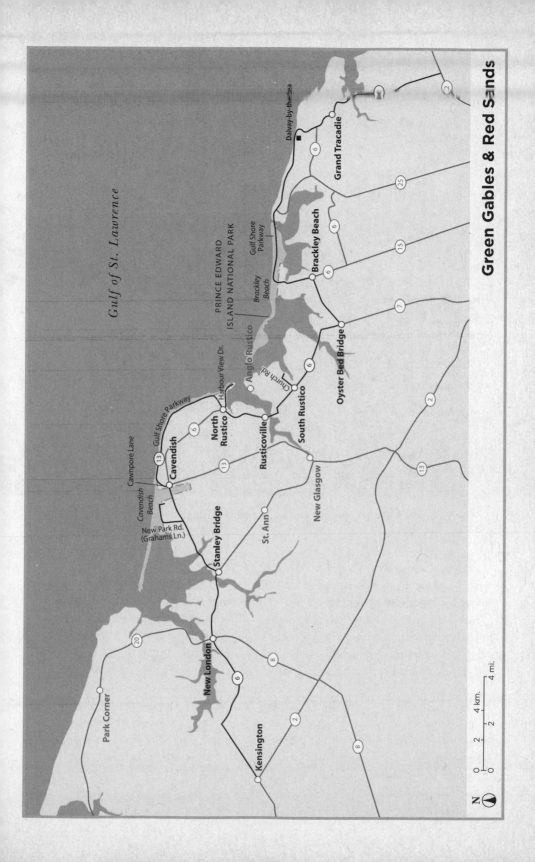

Green Gables & Red Sands

Gulf of St. Lawrence

PRINCE EDWARD
ISLAND NATIONAL PARK

*Brackley
Beach*

Gulf Shore
Parkway

Dalvay-by-the-Sea

Grand Tracadie

Brackley Beach

Oyster Bed Bridge

Church Rd.

Anglo Rustico

Harbour View Dr.

Gulf Shore Parkway

Cawnpore Lane

*Cavendish
Beach*

New Park Rd.
(Grahams Ln.)

Cavendish

**North
Rustico**

Rusticoville

South Rustico

Stanley Bridge

St. Ann

New Glasgow

Park Corner

New London

Kensington

2

2

6

6

25

15

7

6

13

13

6

13

2

20

6

8

2

8

N

0   2   4 km.

0   2   4 mi.

The Green Gables National Historic Site is a favorite with those who love Lucy Maud Montgomery's books.

New London sits at the busy crossroads of Routes 6, 8, and 20. A tour-bus-length parking lot signals the site of an *Anne of Green Gables* attraction, the **Lucy Maud Montgomery Birthplace.** Here, on November 30, 1874, Lucy Maud Montgomery was born. The town was then called Clifton, and Montgomery's parents lived in this wooden home. But before the young Montgomery was two, her mother died from tuberculosis, and her father turned custody over to her maternal grandparents. Exhibits of clothes, writings, and photos fill the two floors.

For more Anne Shirley than one scenic drive can perhaps hold, make a side trip on Route 20 west from New London to Park Corner. Along Cousin's Shore find gardens and the Lake of Shining Waters at the **Anne of Green Gables Museum**—Montgomery's aunt and uncle's home and where the author married Ewan Macdonald. Also nearby, find the **L. M. Montgomery Heritage Museum,** the home of the Montgomery's paternal grandfather.

For beaches, walking trails, and fishing villages, however, continue on the main scenic drive and travel east on Route 6 through Stanley Bridge and Cavendish. Continuing the scenic drive, the route heads toward the national park.

Stop briefly at the small roadside **Panorama Park,** which offers views out over New London Bay and its tributary rivers (although partially obscured by tree foliage).

Stanley Bridge & Cavendish

Less than 5 kilometers (3 miles) from New London, **Stanley Bridge** bestrides its namesake river. Descend the gentle hills to the pretty riverside location. On river left, you first pass **Carr's Oyster Bar and Restaurant,** which serves the locally grown delicacies. Malpeque Bay oysters drew international recognition when they won accolades as the world's tastiest in the 1900 Paris Exhibition.

The **Stanley Bridge Marine Aquarium** at 32 Campbellton Rd. features touch tanks, fish aquariums, and a collection of mounted birds and butterflies that numbers in the hundreds.

But the Stanley Bridge fishing wharf—where boat tours and working fishing vessels come and go—is the most fascinating. Venture from the wharf with a deep-sea fishing tour or just admire the views of seabirds perched on aquaculture buoys. Boats slip out through a narrow, silted-in harbor mouth. See the long stretch of dunes that form the western end of **Prince Edward Island National Park** and shelter the harbor.

The **Stanley Bridge River Days Festival** celebrates the area watershed with events and entertainment in late August.

Driving east from Stanley Bridge, there is an odd intersection at the junction with Routes 254 and 224. Route 6 continues to the left and, as it is the main route, is the only direction without a stop sign.

Crossing the Hopewell River you'll see more aquaculture sites and sand dunes, along with farmland hedgerows and fields. As the road approaches Cavendish, signs for accommodations increase and vacation cabins sit between hayfields and flowering potato plants.

Early on a summer morning **Cavendish** is an empty spot. But as the heat of the day increases, so does the traffic. Allow for "tourist driving" (i.e., drivers slowing down, looking for attractions or accommodations, or turning without using a signal light) as folks navigate a new place.

The attractions they seek are plenty: You'll pass **Ripleys Believe It or Not Odditorium, Avonlea–Village of Anne of Green Gables, Grandpa's Antique Photo Studio,** plus dozens more along Route 6, also called Cavendish Road. Enjoy the tackiness: There are few places in Canada that can match the attention-grabbing appeal you'll see along this stretch.

For many, however, the main draw in Cavendish is **Green Gables National Historic Site.** Amid gardens, barns, and woodland trails sits the **Green Gables House,** its white shingles edged with forest green trim. The house, which belonged to cousins of Lucy Maud Montgomery's grandfather, is now refurbished as the fictional house where orphan Anne Shirley came to live with Matthew and Marilla Cuthbert. Trails lead to **Lovers' Lane,** the **Haunted Woods** and the **Green Gables Golf Course.**

For those more intrigued by the story of Montgomery herself, visit the **Site of Lucy Maud Montgomery's Cavendish Home,** where grandparents Alexander and Lucy Macneill raised Montgomery after her mother died. The home is also where Montgomery penned the legendary tale *Anne of Green Gables*—the internationally famous story of orphan Anne Shirley who comes to live at Green Gables.

At a stoplight Grahams Lane, also called New Park Road, leads left to **Cavendish Beach** and the western end of **Prince Edward Island National Park.** The one-way-in road accesses the campground and the sandy shores of Cavendish. At the shoreline you can follow interpretive trails, relax at the beach, and look out over the dunes.

When near the dunes it's essential to keep on marked paths, as walking on dune or marram grass kills the plant. Grass roots help stabilize the dunes, but once they die the dunes simply drift away. A surprising note in the park brochure says that as few as 10 steps can kill marram grass.

Also fragile in the park are the coastal piping plovers. The endangered black-collared, white-bodied birds nest on the beaches from May through to mid-August. During the nesting season, join the Piping Plover Patrol to monitor nests, see incubated eggs, and watch for predators.

Returning to the main vein through Cavendish, follow Route 6 east for 2.6 kilometers (1.6 miles) before turning left onto Cawnpore Lane or Route 13. On the way in, a large visitor information center is on the left.

You'll need a park pass to stop at lookouts and beaches in the national park. Trees screen the right side of the road, and to the left stand fragile red sandstone cliffs. Boats and birdlife provide lots to watch along the shoreline.

After a 9-kilometer (5.6-mile) scenic drive, Gulfshore Parkway connects again with the Route 6 at North Rustico.

The Rusticos

Although you'll see **North Rustico** when rounding the inland bend of Gulf Shore Parkway, drive back to Route 6 and then turn immediately left on Harbour View Drive to reach North Rustico. Walk along the boardwalk and visit the exhibits at the **Rustico Harbour Fisheries Museum.**

From the heavily silted harbor mouth, the **North Rustico Harbour Lighthouse** beams its navigational signal. Views of distinct red bluffs and the Gulf of St. Lawrence provide a stunning panorama.

Route 6 heads east from North Rustico across the Hunter River, passing through **Rusticoville.**

At **South Rustico,** Church Road travels a short distance to historic Acadian attractions. A stone stronghold, the **Farmers' Bank Museum National Historic Site** at 2188 Church Rd. was the one of the first people's banks in the country. In operation for 30 years, the bank supplied inexpensive credit to the local Acadian population. Tour the solid sandstone bank and learn about the Catholic priest who organized the project, Rev. Georges-Antoine Belcourt.

Neighboring **Doucet House** displays daily life for Acadians during the 1800s through a garden, small wooden house, and guides. Also in South Rustico, **St. Augustine's Catholic Church** is the one of the oldest Catholic churches on Prince Edward Island, having been built in 1838.

A heritage road leads down Rustico Bay to where the harbor, like many along this northern coast, is almost sealed off by the Robinsons Island dunes. In some places along the coast, dunes can close off a saltwater bay, creating a *barachois* that fills with freshwater over time.

Return to Route 6 and follow it east across the Wheatley River. At **Oyster Bed Bridge** see more aquaculture sites in the sheltered bay—oysters and mussels are commonly cultivated and harvested here.

Make a sharp left to continue following Route 6 as it intersects with Route 7.

Brackley to Dalvay

At Route 15, turn left toward Brackley Beach (Route 6 continues to the right). On the 3-kilometer (2-mile) stretch out to the shore, you'll pass the **Dunes Studio Gallery and Café.** Noted for its restaurant and gallery as well as a lush summer garden, stop here to peruse or dine. Then indulge in the soft scents and suds at the **Great Canadian Soap Company.** Ceilidhs at the local community center are a regular summer event.

Through a marshy stretch the road almost seems to dip below the water level and then comes to a T-intersection at the shoreline. Here we pick up another stretch of Gulf Shore Parkway and explore the final kilometers of the drive in this coastal national park. The paved scenic road parallels a cycling and walking path—watch for pedestrians who may be crossing to admire the views.

There are viewpoints down the left road to Robinsons Island, but I prefer the lookouts to the east. A right turn takes you through to **Brackley Beach** where the day-use area includes a beach, picnic tables, and a canteen. The campground provides tent sites only.

Sand dunes and red cliffs make the varied shoreline of Prince Edward Island National Park stunning.

A bridge spans the mouth of **Covehead Bay** and the square **Covehead Lighthouse** serves as a beacon for the fishing boats that return here to dock. At the lighthouse, walk along the beach and visit the fishing shacks on Covehead Bay.

Erosion problems are apparent throughout the park as wind and water shave away the soft red shoreline. Even the Tarmac parking lots are crumbling into the ocean in some places. The PEI coastline erodes about 1 meter (3.3 feet) every year.

Gulfshore Parkway measures 11 kilometers (6.8 miles) from Brackley Beach to Dalvay-by-the-Sea. Stop frequently along this stretch to enjoy the hikes, lookouts, and picnic areas. Although the sand and cliffs are lovely, head inland to hike over marshland boardwalks and through quiet forests. Just be sure to bring bug repellant and long sleeves. The mosquitoes might be the only guaranteed wildlife sighting, but beaver and birdlife also frequent the marshes.

Choose **Stanhope campground** if you're keen to have a campfire. The campground also has serviced sites for RVs.

The last point along this coastal stretch is the impressive summer home turned inn, **Dalvay-by-the-Sea National Historic Site** at 16 Cottage Crescent. The Victorian mansion provides antique-furnished guest rooms with no telephones, televisions, or alarm clocks. The Adirondack chairs under the garden pine trees make the perfect resting spot after a long drive.

Dalvay-by-the-Sea, built in 1895, was once the summer home of Alexander MacDonald. The Scottish-born businessman made his fortune serving as president of Standard Oil Company and a director in the mining, railway, and banking industries.

When MacDonald died, his fortune fell to his two granddaughters, the children of Laura, his only surviving child. But under the management of their father, the granddaughter's million-dollar fortune disappeared with bad investments. Unable to afford the house that had cost $50,000 to build, the MacDonald's granddaughters sold the house to the caretaker, William Hughes, for their debt in back taxes: $486.57.

In 1938 the house and land sold to the government so it could be included in the national park. For the best views, drive past the house to admire the mansion across **Long Pond,** just as Alexander MacDonald did on his last visit to the house in 1909.

Gulf Shore Parkway makes its final connection with Route 6, about a kilometer past Dalvay. After 10 kilometers (6.2 miles) through Grand-Tracadie and past Winter Bay, the route ends at Highway 2.

Side Trip: Lobster Suppers

Prince Edward Island **lobster suppers** are an enduring local tradition, owing to good fishing grounds around the island and the lobster boats that dock in local harbors. Days of an abundant fishery are declining, but it's still possible to get a fresh, PEI lobster dinner.

PEI lobster suppers offer an authentic, down-home feel. Full meals usually include steamed mussels or seafood chowder, homemade rolls, and local vegetables, then are topped off with berry shortcake or pie and a cup of tea.

In June 1958, **New Glasgow Lobster Suppers** served their first lobster dinner as a fundraiser. The cost? $1.50 each. It has since become a private restaurant. The Roman Catholic Church in Hope River started hosting lobster suppers in 1964, and the meal is still a charity fundraiser.

Owing to its popularity as a dining option—many dining rooms can seat hundreds—you can find PEI lobster suppers around the province in Abrams Village, St. Margarets, Cardigan, New London, and (my uncle Tom's favorite) the **Fisherman's Wharf** in **North Rustico.**

21

Ferries & the *Titanic*

Wood Islands to Panmure Island Provincial Park

General Description: Ending at a serene beach, this 70-kilometer (44-mile) scenic drive skirts the southeastern coast of Prince Edward Island. It begins at the Wood Islands ferry terminal—the dock for an endangered May to Dec service between Nova Scotia and the island. En route you'll discover a winery, parks, and lighthouses—one of which was the first land station in Canada to receive the *Titanic*'s SOS call. Take side trips to see a buffalo herd, dine on local mussels, and go seal watching.

Special Features: Wood Islands Ferry, Wood Islands Lighthouse, Northumberland Provincial Park, Rossignol Estate Winery, Cape Bear Lighthouse, Kings Castle Provincial Park, Murray Harbour seal tours, Panmure Island Provincial Park, Panmure Island Lighthouse.

Location: Located in southeastern Kings County, Prince Edward Island.

Driving Route Numbers & Names: Trans-Canada Highway (Highway 1), Route 4 (Shore Road), Route 18, Route 17, Route 347 (Panmure Island Road).

Travel Season: This is another lovely summer drive, although on a clear fall day, walking on the beaches is still an enjoyable activity. Museums and attractions tend to maintain regular hours from June to September only.

Camping: Camp at Northumberland Provincial Park near the start of the drive, where services include washrooms, showers, and laundry. At the drive's end, Panmure Island Provincial Park provides a lovely vantage near sandy beaches and accepts reservations. Private campsites can be found along the way in Murray Harbour and Murray River.

Services: Although gas and basic groceries can be found in Murray River, the closest hospital is in Montague. Most of the accommodations on this stretch are vacation cabins or cottages, requiring a greater self-sufficiency than in better-serviced areas such as Charlottetown, Cavendish, and Summerside.

Nearby Points of Interest: Buffaloland Provincial Park, Garden of the Gulf Museum, Orwell Corner Historic Village, Sir Andrew MacPhail Homestead National Historic Site.

Time Zone: Atlantic time zone (GMT minus 4 hours).

The Drive

If your time schedule allows, arrive on PEI via the ferry. When heading to the eastern end of the island from Nova Scotia, it will cut down on driving time without adding to the overall travel time. Getting to the island is no charge; instead ferry and bridge tolls are collected when you leave.

Northumberland Ferries Limited operates the route from Caribou, Nova Scotia, to Wood Islands, Prince Edward Island. Since 1941 ferries have made the

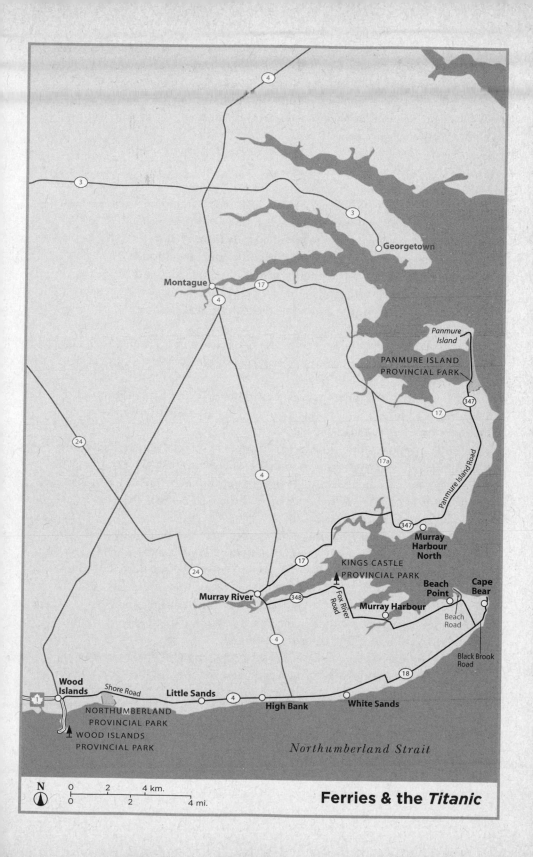

4

3

3
Georgetown

Montague

17

4

Panmure Island

PANMURE ISLAND
PROVINCIAL PARK

347

17

24

17a

4

Panmure Island Road

347
Murray Harbour North

17

KINGS CASTLE
PROVINCIAL PARK

24

17

348
Murray River

Fox River Road

Beach Point

Cape Bear

Murray Harbour

Beach Road

4

Wood Islands

Shore Road

Little Sands

4

High Bank

White Sands

18

Black Brook Road

1

NORTHUMBERLAND
PROVINCIAL PARK

WOOD ISLANDS
PROVINCIAL PARK

Northumberland Strait

N

0   2   4 km.

0   2   4 mi.

Ferries & the *Titanic*

75-minute crossing over the Northumberland Strait, passing Pictou Island on the way. The ferry operates 8 months per year, from May through Dec.

But this 70-kilometer (44-mile) scenic drive doesn't require a ferry trip: Simply follow signs for the Wood Islands ferry on the island, or take the Trans-Canada Highway from Charlottetown.

Wood Islands

After the ferry docks at the terminal in Wood Islands Harbour, the southernmost region of PEI, follow the Trans-Canada Highway that begins at the wharf for 500 meters (0.3 miles). Turn right into **Wood Islands Provincial Park,** which features a museum and interpretive center at the **Wood Islands Lighthouse.** The lighthouse, built in 1876, has ushered the ferry into the harbor since the MV *Prince Nova* made the first crossing in 1941, and it guided iceboats and ships before that.

Learn the tales of the sea: from rum-running during Canada's longest prohibition (1901–1948) to sightings of a phantom ship off the coast. Climb the light station and see the lighthouse-keeper's quarters. Starting in 1775, long before the regular ferry run, iceboats crossed to Nova Scotia with mail and also provided a passenger service.

The provincial park offers a beach, washrooms, picnic tables, play area, and a boat ramp. In July, visit for the entertainment and beach glass treasures at the **Mermaid Tears Sea Glass Festival.**

The Trans-Canada branches west to Charlottetown at the junction with Route 4. Turn right, or east, passing the **Plough the Waves** complex—a collection of services that includes an information center, ice cream shop, liquor store, cafe, and gift store. Ask at the visitor center about the annual **70-Mile Yard Sale,** held in mid-September.

The **Confederation Trail** also passes nearby. Built on the old railway beds after the train service was decommissioned in 1989, an 82-kilometer (51-mile) branch of the trail runs from Iona to Murray Harbour. Traversing the island from tip to tip covers 273 kilometers (170 miles) of walking and biking trails, while all branches of the Confederation Trail cover 357 kilometers (222 miles) total distance.

This scenic drive is a portion of the Points East Coastal Drive, so watch for the blue-and-yellow starfish that mark the route.

As the road follows the coast, you'll pass **Northumberland Provincial Park,** 3 kilometers (2 miles) from Wood Islands. Bluffs look out over the shoreline, where there is a beach and supervised swimming. The campground has good basic facilities.

The straight road sits on an eroding coastline. Farmlands and vacation properties stretch down to the waterfront. Pass through Little Sands where a roadside Winery sign marks the location of PEI's lone winery: **Rossignol Estate Winery.** Widely spaced vine rows slope down to the strait. Although fruit wines are the winery's signatures, it is producing increasing varieties of whites, reds, and special products—like a rosehip liqueur.

After High Bank, Route 4 cuts north in a direct line to Murray River. Instead, continue east and follow Route 18 out to Cape Bear.

Cape Bear

The trees thicken to a forest as the road enters **Cape Bear.** Black Brook Road leads to the **Cape Bear Lighthouse.** Having been moved multiple times away from the quickly eroding cliffs, the lighthouse was scheduled to be moved again as this book goes to print. The old location provided views of the now-demolished Marconi station. The planned location, out on equally heavily eroding Murray Head, was buzzing with dragonflies on my visit. Wherever the lighthouse sits, visit both spots to enjoy the views of the crumbling red cliffs and long sand beaches.

The **Marconi station** at Cape Bear was the first land station in Canada to receive the *Titanic* SOS call. Cape Spear in Newfoundland received the call first, but the rocky province did not join Canada until 1949. Pay a small fee to climb the lighthouse and view the exhibits on past lighthouse keepers.

From Cape Bear, return to Route 18 and follow the road toward Murray River. Beach Point lives up to its name with a local-favorite beach and guiding lights at the mouth of Murray Harbour.

Follow the starfish scenic-drive signs along Fox River Road and Route 348 through Gladstone. A small day-use park, **Kings Castle Provincial Park** at 1887 Gladstone Rd. offers a unique cast of guides: Storybook statues ranging from the Three Bears to Mother Goose decorate the park. Washrooms, a picnic area, a themed playground, and a beach make the park a wonderful budget day trip for families. Check in for details of planned summer activities.

Both Route 348 (Gladstone Road) and Route 18 come to T-intersections with Route 4. Turn right and drive through the small town of Murray River. Seal-watching tour boats dock in Murray River, departing from the wharf to view sea birds and the largest seal colony on the island. Often regarded as pests by fishermen, the harbor seals and gray seals feed on fish and love to bask on rocks, making for easy viewing.

Crossing the Murray River waterway, turn right on Route 17 toward Point Pleasant and Murray Harbour North.

Panmure Island

Cranberry bogs and marshes lie on either side of the Route 17. When sightlines allow, catch glimpses of a small island chain, the Murray Islands, in the sand-spit-protected Murray Harbour. At Murray Harbour North, keep left on Route 17.

About 18 kilometers (11 miles) from Murray River, leave Route 17 and turn right onto Route 347: a no-exit road out to **Panmure Island.** The road soon enters **Panmure Island Provincial Park** at 350 Panmure Island Rd. A campground with washrooms, laundry, water, and a play area are located on the mainland side of the park.

A sandbar connects Panmure Island to the mainland. To the ocean side, enjoy the walks and views from a white-sand ocean beach. Lifeguards supervise the swimming area in summer. On the west side of the road is sheltered **St. Marys Bay,** where a red-sand beach faces mussel aquaculture sites. Enjoy the sand to its fullest with the **Panmure Island Sandcastle Competition**—a fun amateur event held in August.

The **Cardigan Bay** area is also known as Three Rivers for the freshwater tributaries that meet here. The Montague, Brudenell, and Cardigan Rivers flow into the bay.

Atop the northern hill, the **Panmure Island Lighthouse** overlooks the area. Visit the province's oldest wooden lighthouse, built in 1853, where in summer you can view exhibits and climb the tower to see the lantern.

The Mi'kmaq were Panmure Island's first inhabitants, drawn to the rich shellfish grounds where they harvested clams and mussels. Each summer First Nations gather for the **Abegweit Powwow.** Learn ancient teachings, buy crafts, and watch traditional dance during the cultural weekend event, which ends with a feast.

Panmure Island Road runs over to the west side of the island, amid homes and farm fields. Scottish settlers came to the area in the early 1800s and the original one-room schoolhouse, built in 1897 and now used as a community hall, still stands.

From Panmure Island, retrace the road along the sandy causeway. Route 17 continues west 20 kilometers (12.4 miles) to Montague and 37 kilometers (23 miles) to Georgetown—offering the best options for dining and accommodations.

Side Trip: Montague and Georgetown

Continuing west of Panmure Island, Route 17 skirts coves and riverbanks to **Montague,** and then Routes 3 and 4 head out to **Georgetown.** Both small but busy communities, their charm comes from historic architecture, plus riverside and coastal locations.

On the Montague Main Street and housed in a historic sandstone building, the **Garden of the Gulf Museum** delves into pioneer life with exhibits and local photos.

Georgetown is the seat of Kings County. The peninsula on Cardigan Bay was set aside for this purpose when Samuel Holland surveyed the island and divided it into 67 lots and 3 royalties. Theater, storied churches, and many golf courses draw visitors to the area.

Climb the historic lighthouse above Panmure Island beach.

22

Singing Sands in the East

Souris to East Point to New Harmony Heritage Road

General Description: Round the eastern tip of Prince Edward Island on this 75-kilometer (47-mile) scenic loop to discover the famed Singing Sands, lighthouses, and red-dirt heritage roads. Watch for whales and gannets, amble over coastal trails, bike the Confederation Trail, or take a train ride. This drive requires a slower pace: one that includes stopping at beaches, walking out at low tide, and scanning the water of the Gulf of St. Lawrence with binoculars.

Special Features: Souris Beach Provincial Park, Souris East Lighthouse, Magdalen Islands ferry, St. Mary's Roman Catholic Church, Black Pond National Bird Sanctuary, Red Point Provincial Park, Basin Head Provincial Park, Singing Sands, Basin Head Fisheries Museum, East Point Lighthouse, Elmira Railway Museum, Confederation Trail, New Harmony Demonstration Woodlot, New Harmony Heritage Road.

Location: Eastern tip of Prince Edward Island, Kings County.

Driving Route Numbers & Names: Route 16, Elmira Road (Route 16A), Route 302 (Baltic Road), Route 303 (New Harmony Heritage Road).

Travel Season: A perfect summer drive, this route journeys to PEI's eastern beaches. Attractions on this route tend to be open only in the summer months—June to September.

Camping: Red Point Provincial Park lies about halfway through this drive. The park is adjacent to the family-friendly Basin Head Provincial Park, where there is no camping. Red Point has hot showers, washrooms, and RV sites. And the campground also takes reservations.

Services: Souris and Elmira are the best bets for restaurants, supplies, and gasoline. For medical care, head to Souris, where there is a hospital. For extensive shopping, journey the 80 kilometers (50 miles) to Charlottetown—a trip that takes about 1.25 hours. Vacation chalets and cottages are extremely prevalent in this area. Book a stay in St. Peters Bay for a pretty, central location, or in Red Point, which is convenient to parks and beaches. There are also a few large golf resorts on this coast.

Nearby Points of Interest: Myriad View Artisan Distillery, Prince Edward Distillery, PEI National Park—Greenwich.

Time Zone: Atlantic time zone (GMT minus 4 hours).

The Drive

The Singing Sands, great wildlife watching, and the province's easternmost point all delight on this 75-kilometer (47-mile) drive. Arrive in the east via the main roads: Highways 2 and 4. Rather than direct routes, Kings County is filled with farm roads that run parallel to the original land lots—from the northwest to the southeast in this area. With a well-marked road map you can find quick, if not

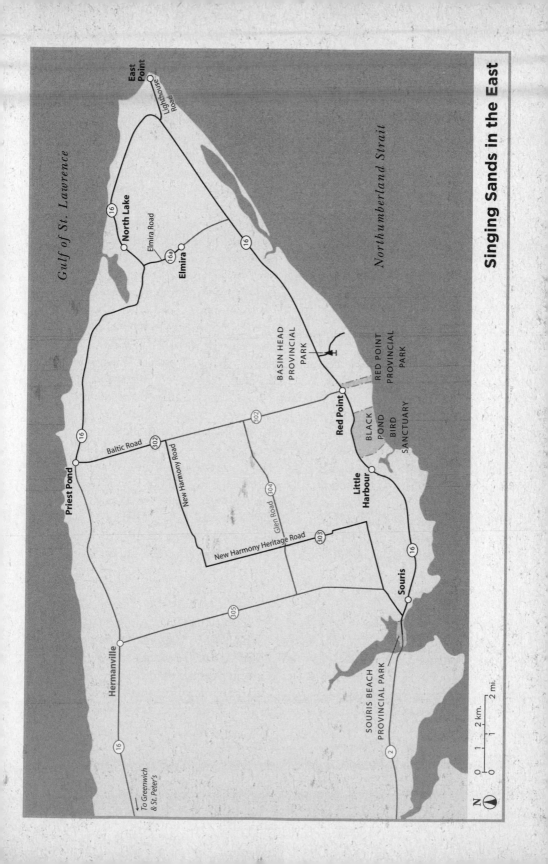

Singing Sands in the East

exactly direct, routes throughout the island. PEI tourism provides above-average highway maps for no charge.

Highway 2 strikes in from the west to Souris in Colville Bay. The Souris River lets out into the bay with the Gulf of St. Lawrence beyond. Between Souris West and Souris, find the sandy shores of **Souris Beach Provincial Park** at 8 Main St. The narrow sand spit protrudes into the harbor mouth, anchored by the pavement of Highway 2. Showers, washrooms, and a play area provide more than the basic day-park services. The area is also popular with boaters—from canoeists and kayakers to windsurfers.

In **Souris,** services cluster (if unattractively) along the main road. The Matthew and McLean Building at 95 Main St. houses the visitor information center as well as some historical exhibits about the Acadian community. In 1727 Acadians established fisheries and farms here. The town's name—meaning "mice" in French—comes from three plagues of rodents that swept through the fields during the 1720s and 1730s.

A hub of the east, a ferry runs from Souris to the **Magdalen Islands (Îles de la Madeleine).** The islands are an isolated network of about 12 sandy islands, about 5 hours offshore by ferry. Part of Quebec, the islands share a similar French-speaking heritage. Most are linked by sand dunes, making the archipelago easy to explore. The islands' history spans shipwrecks and a feudal landlord, but the people—the Madelinots—are perhaps the best reason to visit.

Above the town, the round tower of **St. Mary's Roman Catholic Church** silhouettes a stern profile. The church, first built in 1839 from island sandstone, is a testament to the strong Acadian heritage in the area. The church was rebuilt in 1849, 1902–1903, and 1928 due to fires.

Far to the east end of town, look for the **Souris East Lighthouse.** Dating to 1880, the lighthouse on Knight Point houses a small gift shop. Perhaps most unique, however, is that as recently as 1991 Frank McIntosh was a lighthouse keeper here. When he retired, McIntosh became the last lighthouse keeper on Prince Edward Island.

Singing Sands

Follow Route 16 through Souris, east past Chepstow and Deane Points, and toward Little Harbour. The road bridges the **Black Pond National Migratory Bird Sanctuary,** first established in 1936. Hundreds of bird species have been spotted in the province, but Canada geese are most prevalent here. Great blue herons nest in eastern PEI, as do ospreys, kestrels, hummingbirds, and sandpipers. A community website, Eastern Kings Meeting Place (http://ekpei.ca/bw1.html), has a full checklist for birders.

Although Route 16 sits inland from the coast, you'll find the best views at the provincial parks and stops along the way. The first, **Red Point Provincial Park** at

Swimmers thrill at bridge jumping in Basin Head Provincial Park.

249 Red Point Park Rd., features more than 100 campsites plus washrooms, showers, fire pits, and a playground. A dump station and serviced sites accommodate RVs. The park is situated on the beach—a great spot for swimming in the supervised area.

Better for a day trip, continue 2 kilometers (1.2 miles) past the Red Point turnoff and then make a right to **Basin Head Provincial Park.** Known for its **"Singing Sands,"** scuffing your feet along the beach produces a so-called singing sound—a noise that hits a pitch somewhere between a squeak and the zip of a tent fly closing. Scientists haven't determined what causes the sand's sound, although speculations identify the high amount of silica or perhaps the amount of quartz in the sand. The beach is a summer frenzy of activity as kids jump from the pier into the basin's small mouth, also known as the run. Families picnic on the busy beach and make use of the good facilities.

At the park visit the **Basin Head Fisheries Museum,** which sits above the beach on a bluff. It tells the history of the inshore fishery: the boats, workers, and the cannery. A harbor to Basin Head was dredged in the late 1930s and a wharf built to maintain access to the basins. You won't likely see it, but the lagoons at Basin Head are the only place where **giant Irish moss** grows. The moss contains high amounts of carrageenan, a thickening agent used in ice cream and toothpaste. Unlike other types of Irish moss, the strain that lives in Basin Head never roots to the ocean floor and has an even higher concentration of carrageenan.

From Basin Head, follow PEI's coast of sand dunes for 12 kilometers (7.5 miles) to reach the island's eastern tip.

East Point

In **East Point** turn right on Lighthouse Road to reach the **East Point Lighthouse.** Built in 1867, the octagonal light station is one of the oldest on the island. (Newer beacons are four sided.) Three tides—from the Atlantic Ocean, Gulf of St. Lawrence, and Northumberland Strait—meet off this point. Add in reefs and a foggy day, and shipwrecks were common here in earlier days. Across the Gulf of St. Lawrence when the day is clear, you'll see the Cape Breton Highlands rise up from the lowlands of the Margaree Valley. Use the stationed binoculars to spot whales or nose-diving gannets.

Across from the lighthouse a gift shop is well stocked with local, handmade goods. It's also the spot to get your Tip-to-Tip recognition: For visiting both East Point and North Cape, the tourism bureau offers ribbons and certificates.

Walk along the bluffs and down to the shore: A large, empty, red-sand beach stretches to the horizon.

From East Point, Route 16 continues around the coast. You'll spot a string of white wind turbines on the horizon that form **East Point Wind Farm.** At North Lake, Route 16A is a shortcut across the eastern tip through to Elmira. The terminus of the Confederation Trail, which was reclaimed from railway line abandoned in 1989, Elmira focuses on its locomotive history. The **Elmira Railway Museum** lies on the north side of town, directly on Elmira Road. With photos and artifacts, it revives the glory days of the train. Take a miniature train ride, size up the model train collection, and enter the stationmaster's office.

The Confederation Trail ends (or begins) in Elmira, connecting to Tignish in the west via 273 kilometers (170 miles) of gravel paths. The trail is a favorite with cyclists as the hills are well graded.

Returning to Route 16, follow the shore to my personal favorite section of the drive: a scenic heritage road.

New Harmony Heritage Road

Turn left at Route 302, or Baltic Road. After about 4 kilometers (2.5 miles) make a right turn onto the packed-dirt **New Harmony Heritage Road,** or Route 303. One of a dozen or so scenic heritage roads on the island, the route follows old farm lanes and takes visitors back to a long-lost Prince Edward Island.

In hot, dry weather the dust can be bad if traveling behind another vehicle, plus it reduces visibility. Conversely, after the spring thaw the roads are muddy, and wheels easily rut the soft, soggy clay. Stick to clear, dry summer days for this section of the drive.

Bicycles, tractors, and other vehicles also use these roads, as do animals. Enjoy the quiet of the heritage road by driving slowly—hedgerows often grow close to the road edges, so scan them for wildlife and farm animals.

The first stretch of the 14-kilometer (8.7-mile) scenic road passes through farm fields of grains and potatoes. The scene is void of power lines and houses. During PEI's long prohibition, which stretched from 1901 to 1948, rumrunners used this route as they unloaded boats off the shore.

After 5.5 kilometers (3.4 miles) on New Harmony Road, Kelly Road meets it from the right. Hang left here to continue following Route 303. As the red clay road crosses the **Confederation Trail,** it enters a tunnel of tree canopies. The mixture of foliage makes this drive a lovely trip on a clear fall day.

Glen Road, Route 304, intersects the heritage road about 3 kilometers (2 miles) after the last left.

While the full distance from Route 302 through to Route 16 stretches 14 kilometers (8.7 miles), it's this section from Glen Road (Route 304) to Greenvale Road that is the officially designated heritage section. The diverse, mature hardwood stands at the **New Harmony Demonstration Woodlot** add to the appeal, with a canopy of yellow birch arching over the road.

At the junction with Route 335, turn right to head back into Souris. Alternately, follow the heritage road as it bends left and meets Route 16 at Little Harbour.

Side Trip: St. Peters and Greenwich

The rural, low-trafficked roads of eastern Prince Edward Island make exploring farther a welcome option. **St. Peters,** noted as one of the prettiest destinations to enjoy the Confederation Trail, is also the access point for the Greenwich section of Prince Edward Island National Park.

Separated from the family beaches and red dunes of the western and largest section of the national park, **Greenwich** features marshlands, bird-watching opportunities, and a floating boardwalk. The park interpretive center enlightens visitors about the protected habitat, while the supervised beach escapes the crowds.

NEWFOUNDLAND
& LABRADOR

Mantle in the Tablelands

Wiltondale to Woody Point to Trout River

General Description: Through forested roads to the vast mountain plateau of the Tablelands, this 60-kilometer (37-mile) scenic drive along Route 431 enters a lesser-visited side of Gros Morne National Park. Fishing villages on Bonne Bay, a national park discovery center, and short hikes provide a day or two of explorations. Nearby lies the northern shore of Gros Morne National Park with its looming inland fjords and slopes of the Long Range Mountains.

Special Features: Lomond River, St. Patrick's Church, Gros Morne Discovery Centre, Green Gardens, Tablelands, Trout River Fishermen's Museum, Jacob A. Crocker House, Trout River Interpretation Centre, Big Pond, hiking, geology.

Location: On the Gulf of St. Lawrence coast, west of Deer Lake.

Driving Route Numbers & Names: Route 431, Water Street, Main Street.

Travel Season: Boat tours to Western Brook Pond run three times daily in July and August, which is also the most pleasant season for hiking and camping. June and September are shoulder seasons along this coast of changeable weather. But perhaps more than the weather, you'll want to check in on a bug forecast—late August often fares the best in this respect.

Camping: Throughout the national park find well-equipped campgrounds for tents and RVs. Closest to Route 431, Lomond campground includes sites on the shore of Bonne Bay and has a wharf and boat ramp. At the end of this scenic drive, Trout River campground offers the benefit of services in the nearby community, including excellent restaurants. In the larger section of the park, you can camp at the wooded Berry Hill or along the coast at Shallow Bay or Green Point. Some campgrounds even offer wireless Internet—ask when you buy your park pass for an updated list.

Services: Fuel up in Rocky Harbour across Bonne Bay or grab supplies and seek medical attention in Norris Point. National park staff members are best equipped to direct you to the closest services. Wiltondale, Lomond, and Trout River offer a greater selection of cabins, while heritage homes in Woody Point have been converted to comfortable bed-and-breakfasts.

Nearby Points of Interest: Bonne Bay Marine Station, Jenniex House, Dr. Henry N. Payne Community Museum, Lobster Cove Head Lighthouse, Western Brook Pond, hiking, camping, wildlife watching.

Time Zone: Newfoundland time (GMT minus 3.5 hours).

The Drive

A one-way-in scenic road travels 60 kilometers (37 miles) along the shore of Bonne Bay, through the Tablelands, and out to the clustered community of Trout River. Hikes branch off the main route and lead to a stark but geologically rich landscape and rugged coastline. Visit a heritage church, fisheries museum, or impressive exhibits at the park Discovery Centre.

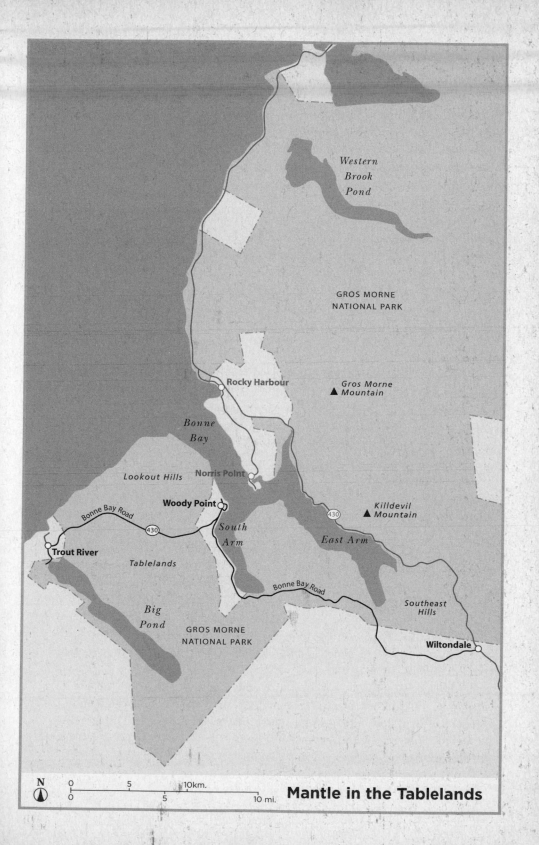

Western
Brook
Pond

GROS MORNE
NATIONAL PARK

Rocky Harbour

Gros Morne
▲ Mountain

Bonne
Bay

Lookout Hills

Norris Point

Woody Point

Killdevil
▲ Mountain

430

Bonne Bay Road

430

South
Arm

East Arm

Trout River

Tablelands

Bonne Bay Road

Southeast
Hills

Big
Pond

GROS MORNE
NATIONAL PARK

Wiltondale

N

0   5   10km.

0   5   10 mi.

Mantle in the Tablelands

From Deer Lake on the Trans-Canada Highway, drive north on Highway 430 for 30 kilometers (18.6 miles) toward **Wiltondale.** Visit the park gate to purchase a visitor pass and pick up a guide to the national park. From the Southeast Hills, Route 431 or the Bonne Bay Road cuts west, leading out to Woody Point and through the Tablelands to Trout River.

Thick coniferous forests smother the bulging rock mountains, which bear down on the road like guards. A 5-kilometer (3-mile) stretch of road edges the narrow but long Bonne Bay Little Pond. The skyline of knobby mountains continues to change as the road twists west.

About 13.5 kilometers (8.4 miles) from Wiltondale, Lomond Road leads down to a national park campground on the right. With a mix of drive-in and walk-in sites, the campground accommodates all. The usual amenities—showers, washrooms, a kitchen shelter, and playgrounds—make for a comfortable stay, while the wharf and boat ramp provide access to the water.

Hikes follow old logging roads. A 4-kilometer (2.5-mile) hike leads through forest to the abandoned community of **Stanleyville.** The loggers have moved on, and it's now just the garden plants that live here on **East Arm of Bonne Bay.**

Other hikes follow the **Lomond River** or circumnavigate heart-shaped **Stuckless Pond.**

The main route begins to climb at Tappers Mountain, just past the Lomond Road. The scenery closes in with larger multipeaked hills. It's a 9-kilometer (5.6-mile) drive through to **MacKenzie Brook,** where a picnic site marks the head of Bonne Bay's South Arm. Treed slopes and ponds giveaway to residential houses as the park boundary ends.

Woody Point

The park boundaries end just before the coast to accommodate the communities of Glenburnie, Birchy Head, and Shoal Brook. The houses of one abut the next, and the road twists severely along the coast. Take it slow, and pull over for the locals to pass if you're being followed closely.

At the turnoff to the Tablelands and the continuation of Route 431, either turn left now and head west to explore the Tablelands and Trout River first, or head to Woody Point for lunch and return shortly. Here, I describe the Woody Point tangent first.

After following the main route into **Woody Point,** 20 kilometers (12.4 miles) from the Lomond Road, turn right onto Water Street. Heritage buildings and homes line the waterfront, looking out across Bonne Bay to Norris Point. Fishing vessels recall the days when Woody Point was a commercial fishing center, vaulted by the wealth of the offshore waters.

The region was originally home to First Nations people, then ceded to the French as part of a treaty with the British. Used as a seasonal fishing base for the British in the 1800s, it wasn't until those seasonal fishermen started to overwinter in Bonne Bay that the area was considered permanently settled. As the herring fishery boomed so did Woody Point, growing to include a telegraph station, customs office, tinsmith, and bank, among other services. But a raking fire in 1922 burned much of the town, and Woody Point never totally recovered its former prosperity. Today, seafood restaurants, heritage bed-and-breakfasts, and gift shops stand in strong force along this short waterfront street.

Particularly notable is the **Old Loft Restaurant.** In a gleaming refinished fishing loft complete with barrel chairs and historic photos, the restaurant serves fresh and local seafood. Downstairs a craft gallery presents some handmade souvenirs as well as dessert—an ice cream shop. The building dates postfire to 1936.

On the upper street, Bonne Bay Road, find St. Patrick's Church. The tiny white structure was built in 1875 and is one of the oldest in the diocese. Nearby the Woody Point Heritage Theatre may be hosting music or a show. The theater is the former Lord Nelson Orange Lodge No. 149, originally a meeting place for a Protestant fraternal order, but the hall was also used for local weddings and dances.

In August, wordsmiths gather for **Writers at Woody Point**—a literary festival showcasing writers and musicians. **Gros Morne,** in fact, is a center for arts festivals and also hosts theater and music events during the summer.

Tablelands

From Woody Point, backtrack to Route 431 and turn uphill toward the Discovery Centre, the Tablelands, and Trout River. The national park **Discovery Centre** sits overlooking Bonne Bay. Stop at the yellow building, the biggest visitor center in the park, to view exhibits on the importance of the national park environment, wildlife, and human history. Due to the rich geology, inaccessible wilderness, and rugged coast, **Gros Morne National Park** became a UNESCO World Heritage Site in 1987.

A 5-kilometer (3-mile) loop hike climbs behind the Discovery Centre to a lookout over the bay.

Continue driving west as the route climbs from near sea level to more than 200 meters (656 feet) elevation at a roadside lookout. The road then cuts a fairly straight but dramatic path between the Lookout Hills to the right and the Tablelands to the left.

In some ways it's not hard to imagine the forceful collisions that created this scenery. The **Lookout Hills** share the rocky gray and deep forest green of other Gros Morne landscapes. But to the south, the stark dryness of the orange Tablelands overpowers.

Boat tours explore the inland fjord of Western Brook Pond in Gros Morne National Park.

From 570 to 420 million years ago, the **Tablelands** lay below sea level, part of an ocean bed. Moving plates forced Africa and North America together, thrusting up the ocean floor to create the Appalachian Mountains. Rising to 719 meters (2,359 feet), the Tablelands have steep edging slopes and a far-reaching plateau at the top. The orangey rock is peridotite, part of the earth's mantle. The Tablelands are a rare opportunity to see the mantle, and they have provided evidence to help develop the theories of plate tectonics.

If available, take a guided hike on the 4-kilometer (2.5-mile) return trail in this area of the park. A rocky landscape leads to the entrance of **Winterhouse Brook Canyon.** Fragile flowering plants and engaging geology define the explorations.

Continuing the drive along Route 431, two trailheads provide hikes to the shoreline at Green Gardens. Sea stacks, an ocean cave, and primitive camping provide destinations for a longer hike over steep terrain.

Trout River

Follow Route 431 through the barren landscape to its terminus at **Trout River,** 18 kilometers (11 miles) from Woody Point and 50 kilometers (31 miles) from Wiltondale. This is the western edge of the national park, where it meets the Gulf of St. Lawrence.

The road exits the boundaries of the park as it reaches the community. Follow Route 431 to a T-junction with Main Street.

A left turn away from the town leads inland to **Big Pond,** also called Trout River Pond. Big Pond is deceptive in its size—measuring about 15 kilometers (9 miles) long but rarely more than a kilometer wide. The glacier-carved pond features a boat ramp and is a popular with anglers. A campground provides excellent services for walk-in and drive-in campers; however, there is no dump station.

Return on Main Street to the commercial center of Trout River along the waterfront. The town wharf juts out on a finger at the river mouth. Tucked in a wharf building amid working fishing boats, find the **Trout River Fishermen's Museum.** A series of displays cover the local cod, crab, and lobster fisheries. From the museum a boardwalk trims the edge of Trout River Bay to pass the beach where caplin (a small saltwater fish) wriggle onto the sand to spawn.

From 1815 to 1880, Crocker families were the only residents in Trout River. Built in 1898, the **Jacob A. Crocker House** at 221 Main St. shows a traditional fisherman's home. In the same stretch the **Trout River Interpretation Centre,** 245–257 Main St., provides hands-on and interactive exhibits that include a touch tank and a three-dimensional geology display.

From its days as a one-family community, Trout River has grown to include restaurants and cabins that accommodate the visitors drawn to the outstanding national park.

Side Trip: Route 430

Route 430, also called the **Viking Trail,** leads through the most-visited portion of Gros Morne National Park. It is also the route to the Northern Peninsula and southern Labrador, featured in Drives 25 and 24 respectively. The **Long Range Mountains** create an intimidating scene as they meet the boggy coastal plateau.

Traveling from Wiltondale, **Killdevil Mountain** is the first great height along East Arm. The road then journeys inland past the bare mound of Gros Morne. The mountain's name translates literally from French as "big gloomy," but *morne* is also a Creole word meaning "rounded hill."

Side streets lead to the communities of **Norris Point** and **Rocky Harbour,** where you'll find supplies and accommodations. The national park visitor center is located close to the main highway, and the **Bonne Bay Marine Station** sits on the waterfront in Norris Point.

Follow side roads through Rocky Harbour and out to **Lobster Cove Head Lighthouse**—a light station at the entrance to Bonne Bay. Walk along trails edged with weather-twisted branches and trunks of tuckamore—the name given to stunted conifers.

Daily summer boat tours are the most dramatic way to experience the high cliffs and waterfalls around **Western Brook Pond.** Well, that is unless you're prepared for a multiday wilderness trek using only a compass and map to find the route. The stunning inland fjord is the park's most famous feature.

Various museums in park communities recall the commercial-fishing lifestyle that first saw settlements take root along this coast. The **Jenniex House** in Norris Point caters to photographers with tea and muffins, while the **Dr. Henry N. Payne Community Museum** in Cow Head explores outport history.

Travel the coast with trails at Green Point, Broom Point, and Shallow Bay. But throughout these adventures, you'll not escape the panoramic view of the grand Long Range Mountains—which are the northern end of the Appalachian chain.

24

Labrador Coast & Basque Whalers

St. Barbe to Point Amour to Red Bay

General Description: A taste of Labrador, this 140-kilometer (87-mile) scenic drive explores the coast along the Strait of Belle Isle. It's an isolated shoreline of icebergs and whales. Cross from Newfoundland to Labrador by ferry and follow the barren highway through small communities. Lighthouses, rivers, and dramatic bluffs mark the coastline. With few trees, your gaze travels farther to the horizon. In the 1500s Basque sailors made the long journey across the Atlantic to hunt whales in Red Bay. The Basques set up seasonal communities where they rendered blubber into whale oil. The national historic site at the end of the paved road looks at what they left behind.

Special Features: St. Barbe–Blanc-Sablon ferry, Gateway to Labrador visitor center and museum, Point Amour (Canada's second tallest lighthouse), Maritime Archaic Burial Mound Historic Site, Labrador Straits Museum, Pinware River Provincial Park, Boney Shore Trail, Red Bay National Historic Site, hiking, iceberg watching.

Location: Southern Labrador coast.

Driving Route Numbers & Names: St. Barbe–Blanc-Sablon ferry, Route 138, Route 510 (Trans-Labrador Highway), L'Anse-Amour Road.

Travel Season: In spring and early summer, icebergs often float through the Strait of Belle Isle, grounding themselves on the

bays and becoming visible from shore. The provincial ferry runs from Apr through late Jan, although it is susceptible to winter ice conditions. In fall and winter the northern lights are visible along this coast, making it a special but cold and unpredictable season to visit. The few attractions—Red Bay and Pinware Provincial Park—have the longest hours during the height of the season, usually June through September.

Camping: Pinware Provincial Park has camping facilities along with a day-use area and a lovely beach. Campers have access to flush toilets, showers, drinking water, fire pits, and garbage disposal while staying at one of 22 campsites.

Services: Find medical services at the regional hospital in Lourdes-de-Blanc-Sablon, Quebec, west of the ferry terminal. Fuel up while in L'Anse-au-Clair, L'Anse-au-Loup, or Red Bay. L'Anse-au-Loup is the largest community on this drive, and the best bet for supplies and accommodation.

Nearby Points of Interest: Thrombolites at Flower's Cove, Deep Cove Winter Housing Site, Musée Scheffer, Battle Harbour National Historic Site, highway to Happy Valley–Goose Bay.

Time Zone: Atlantic time zone (GMT minus 4 hours; does not observe DST) and Newfoundland time zone (GMT minus 3.5 hours).

The Drive

Cross the Strait of Belle Isle on the Newfoundland provincial ferry to the Labrador coast. The bare coast of bluffs, coves, and tiny communities (some just six

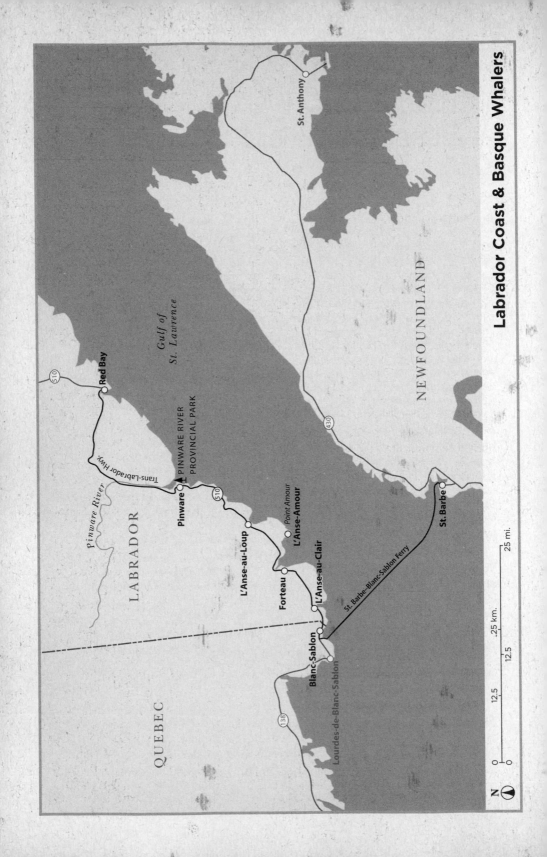

Labrador Coast & Basque Whalers

NEWFOUNDLAND

QUEBEC

LABRADOR

Gulf of
St. Lawrence

Pinware River

Trans-Labrador Hwy.

510

Red Bay

PINWARE RIVER
PROVINCIAL PARK

Pinware

510

L'Anse-au-Loup

Point Amour

L'Anse-Amour

Forteau

L'Anse-au-Clair

Blanc-Sablon

Lourdes-de-Blanc-Sablon

138

St. Barbe-Blanc-Sablon Ferry

St. Barbe

430

St. Anthony

N

0
0
12.5
12.5
25 km.
25 mi.

houses large) create an empty yet engaging landscape. The final portion of the drive follows the Pinware River before reaching Red Bay—the end of the paved road.

Begin by catching the ferry in **St. Barbe,** Newfoundland—about 200 kilometers (124 miles) from the northern end of Gros Morne National Park and 120 kilometers (75 miles) from St. Anthony. It's best to make reservations for the Labrador Marine ferry, which runs two to three times daily in summer. Those with reservations must arrive at the terminal and check in a full hour in advance, or lose the reservation. The 1.5-to-2-hour trip crosses the **Strait of Belle Isle,** providing great views of both coasts.

Quebec to Labrador

The provincial ferry actually arrives in Quebec. The terminal in **Blanc-Sablon** is located in the Atlantic time zone, in an area that doesn't observe daylight savings time. In summer, that puts Blanc-Sablon 1.5 hours behind Newfoundland. Thankfully, despite docking in Quebec, the ferry runs on Newfoundland time—making the schedule far less befuddling.

After exiting the ferry, follow Jacques Cartier Avenue to a T-junction with Route 138 or Dr. Camille Marcoux Boulevard. Head east, crossing the Blanc-Sablon River and passing through the small Quebec community.

Route 138 leads to the Quebec-Labrador border, where a sign welcomes visitors to the "Big Land." Begin the eastward trek over the vast Labrador landscape. It's a challenge to spot a tree on this vast panorama of rocky hills and coastal bluffs. Just imagine trying to build a house or collect firewood.

Climb and descend the bluff above **Charles Point** on what is now **Route 510,** or the **Trans-Labrador Highway.** The village of **L'Anse-au-Clair** centers on a wide beach tucked in a narrow cove—the poetic **Belle Amours Bay.**

The **Gateway to Labrador Visitor Centre** and museum is located on the right when arriving in town. Housed in a 1909 church that was constructed with volunteer labor, the visitor center serves equal parts historical tales and local information.

Over the 11-kilometer (6.8-mile) stretch from L'Anse-au-Clair to **Forteau,** the slightly inland road still affords excellent views of the coast. The highway rounds Forteau Bay, where houses cling to the road. Forteau celebrates the hardy orange **bakeapple berry**—elsewhere known as a cloudberry—with an August festival.

About 5 kilometers (3 miles) after English Point, watch for a right-hand turn to **L'Anse-Amour.** The dusty 4-kilometer (2.5-mile) road leads out to Point Amour but first passes through L'Anse-Amour, where six homes lie along the bay and a sandy beach.

Keep following the cliff-side road around the hill, toward the water, and **Point Amour Lighthouse** soon comes into view. The tallest lighthouse in Atlantic Canada and the second tallest in Canada, Point Amour stands 33.2 meters (109 feet) tall. In summer, costumed guides provide tours of the lighthouse and keeper's quarters, which have been restored to the 1850s period. First lit in 1858, the lighthouse has walls that measure about 1.8 meters (6 feet) thick at the base.

Continue past the lighthouse on the lone road to visit the **Maritime Archaic Burial Mound Historic Site.** The oldest funeral monument in North America dates back about 7,500 years. Excavated in the 1970s, the burial mound featured a wide pit where an adolescent had been wrapped and placed facedown, her/his head pointed west. The adolescent was buried with tools and weapons, and with a flat stone on the lower back. Rocks were piled in a mound over the grave.

A graveyard of another kind lies off the coast. In 1922, HMS *Raleigh* grounded on Point Amour while en route to Forteau Bay to fish for salmon. Measuring 184 meters (605 feet) overall, the light cruiser sat stalled for four years before the British navy used explosives to demolish it.

Return along the dirt road to Route 510, where rolling hills and sparse forest stretch to the inland horizon.

The **Labrador Straits Museum,** between Forteau and L'Anse-au-Loup, displays a vast array of exhibits. From reproductions of the excavated Maritime Archaic burial mound artifacts to stories of the first nursing station on the coast, the museum tells deeply local stories. Run by the Women's Institute, the museum highlights the often-overlooked role of women in the region's history.

Continuing east on Route 510, **Schooner Cove hiking trail** lies on the coastal side of the highway, just before L'Anse-au-Loup. The hike visits a site where the Maritime Archaic peoples first lived, Basque whalers rendered whale oil, and a whaling factory was built in the 1900s.

Stock up on supplies in L'Anse-au-Loup, and then drive over the Red Cliffs and through Diable Bay, Capstan Island, and West St. Modeste.

Pinware River

At Ship Head the **Pinware River** meets the Strait of Belle Isle. **Pinware River Provincial Park** features a smooth, sandy beach, abundant trout fishing, and short hiking trails. A campground and day-use area provide running water, pit toilets, and fire pits. The nearby **Pinware Hill** has yielded artifacts dating to about 9,000 years ago, making it one of the province's oldest Paleo-Indian archaeological sites.

The provincial parks hosts Canada Day celebrations in July, with family-friendly activities.

Point Amour Lighthouse is the tallest in Atlantic Canada and lies near an ancient burial site of the Maritime Archaic people, dating back 7,500 years.

From the park, Route 510 follows the Pinware River for about 20 kilometers (12.4 miles) through to **County Cat Pond.** Midway the treed scenery ends briefly at a bridge over the stunning **Pinware River gorge.** Often visitors will stop mid bridge to photograph and admire, but for the safety of all, continue to the eastern side of the bridge where a sandy dirt road provides short-term parking.

The Pinware River, stocked with a healthy supply of salmon traveling upstream to spawn, is popular with anglers. As the road cuts east, glimpse views of large pond-lakes carved by glaciers and where hills dip down to the coast.

At County Cat Pond, where a few homes sit within this mostly uninhabited landscape, the Pinware River tracks north. More ponds abut the road as the route cuts through a glacial landscape scattered with boulders.

Red Bay

The road meets **Red Bay** on the west side of the harbor, where two trails branch off to the shoreline. The 3-kilometer (2-mile) return **Tracey Hill Trail** is notable for its 689 steps to the top of its namesake hill. Picnic tables make mid-hike rests easier. An easier route, the **Boney Shore Trail** follows the coast to a **whale graveyard.** Bones mark the location where the carcasses of whales, killed by the Basque, washed ashore. A small interpretive site with a model right whale sits alongside the main road and marks the entrance to Red Bay.

On the east side of the bay, you'll see a dirt road twisting up into the hills. It heads north for 340 kilometers (211 miles) to Cartwright.

At the town center, the **Right Whale Exhibit** explores the underwater world of endangered bowhead and right whales. The exhibit, at 50 Main Hwy., displays a **400-year-old whale skeleton,** scavenged from the sea floor of Red Bay.

Alongside a white church on the east side of the harbor, find the two visitor centers/museums for the **Red Bay National Historic Site.** In the 1500s whalers from Basque Country in northern Spain spent summers on the Labrador shores, hunting bowhead and right whales. The Basques rendered the whale blubber into oil, barreled it, and shipped the oil back to Europe. Whale oil was valuable in Europe for use as fuel, and in soaps and pharmaceuticals.

Making summer-season journeys, the whalers would return to the Bay of Biscay for the winter. But harsh winters, when the ice moved in early, could strand the whalers. Unprepared for the long, cold season, many of the whalers would not survive the Labrador winter.

Around **Red Bay Harbour,** archaeologists have uncovered more than 20 whaling stations. The visitor center shows a film on the Red Bay discoveries, and displays excavated whalebones and a *chalupa,* or small wooden whaling boat built

The Pinware River gorge is not only scenic, but the river is excellent for salmon fishing.

by the Basques. The main museum, however, sits on the waterfront. From the nails to clothes to graves, much has been uncovered in the Red Bay area. Model ships and interpretive panels retell the Basque story.

Climb to the viewing tower in the waterfront museum to see the panorama of the bay. Drawings show the location of Basque-era tryworks (cauldrons used for rendering the fat from the blubber) and the cemetery. Look out to the lighthouse keeper's quarters at Bay Lighthouse and Saddle Island. A shuttle boat takes visitors out to Saddle Island where trails lead to the sites of tryworks and cooperages. To the northwest of the island, archaeologists have uncovered a cemetery containing the remains of 140 bodies in 60 graves.

Mid harbor you'll see a beached and rusting steel hull of a shipwreck.

Side Trip: Battle Harbour Historic District

About 90 kilometers (56 miles) north along the coast, take the ferry from **Marys Harbour** to visit a historic island-bound fishing settlement at Battle Harbour. The **Battle Harbour Historic District** is a re-created 1800s fishing station. During the height of the fishery, the community was called the "Capital of Labrador." A fire and decline of the fisheries crippled the community, but today costumed guides, hundreds of artifacts, and restored buildings bring the island outport back to its busiest days.

From Marys Harbour the dirt-road highway pierces farther into the vast territory of Labrador, through to Port Hope Simpson and then Cartwright. The newest phase of the Trans-Labrador Highway connects Cartwright Junction to Happy Valley–Goose Bay: a total of about 550 kilometers (342 miles) over unpaved surface from Red Bay.

25

Vikings

St. Anthony to L'Anse aux Meadows

General Description: Drive back in time a thousand years as this 30-kilometer (18.6-mile) scenic route travels out to the L'Anse aux Meadows National Historic Site. Empty coastal scenery, jam stands, and Viking interpreters create an eclectic but end-of-the-world feel at this northernmost end of the Northern Peninsula. Perhaps the Vikings also felt that they were reaching the end of the world as they landed on these shores more than 1,000 years ago. The glacier-raked scenery yields shallow ponds and frequent moose sightings. In fact Roddickton, just down the coast from St. Anthony, is known as the "moose capital."

Special Features: Dark Tickle Economuseum, Norstead: A Viking Port of Trade, L'Anse aux Meadows National Historic Site, Pistolet Bay Provincial Park, Burnt Cape Eco Reserve.

Location: Northern Peninsula, Newfoundland.

Driving Route Numbers & Names: Route 430, Route 436, Route 437.

Travel Season: Summer rates as the best time to travel with the attractions at their peak: Interpretive sites are filled with guides demonstrating ancient chores, and the local restaurants are serving bakeapple and partridgeberry desserts.

Camping: Pistolet Bay Provincial Park makes a lovely, quiet campground for visitors. There is a small RV campground outside L'Anse aux Meadows. While Triple Falls RV Park is close to the services in St. Anthony, I found it excessively noisy (music playing until 3 a.m. on a weekday).

Services: St. Anthony, while not the prettiest town, offers plenty of services, including gas stations, medical care, and groceries. Hay Cove features historic bed-and-breakfasts close to the Viking attractions, while St. Anthony offers a mix of motels and inns.

Nearby Points of Interest: Grenfell Interpretive Centre, Dock House Museum.

Time Zone: Newfoundland time (GMT minus 3.5 hours).

The Drive

An amble through a bare and glacier-carved landscape, the 30-kilometer (18.6-mile) trip to L'Anse aux Meadows takes on a dreamlike quality. It's a barren landscape, like in so many areas of Newfoundland, but without the sweeping views the hillocks give the feeling of finding a hidden destination. Ponds and stunted conifers are slipped between massive granite boulders.

Begin this route from Route 430, the Viking Trail. The turnoff is about 300 kilometers (186 miles) from the northern end of Gros Morne National Park—first along a coastal road then through a horizon-filling view of bog, ponds, and barren.

St. Anthony lies at the precarious end of the Northern Peninsula, lightening the severe winter weather with celebratory festivals. **The Grenfell Ride,** in March,

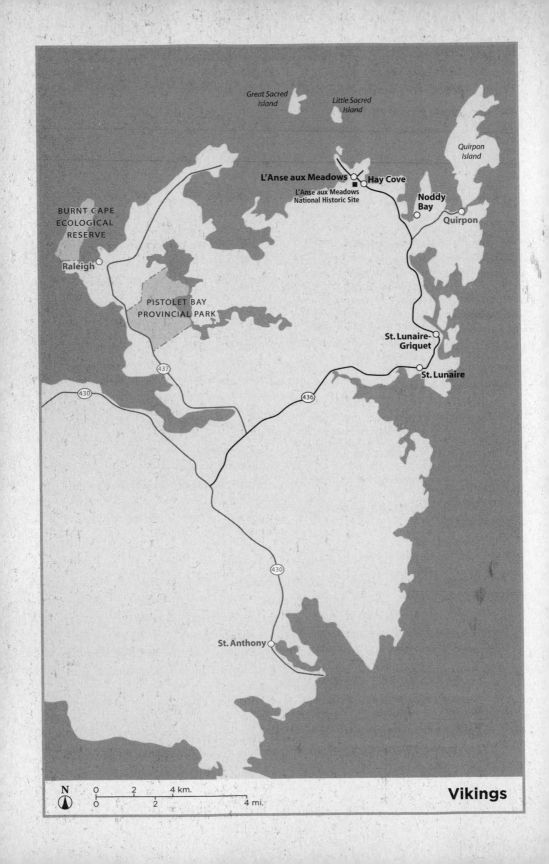

Great Sacred
Island

Little Sacred
Island

Quirpon
Island

L'Anse aux Meadows ◻ **Hay Cove**
L'Anse aux Meadows
National Historic Site

**Noddy
Bay**

Quirpon

BURNT CAPE
ECOLOGICAL
RESERVE

Raleigh

PISTOLET BAY
PROVINCIAL PARK

**St. Lunaire-
Griquet**

437

436

St. Lunaire

430

430

St. Anthony

N

0   2   4 km.
0   2   4 mi.

Vikings

Fishing huts and coastal cliffs form the rugged scenery of the Northern Peninsula.

recalls the journey of renowned physician Dr. Wilfred Grenfell from *Adrift on an Ice Pan* and turns it into the world's longest chain of snowmobiles. **The Iceberg Festival** in June offers boat tours, nature walks, and music, plus the giants of **Iceberg Alley.**

From this northern commercial center, you'll travel just 10 kilometers (6.2 miles) west over a forested, unscenic road to Route 436.

Whichever way you arrive, be sure to watch carefully for moose that like to hang out eating the foliage near the highway.

St. Lunaire-Griquet

Route 436 winds through the landscape of ponds, coniferous scrub, and irregular hills, haphazard in their placement. About 10 kilometers (6.2 miles) past the junction with Route 430, the road meets the saltwater in St. Lunaire Bay. Small islands mark the inside harbor and mouth of the bay, including **Granchain Island**—its rocky headlands protecting the bay from the harshest winds. Flocks of seabirds circle above the fishing community and the bay, where fishing boats are docked at wharves along the shore.

The **Dark Tickle,** one of Newfoundland's most recognizable makers of home-made goods, is located in St. Lunaire. Dark Tickle produces jams, chocolates, teas, vinegars, and other items from the local berries. The shiny orange **bakeapple berries** (cloudberries) and tart **partridgeberries** (lingonberries) are two Newfoundland-favorite varieties.

The shop, which takes its name from a narrow channel of water called a tickle, also operates as an economuseum—where traditional crafters share their processes with visitors. Trails, a tearoom, and the berry patch make for a satisfying visit.

Although French fishermen plied these waters in the 1500s and the Vikings before that, the area was not mapped until 1784. It was then that **Liberge de Granchain,** a French sailor, charted the waters while stuck in the bay. On the island named for him, bread ovens from the 16th-century visits of French fishermen are still visible. The Dark Tickle features an exhibit on Granchain and his work.

As the road approaches Gunners Cove on Griquet Harbour, the landscape evens out into larger hills. A sheer cliff marks White Cape and the protected entrance to the narrow waterway. In the tangled bay of Griquet Harbour, Griquet is an island community.

A right turn onto the next peninsula takes you on a circuitous route along the coast and through the residential community on **Quirpon Harbour.** Fishing boats, wharves, and vinyl-sided homes line the shoreline.

L'Anse aux Meadows

In **Noddy Bay,** the protected national historic site begins. More than the archaeological site alone, the grounds encompass 80 square kilometers (31 square miles) of islands, bay, and bogs. Windswept bluffs, lush islands, and a changing ocean create a wild scene.

Between Hay Cove and L'Anse aux Meadows, turnoffs lead to **Norstead: A Viking Port of Trade** and **L'Anse aux Meadows National Historic Site.** But first follow Route 430 to its end.

In the community of **L'Anse aux Meadows,** the road forks around Medee Bay. Both routes are dead ends and lead to wild views. Seagulls drop sea urchins on the pavement to break open the tough shells. Off the coast Great Sacred, Little Sacred, Warren, and Green Islands are clearly visible, with the larger but fainter Belle Isle farther offshore.

L'Anse aux Meadows National Historic Site features a Viking leader's hall, built from sod.

At **L'Anse aux Meadows National Historic Site,** a large visitor center overlooks the archaeological site, reconstructed leader's hall, and coastal walking trails. Helge Ingstad, an explorer and writer from Norway, discovered the site in 1960, in part by following the ancient sagas of Vinland. Local George Decker, who knew the humped ground as an old First Nations camp, led him to the site.

L'Anse aux Meadows is the earliest evidence of Europeans arriving in North America, and so predates the infamous journey of Christopher Columbus in 1492 and Prince Henry Sinclair's possible voyage in 1398. At the visitor center interpretive panels lead you through the tales of **Vinland**—of exiled murderers and Viking explorers. About 1,000 years ago Vikings from a colony in Greenland landed here and established an outpost. They explored farther south, seeking hardwood, but the base was burnt and abandoned a few seasons after.

L'Anse aux Meadows was protected as a historic site in 1969 and added to the World Heritage Site list in 1978.

Walk along a boardwalk to the reconstructed Viking base. A large sod hall is filled with weapons, sheepskins, and a flickering hearth. Bearded Viking interpreters sit around the fire, telling stories and answering visitors' questions. A group of crafters weave sail cloth, spin wool thread, and tie knotted belts. Around the hall, workers build a replica boat and shape nails in the forge. Slaves go out to the stream to fetch water and cook meals.

You can interact with all these characters, who explain their tasks or tell mythical stories. Dress for photos with helmets, swords, and shields.

After exploring the living-history portion, head over to the ruins, now showing as grassed-over bumps. Rectangular shapes faintly show where the buildings of the Viking encampment stood 1,000 years ago. The leader's hall, the largest building, is about the same size as a chieftain's hall in Iceland.

Also along Medee Bay, Norstead recreates a Viking port of trade. The boathouse features a **full replica Viking cargo ship,** the *Snorri*, while the forge shows how nails were made. Enter the chieftain's hall to hear stories, or walk the grounds and watch a Viking battle. The site is similar to that at L'Anse aux Meadows, but with more hands-on activities. Norstead celebrates the **Summer Solstice Viking Festival** in June.

Side Trip One: Raleigh

Just 4 kilometers (2.5 miles) in from the junction of Routes 430 and 436 (the road to L'Anse aux Meadows), another road branches off to a provincial park and nature reserve. Route 437 follows Milan Arm to Pistolet Bay, Ha Ha Bay, and out to Ship Cove at its end.

Halfway to Raleigh, stop in at **Pistolet Bay Provincial Park.** The park is situated near a salmon river, and the campground offers 30 sites serviced with fire pits, washrooms, showers, laundry, and drinking water. The day-use area has access to a freshwater pond for swimming.

At **Raleigh,** the main road off Route 437 leads to **Burnt Cape Provincial Ecological Reserve.** A naked landscape of limestone, the reserve is the rooting ground for rare plant species. The growing season is short here, with frosts occurring year-round, but the plants survive despite the peninsula's harsh climate. Guided hikes are available, or hike independently keeping on the reserve roads so as not to disturb the arctic plants.

A further 11 kilometers (6.8 miles) on Route 437, the road heads out to Ship Cove and Cape Onion, on the western edge of the national historic site. Look out to island and ocean views from the rugged shore where Vikings once anchored.

Side Trip Two: St. Anthony

A town of perseverance, **St. Anthony** has attractions that center on a hardy character, **Dr. Wilfred Grenfell**—a medical doctor who practiced here in the late 19th and early 20th centuries. In 1892 Grenfell arrived to evaluate life on the Labrador coast and then established a medical service. In 1900, he became the first doctor in St. Anthony—an area that had been settled by migratory fishermen since the 1500s.

The extent to which Dr. Grenfell went to treat his remote patients can perhaps be best examined in his tale *Adrift on an Ice Pan*. In the epic, Dr. Grenfell and his dog team are stranded offshore on an unstable slush of ice. He survived by killing three dogs before being rescued.

ıuks & Icebergs

Lew.... te to Boyd's Cove to Twillingate

General Description: Traverse causeways, islands, and historic Beothuk territory to travel to Twillingate, Newfoundland's most renowned iceberg-watching destination. A 125-kilometer (78-mile) scenic drive ventures from the calm waters of Lewisporte, skirts the Bay of Exploits, and then island-hops out to Twillingate. Along the way, visit museums that explore historic fishing methods, recall outport life, and present the scant-known information about the extinct Beothuk peoples.

Special Features: Lewisporte Train Park, By the Bay Museum, Boyd's Cove Beothuk Interpretation Centre, Dildo Run Provincial Park, Prime Berth–Twillingate Fishery Museum, Twillingate Museum, Durrell Museum, Long Point Lighthouse, iceberg watching, whale watching, hiking, bird watching.

Location: Along the Bay of Exploits, on the northern coast midway between Grand Falls–Windsor and Gander.

Driving Route Numbers & Names: Route 340, with many side trip options.

Travel Season: Travel in May or June for the best chances of seeing icebergs—although to catch the cold giants, it's essential to phone in advance or track the bergs at www.icebergfinder.com. Museums and attractions keep the longest hours from June through September.

Camping: Camp in Lewisporte for full services, or en route at Dildo Run Provincial Park, where there are pit toilets, showers, drinking-water taps, and fire pits. Notre Dame Provincial Park, located near the Trans-Canada Highway, has washrooms, showers, and laundry facilities.

Services: Gander and Grand Falls–Windsor are the easiest places to make a supply run before embarking on this scenic drive. Lewisporte offers groceries and gas, as does Twillingate at the road's end. Find medical assistance in Twillingate.

Nearby Points of Interest: Change Islands, Fogo Island, Pikes Arm Museum and Lookout, Moreton's Harbour Community Museum, Notre Dame Provincial Park, Silent Witness Memorial in Gander.

Time Zone: Newfoundland time (GMT minus 3.5 hours).

The Drive

This route is a 125-kilometer (78-mile) tangent north from the Trans-Canada Highway, the starting point for many drives in central Newfoundland. Following the coast along the **Bay of Exploits,** causeways link islands and lead out to the frigid northern coast where icebergs meander by.

Whether traveling east or west on the Trans-Canada Highway, take the Lewisporte-Twillingate exit at Notre Dame Junction. Nearby **Notre Dame**

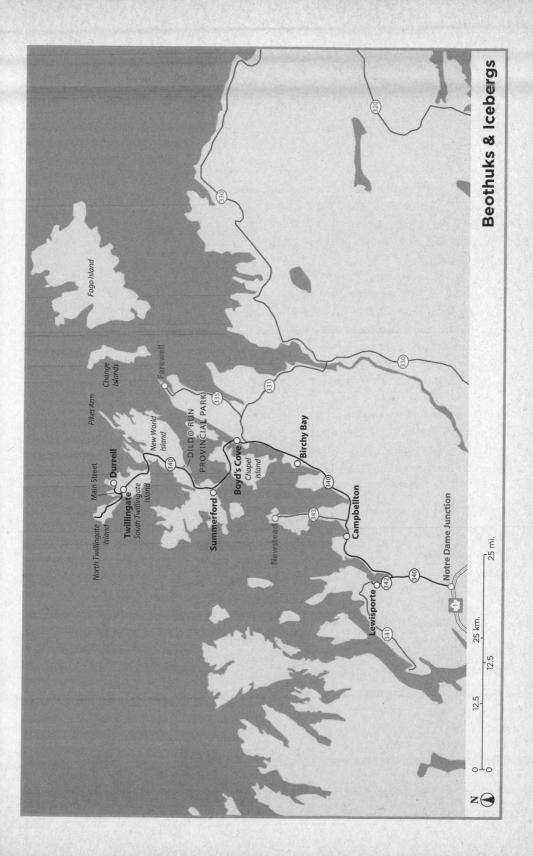

Beothuks & Icebergs

Provincial Park offers campsites, flush toilets, showers, and laundry facilities—a few more comforts than the campground at **Dildo Run** mid route.

From the highway exit, Route 340—also know as the Road to the Isles—heads north.

Lewisporte

An unscenic, 11-kilometer (6.8-mile) stretch cuts through forest to the head of Burnt Bay. For a break, stop in at the roadside **Lewisporte Train Park** on West Main Street, which features a passenger car, caboose, and interpretive railway displays. A large orange snowplow hints at the climate challenges the railway faced in Newfoundland.

The Newfoundland Railway connected Port aux Basques to St. John's, linking small settlements across the province. From the late 1890s to 1969, a passenger service ran across the province on the line, and then freight only through 1988. After Canadian National decommissioned the narrow-gauge rail lines, they became a provincial park—the 883-kilometer (548-mile) **T'railway.** Walkers, runners, and cyclists use the trail, and the recreational corridor crosses the island.

Main Street heads straight into downtown Lewisporte, while Route 340 continues to the right.

Head first into **Lewisporte,** via Main Street, where the **By the Bay Museum** shows local exhibitions, thoughtfully illuminating the history of the Bay of Exploits. Located in an old school, a craft gallery provides handmade wares, from Newfoundland hand knits to jams. The town has a sheltered marina, and the wide waters of Burnt Bay are an attractive sight when filled with boats under sail.

Lewisporte was once a rich timber region, its hills thick with spruce, birch, and the now-rare white pine. The forest resources drew shipbuilders to establish operations here. Sheltered ocean access and the nearby railway at Notre Dame Junction made Lewisporte a shipping center. During World War II, the port provided supplies to Canadian Forces Base Gander. Due to logging and fungal disease, however, the stands of white pine have been largely reduced.

Leaving Lewisporte, follow Main Street back to Route 340, which then cuts north for about 50 kilometers (31 miles) to Boyd's Cove. The road follows bays and passes through low, forested hills. En route in **Campbellton,** fishing wharfs make the area look more like a Nova Scotia coastal village than the usually rugged Newfoundland coastline.

Islands in Indian Arm—Sivier, Birchy, and Camel—are visible along with the peninsula town of Newstead. Dozens of named islands lie in the Bay of Exploits, and you'll see many more exposed at low tide that put the overall tally in the hundreds.

Side routes like Route 343 to **Newstead** are scenic to explore but offer no definitive attractions beyond the views. Coming to Loon Bay the road crosses a narrow section of water and then continues along the eastern side of the bay. At Birchy Bay, the main street provides another scenic detour and a snack stop.

Finally, 50 kilometers (31 miles) from Lewisporte, the route arrives at Boyd's Cove on the shore of an undescriptively named water channel known as the Reach.

At **Boyd's Cove,** Route 340 crosses a causeway en route to Twillingate in the northwest, while to the northeast, Routes 331 and then 335 head to the ferry terminal at Farewell on the tip of the Port Albert Peninsula. The ferry service connects to Change Islands and the large Fogo Island. The latter first appeared on French maps and was settled by English and Irish settlers. In fishing outports along the coast, Fogo Island residents refused to move inland during resettlement. The island is a favorite destination to experience Newfoundland culture.

Boyd's Cove

Driving on Route 340, follow signs along Boyd's Cove South Road to the **Beothuk Interpretation Centre.** The interpretive center pieces together what is known about the now-extinct Beothuks, the original native inhabitants of Newfoundland. Through a combination of European conflicts, European diseases, and loss of territory, the Beothuk population was decimated; the last Beothuk—a woman in her late 20s named Shanawdithit—died in 1829.

At the interpretation center a short video shows interviews with Dr. Ralph Pastore, who excavated 4 of the 11 Beothuk dwellings here in the 1980s. See the powdered red ochre that the Beothuk used for ceremonies, which also acts as a fly repellent. View artifacts the Beothuk fashioned from European iron implements, such as nails that they flattened and sharpened into arrowheads.

The Beothuks avoided trade with the Europeans, and instead preferred to visit the abandoned fishing communities in winter. When the fishermen returned to the seasonal outposts each spring, their encounters with the Beothuks escalated to violence because of the missing items and overlapping territories.

From the visitor center a trail and boardwalk lead down to the shoreline archaeological site and former Beothuk village. The sites have been filled in again after the excavations, showing as mere numbered depressions in the grass. Perhaps more special to see is Newfoundland artist Gerald Squires's bronze sculpture of a Beothuk woman. Proud and silent, the statue brings home the emotions that we can only imagine Shanawdithit felt in 1829: being the presumed last of your people.

Leaving Boyd's Cove, and still on Route 340, cross the first causeway—Reach Run Causeway—to Chapel Island. The L. R. Curtis Causeway connects Chapel Island to a smaller island, a stepping-stone in Dildo Run en route to Summerford on New World Island.

Route 344 ventures through **Summerford,** which offers a few supplies. Farther north at **Virgin Arm,** find a side trip on Route 345 out to **Moreton's Harbour,** where there is a community museum.

Views of North and South Trump Islands in Friday Bay linger to the left, while the main route passes alongside **Dildo Run Provincial Park** on the right.

More than just its snicker-worthy name, the protected area has hiking trails and viewpoints that look out to Dildo Run. Among the twisted peninsulas, there are hundreds of teeny islands. Seemingly countless, the islands number about 365 according to the provincial park literature. For facilities, the park offers a campground with pit toilets, showers, drinking water, laundry, and a sewage dump station.

Traveling north, Route 340 is surrounded with interesting scenery: Steeply mounded hills show rocky bedrock between thick coniferous forests, while small lakes and bays pierce the tree line.

Just after Newville, a side trip on Route 346 takes you east to **Pikes Arm Museum and Lookout**—a detour of 11 kilometers (6.8 miles) one-way.

Twillingate

Leaving New World Island, cross the Walter B. Elliott Causeway to arrive on South Twillingate Island. **Prime Berth–Twillingate Fishery Museum** sits immediately to the left when arriving on the island. At the collection of buildings on the shore, interpreters demonstrate the treasured techniques of fishing, including splitting and salting the cod and drying squid. Stories, song, and photos piece together the mostly lost way of outport life. The museum introduces you to Twillingate's history—that of a fishery that prompted men to build wharves and boats and head out to sea.

In all directions Route 340 affords gorgeous views of a convoluted coast. Coves and communities lie along the water in the dozens, giving testament to the rich fishing grounds that once sustained the area. But as the route enters into **Twillingate,** the scenery starts to empty, and the windswept coastal barrens begin.

At a T-junction, head left to North Twillingate Island or right into Durrell. Both routes are not to be missed—the former will deliver the most stunning views, and the latter offers an interesting museum.

First turn right to **Durrell,** following the South Twillingate Island coast past Jenkins Cove. At Museum Road, look for the single-story red building that was built as an Arm Lads Brigade armory in 1910. Today the **Durrell Museum** displays a slice of Twillingate life, ranging from the old brigade uniforms to a stuffed polar bear that traveled to the town on the ice flows in 2000. More exhibits revive the

A bronze statue in Boyds Cove is a silent reminder that the last Beothuk died in 1829.

Icebergs often float south to Twillingate, where the Long Point Lighthouse and a viewing deck allow great views.

day-to-day of outport life, famed in movies and books such as *Random Passage* and *The Shipping News*. The museum overlooks Durrell Arm.

Follow Main Street back to Route 340, this time crossing the causeway to **North Twillingate Island.**

On the northern island, history is not forgotten. A Women's Institute—a nonsectarian educational organization—sits near the **Twillingate Museum.** The museum is housed in a 1913 cream-colored, two-story home with a wide porch overlooking the main street. Exhibits feature local stories, such as that of opera soprano Marie Toulinquet, who was born in Twillingate as Georgina Stirling. Other histories range from First Nations to mining and the Alphabet Fleet.

Made into near-legends in folk songs and paintings, the **Alphabet Fleet** were boats owned by the Reid Newfoundland Company. The boats ran mail, passengers, and supplies to remote Newfoundland outports—thereby connecting the communities to the inland world. The 13 boats were named for Scottish towns, from the SS *Argyle* to the SS *Meigle*.

Stop in **Twillingate** for lunch where wharf-side restaurants serve local seafood. Whale-watching and iceberg tours depart from the town. The **July Fish Fun & Folk Festival** in Twillingate hosts a party with Newfoundland music and fireworks.

From the commercial center, Route 340 continues north past fishing stages and heritage homes to the viewpoint at Devils Cove Head. The narrow twisting road with steep inclines ends at rocky cliffs. From the viewing platforms icebergs are sometimes visible in May and June, but don't come to town without checking on the icebergs first (www.icebergfinder.com).

The blocky Lego-like **Long Point Lighthouse** stands more than 100 meters (331 feet) above sea level and marks Newfoundland's **"Iceberg Alley."** The lighthouse, built in 1876, and interpretation center display exhibits, antiques, and crafts.

The small, gray **Gull Island** is shaped almost like an iceberg. But whatever the season, use the stationed binoculars to spot seabirds feeding around the island or perhaps whales breaching on the horizon.

Side Trip: Change Islands & Fogo Island

From the prettily named community of **Farewell,** a ferry connects the tangled peninsulas of central Newfoundland to **Change Islands** and **Fogo Island.**

Fogo, the largest offshore island, was first settled by the Beothuks and then seasonally by European fishermen in the 1500s. The isolation of the culture and the refusal of locals to move during resettlement has developed a distinct island spirit. Fishing has been the main industry since its settlement.

Theater productions, heritage fishing stages, age-old cemeteries, and a stunning coastline spin the weathered tales of Fogo Island.

27

Hidden Beaches & Abandoned Outports

Terra Nova National Park to Eastport to Salvage

General Description: This 38-kilometer (23.6-mile) scenic drive provides a short detour from the national park to a historic fishing community. Dramatic views of the national park, a water-bound causeway, beaches where access is restricted by the tides, and hikes to abandoned outports all allow visitors to explore a mostly uninhabited coast.

Special Features: Glovertown Museum, Terra Nova National Park, Eastport beaches, Beaches Heritage Centre, Burnside Archaeology Centre, Salvage Fishermen's Museum, historic fish stages, hiking trails.

Location: On the northern shore of central Newfoundland, west of the Bonavista Peninsula.

Driving Route Numbers & Names: Route 310 (Road to the Beaches).

Travel Season: July and August offer the best weather to enjoy the beaches that give this route its name.

Camping: Two campgrounds in Terra Nova National Park—Malady Head and Newman Sound—offer full facilities including showers and bathrooms. The wooded campgrounds, generally quiet and patrolled by security, have fire pits and picnic tables. Washrooms, however, are not as nice as the comfort stations at many private campgrounds.

Services: Glovertown near the park entrance has full services including firewood, gas, and supplies. The park is midway between hospitals in Clarenville to the east and Gander to the west. Fuel and basic supplies are available along the drive in Sandringham and Eastport.

Nearby Points of Interest: Salvage and Terra Nova National Park lie alongside the Bonavista Peninsula, where the heritage fishing villages are renowned for their scenic charm. In Bonavista find the Ryan Premises and Mockbeggar national historic sites, Bonavista Museum, Abbott's Wildlife Museum, and Elliston's Root Cellars. On the southeastern side of the peninsula, visit the Trinity Historical Museum and Hiscock House.

Time Zone: Newfoundland time (GMT minus 3.5 hours).

The Drive

Tucked above the **Bonavista Peninsula** sits an often-overlooked area. Accessible only through a stretch of Terra Nova National Park, this 38-kilometer (23.6-mile) scenic route along the Eastport Peninsula is also known as the **Road to the Beaches.**

The sandy shores in Eastport alone are worth the trip. Liven the mix by adding explorations in the quaint fishing town of Salvage, with its red fishing stages and trail network to abandoned communities.

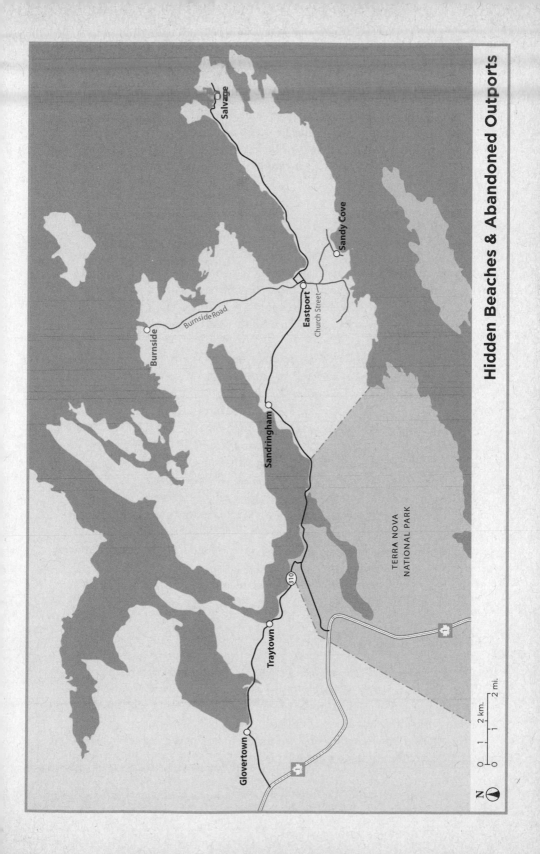

Hidden Beaches & Abandoned Outports

Salvage

Sandy Cove

Eastport
Church Street

Burnside Road

Burnside

Sandringham

310

Traytown

Glovertown

TERRA NOVA
NATIONAL PARK

N

0   1   2 km.
0   1   2 mi.

From the Trans-Canada Highway, take the turnoff for Glovertown and follow Route 310 through a string of commercial and residential buildings, stopping perhaps at the Glovertown Museum—The Janes House to learn about the resettlement of the Bonavista Bay islands to more central towns.

After Traytown, Route 310 begins to follow the coast of Terra Nova National Park and a bend of the far-reaching Northeast Arm. For a faster route, stay on the Trans-Canada Highway for an extra 9 kilometers (5.6 miles) to take the exit for Traytown and Malady Head.

Terra Nova National Park

Set aside in 1957, **Terra Nova National Park** was the province's first national park. A labyrinth of rocky peninsulas juts out into Bonavista Bay, creating sheltered boating areas and a diverse coastline. Hilly scenery of boreal forest forms an untouched backdrop to the water. Throughout the park hiking trails lead to abandoned outport communities and lookouts, while boat ramps and beaches provide access to the water.

Driving east on Route 310, find **Malady Head campground.** The quiet, forested sites are family friendly and well maintained. All have picnic tables and fire pits, plus access to showers, washrooms, and a playground. To reach the park visitor center—where a touch tank, film, and exhibits introduce the park and its wildlife—and the larger Newman Sound campground, backtrack to the Trans-Canada Highway and continue south to the center of the park.

But to continue the scenic drive on Route 310, follow the Northeast Arm of Alexander Bay. The road crosses a causeway, which divides the arm from Broad Cove in Southeast Arm. The sheltered waters to the right are favored with canoeists.

With water on both sides, the kilometer-long causeway is achingly pretty. Either stop on the east side of the causeway to look back at the glacier-rounded Appalachian hills, or plan to return close to sunset to see the silhouetted skyline of Terra Nova National Park.

Just before it leaves the park boundaries, the road passes a beach and picnic area.

Sandringham and Eastport

Route 310 follows the Northeast Arm through to **Sandringham.** Strung along the highway, the town provides options to fuel and stock up. Follow the road through a forested section to reach **Eastport,** the center of the peninsula, and a junction of routes to Burnside, Sandy Cove, and Salvage.

The **Road to the Beaches**—named for Eastport's delightfully sandy shores—passes the **Beaches Heritage Centre** in Eastport, about 15 kilometers (9 miles) from the Trans-Canada Highway. Housed in the old community school, the heritage center hosts art exhibits and theater performances, as well as the annual Winterset in Summer—a literary festival.

Stop in for hiking maps and information about **the Old Trails,** which follow the traditional paths between outport fishing communities on the peninsula. The hiking trails connect the beach community of **Sandy Cove** (just south of Eastport on Church Street) to the saltbox houses of **Salvage.** Along the approximately 20 kilometers (12.4 miles) of old footpaths and cart roads, the trails pass ponds, wildflower meadows, and coastal viewpoints.

At the head of rectangular, sandy **Eastport Bay** (also called Salvage Bay), find the **Eastport beaches.** A rarity amid the rugged Newfoundland coastline, the beaches have made the area a favorite summer destination for locals. Along the shore find easily accessible Eastport Beach, tiny but quiet Seal Cove Beach, and the largest of the three—kilometer-long Northwest Beach. While all the beaches are accessible along the shoreline at low tide, the High Tide Trail connects them at high water. Eastport Beach, also called Southwest Beach, has a large parking area with change rooms and picnic areas.

Settlers first arrived in Eastport in the mid-1860s, having left crowded Salvage at the end of the peninsula (so desirable because of its proximity to fishing grounds). Besides the beaches, the arable land on the Eastport Peninsula is another Newfoundland rarity, as topsoil is barely apparent in some areas of the province. The **Eastport Peninsula Agriculture Exhibition** celebrates this legacy with events ranging from pie eating to strong-man competitions.

In the 1960s Eastport Beach saw houses floated in from island communities—part of a resettlement plan to consolidate communities so the government could more easily provide health care and education.

From Eastport, take a drive south along Church Street and then follow Main Street to Sandy Cove—a fitting name for a community with such a wide stretch of sand. The beach looks out on Newman Sound and Swale Island in Terra Nova National Park.

North from Eastport, Burdens Road becomes Burnside Road (officially Route 310-32) and leads out past St. Chads on Damnable Bay—often pronounced "Damn the Bell." At the end of the road lies the community of Burnside, situated on Fair and False Bay. The drive, 8 kilometers (5 miles) one way, gives access to the **Burnside Archaeology Centre,** where artifacts provide insight into the ancient peoples who fished and hunted on this coast of islands. Discoveries show that Maritime Archaic, Paleo-Eskimo, and Beothuk people lived on the peninsula dating back at least 5,000 years. Known as the Bloody Reach archaeological sites, the area includes a Beothuk burial ground and rock quarry. The region is accessible by boat only; guided tours can be arranged through the center.

Burnside is also the departure point for the 45-minute ferry to St. Brendan's on Cottel Island.

Salvage

The Road to the Beaches keeps close to the coast as it follows Eastport Bay toward Salvage. Beyond the island-sheltered harbor, see the rocky bulge of Cow Head on the ever-nearing horizon. Islands—Sailors, Bakers Loaf, Petty, and Hart—scatter the bay. Before reaching town you'll pass picnic tables and a small park area at Wild Cove.

The saltbox houses and ochre-red fishing stages of Salvage hug Bishops Harbour. First settled in the 1600s, the community is often noted as one of the oldest continually settled places in the area. Migratory fishermen initially used the sheltered harbor as a base, and permanent settlement followed. From the mid-1800s through the 1930s, men and fishing schooners left for the summer Labrador fishery. They would return laden with salt cod for winter stocks and selling.

The local **Salvage Fishermen's Museum** on the main road lays out the history of the area and is located in the community's oldest building, a white two-story house dating to 1860. The preserved fishing stages and boathouses cluster on the shore, alongside wharves and docked vessels. A seafood packaging company is stationed on the large community wharf, making Salvage a working fishery still.

In 2001, the fish plant burnt down, putting many workers out of a job. But restoration of the **Salvage Trails** provided employment after the fire. The trails are derived from old footpaths and rural roads between outports along this coast. Trails venture out to Net Point and other lookouts around the town.

The trail network also connects to the Old Trails, which lead back to Sandy Cove via abandoned Broomclose, Barrow Harbour, and Little Harbour along Bonavista Bay.

In September 2010, Hurricane Igor lashed the peninsula, washing away roads and damaging infrastructure.

Side Trip: Terra Nova National Park & the Bonavista Peninsula

Terra Nova National Park offers many days of exploration by boat tour, paddle, and hiking trail. Newman Sound and Clode Sound are the largest saltwater channels into the park, and **Bonavista Peninsula,** with many well-known heritage attractions, sits to the south.

A fishing outport with historic ochre-red fishing stages, Salvage rates as a picturesque spot.

Routes 230 and 235 trace the shorelines of the hook-shaped Bonavista Peninsula. At its point, the town of Bonavista features fishing heritage sites. The **Ryan Premises National Historic Site, Mockbeggar National Historic Site, Bonavista Museum, Abbott's Wildlife Museum,** and **Elliston's Root Cellars** all explore the town's history as a commercial and fishing center.

On the southeastern side of the peninsula, Trinity is perfectly picturesque. The **Trinity Historical Museum** and **Hiscock House/Lester Garland Premises Provincial Historic Site** provide background to the photo-worthy setting. South along the coast, visit the ***Random Passage* film set**—where sod-roof houses perched on the rocky shore re-created early-1800s outport life for the television miniseries.

28

Bell Island

Portugal Cove to Wabana, Bell Island

General Description: This 36-kilometer (22.4-mile) loop crosses the Bell Island Tickle between Portugal Cove and Bell Island, Conception Bay's largest island. Once home to 12,000 people, the island grew prosperous by mining iron ore from its heavy rocks—originally used as boat ballast and to give weight to traditional killicks, or anchors. Tour a submarine mine or admire the painted murals depicting mining life. Visit the dock in Lance Cove that saw the only German land attack in North America during World War II. See the memorial to the lost sailors, hike to artillery guns, and discover secret beaches below towering cliffs.

Special Features: Bell Island Ferry, Bell Island Gunsite, Lance Cove memorial, shipwrecks, Bell Island Community Museum, Underground Mine Tour, Bell Island Sports Hall of Fame, Grebes Nest, Bell Island Lighthouse.

Location: Conception Bay in the Avalon Peninsula.

Driving Route Numbers & Names: Bell Island Ferry, Beach Hill, the Front, Lance Cove Road, Middleton Avenue, West Mines Road, Main Street, Quigleys Line, Lighthouse Road, Long Harry Road.

Travel Season: Although the ferry runs year-round, ice can hamper crossing from February through June. The Bell Island Community Museum, which gives underground mine tours, opens June to Sept. As it is the island's main attraction, a visit is best timed during the summer months.

Camping: There are no camping facilities on Bell Island, but the island is a good day-trip distance from Pippy Park in St. John's or Butter Pot Provincial Park near Holyrood. Both are fully equipped campgrounds for tents and RVs.

Services: Wabana, the largest town on Bell Island, features all the basics, including a hospital, grocery store, and a gas station. There is a bed-and-breakfast on the island—Belle of the Bay Inn—and more accommodation options in Portugal Cove.

Nearby Points of Interest: Visit Bell Island as part of a coastal drive from St. John's, exploring Conception Bay's rich historical and natural sites: Pouch Cove Museum, Butter Pot Provincial Park, Hawthorne Cottage National Historic Site, Cupids Archaeology Dig, Cupids Legacy Centre, Conception Bay Museum, and Harbour Grace Airstrip.

Time Zone: Newfoundland time zone (GMT minus 3.5 hours).

The Drive

World War II history, submarine mines, and a controversial ball-lightning strike provide a magnetic complement on **Bell Island.** With one main road that trims the island, you'll spend little time driving on this 36-kilometer (22.4-mile) island loop and lots touring an iron-ore mine and spotting the wartime shipwrecks.

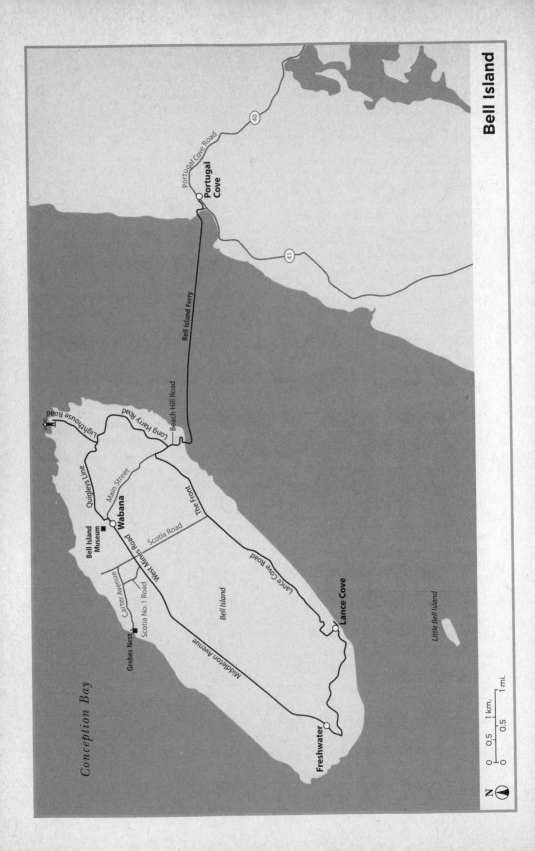

Bell Island

Conception Bay

Lighthouse Road

Quigleys Line

Main Street

Bell Island Museum

Wabana

Carter Avenue

Grebes Nest

West Mines Road

Scotia No. 1 Road

Scotia Road

The Front

Middleton Avenue

Bell Island

Lance Cove Road

Lance Cove

Freshwater

Little Bell Island

Long Harry Road

Beach Hill Road

Bell Island Ferry

Portugal Cove Road

Portugal Cove

40

41

N

0   0.5   1 km.
0   0.5   1 mi.

Unfortunately, on summer weekends you'll also spend time in ferry lines. The ferry operates on a no-reservations policy, so if at all possible arrive during off-peak times. Avoid weekday rush hours and midmorning to early evening on weekends. Ferries run daily, with more than a dozen trips; however, in winter conditions the tickle—a narrow channel of water—can pack with ice, making the crossing impassable.

Bell Island Tickle

Portugal Cove Road, Route 40, leads from St. John's and passes the airport en route to **Portugal Cove** on the shore of Conception Bay. You may see the ferry "lineup," along the right shoulder of the road before the ferry. Avoid blocking driveways and keep in mind that the line moves quickly for the short 20-minute crossing.

Board either the MV *Flanders* or the MV *Beaumont Hamel* in Portugal Cove. Transportation regulations require passengers to head to the upper decks—an appreciated opportunity to admire the views during the crossing. There are washrooms and a small canteen on board.

In 1940 a tragic accident saw two ferries—the *W. Garland* and *Little Golden Dawn*—collide just off the Bell Island shore. The *W. Garland,* carrying 24 passengers plus crew, sank in four minutes. The mostly empty *Little Golden Dawn* stayed afloat longer. Twenty-two died, and a memorial to the disaster stands near the beach at the island ferry dock.

Bell Island's vertical cliffs, rising up to about 45 meters (148 feet) in places, give a stony welcome to the island.

As the ferry docks at Beach Hill, look to the left to see the **Bell Island Gunsite.** A hiking trail leads up to the promontory where you can see guns that fired on German U-boats during World War II.

A testament to the small size of the island, which measures only 3.5 kilometers (2.2 miles) wide and less than 10 kilometers (6.2 miles) long, is the sight of the **Wabana water tower.** The town is the final stop for this drive.

Drive up the steep hill from the ferry and take a left at the Y-intersection, then another left at the stop sign onto a route known as the Front. The road quickly clips along at about 90 meters (295 feet) in elevation. Despite the road being set slightly inland, the high vantage allows clear views of Conception Bay. Heading southwest along the road, look out to Little Bell and Kellys Islands. Bell Island was once called Great Belle Isle, but the name was shortened over time.

Follow the road through farm fields. Irish and English, drawn to the arable soil here, first settled Bell Island in the 1740s.

About 6.5 kilometers (4 miles) from the ferry terminal, turn left onto Lance Cove Road and head down to the waterfront.

Old mine collars still poke above the ground, a testament to Bell Island's history of mining iron ore.

Follow the roads as they twist down to a bayside monument. An anchor memorializes the torpedoing of four ships that were transporting iron ore from the island during World War II. On September 5, 1942, a German U-boat attacked and sank the SS *Sargarnaga* and SS *Lord Strathcona*. Less than two months later on November 2, 1942, a second U-boat attack was launched against the SS *Rose Castle* and freighter PLM. *27.* In the second attack one of the torpedoes missed its target, hitting Scotia Pier. The explosion was the only land attack on North America during the war. At low tide the ship wreckage is still visible along the shore.

Lance Cove is also the site of a very different blast. In 1978, a 10-megaton explosion shocked residents. Reported to be ball lightning—a rarely observed phenomena that has a longer duration and more globular appearance than streak lightning—it left blast holes in the ground, exploded television sets, and melted the insulation on power lines. Happening mid Cold War, the blast is said to have drawn investigations from Canadian, US, and Russian military personnel.

From Lance Cove, follow the main road as it rounds a sharp right bend at Freshwater and becomes Middleton Avenue. There are places named **Freshwater Cove** on both sides of the island, owing to sailors stopping on Bell Island to replenish their stocks of potable water.

Although not visible from the road, Bell Rock sits off the island cliffs here at the western edge of the island.

From Freshwater the straight road cuts through a forested path along the northwestern edge of the island toward Wabana.

Wabana

Arriving on the outskirts of **Wabana**—which is derived from an Abenaki First Nations word that means "place of first light"—you'll first pass one of the two schools on the island. The school walls serve as canvas for large, vivid murals showing mining scenes. Historic murals feature on many buildings throughout the town.

Rich in red hematite, or iron ore, the first mine opened on Bell Island in the 1890s. The heavy rock was used historically as ship ballast and as the weight for killicks, or anchors made from wood and rock. First a surface mine operation, and later submarine mines, extracted some of the more than 3 billion tons of iron ore from Bell Island.

The houses of Wabana splay out amid a spacious scribble of roads. The maze-like streets are untypical of the bay-clustered houses you'll see in most Newfoundland communities. Old mineshafts, like the collar of No. 4 Mine, occasionally break the surface from below the depths, and piles of waste ore give the feeling of a quarry pit.

Heading northeast into town, follow signs for the No. 2 Mine to the **Bell Island Community Museum.** One of six mines on the island, the No. 2 mine is open for tours, taking visitors into the submarine shaft. See the iron ore carts where the miners loaded ore, hear about horses that lived in belowground stables and pulled the carts, and feel the chill of the shafts that miners first navigated by candlelight. The temperature in the mines is about 8 degrees Centigrade (47 degrees Fahrenheit).

Piles of rust-colored waste ore surround the museum. The small one-story building houses an array of donated local artifacts as well as a large collection of Bell Island mining photos by famed portrait photographer Yousuf Karsh.

Fueled by a strong industry, the Bell Island population quickly grew in the first half of the 20th century. By 1961 more than 12,000 lived on the island. The No. 2 mine closed in 1949, and Bell Island's last mine closed in 1966, owing to the increasing costs to excavate the iron ore.

Rocky trails lead from a rock stack to a blasted tunnel—the Grebes Nest—on Bell Island.

On **Petrie's Hill,** find the local curling club where the **Bell Island Sports Hall of Fame** retells the island's sport triumphs. Wabana also has services such as a hospital, grocery store, and gas station. More murals provide vivid reminders of mining life. North of Wabana you'll see the dark peninsula that is capped with the community of Biscayan Cove beyond Pouch Cove.

For an adventurous detour (over Bell Island's roads that often sport multiple names), turn off West Mines Road onto Scotia No. 1 Road (by the West Mines Sports Bar). Nearby the close-in-name Scotia Road cuts clear across the island, a direct route to transport ore from the Wabana mines to the loading dock at Scotia Pier.

Follow Scotia No. 1 Road past Foleys Road and McCarthy Street, and then bear left on Carter Avenue. The dirt road parallels the shoreline. For some vehicles it may be best to pull off, park, and then walk the short distance down to the cliffs by foot.

From the cliff tops at the end of the road, you'll see the rock stack that divides the beaches. A trail leads under questionably stable cliffs down to sea caves, a beach, and a tunnel blasted through the rock. Both sides of the sea stack provide coast to explore.

To the northeast, waves have carved dramatic sea caves in the island's cliffs.

To the southwest, the trail approaches a head-high tunnel opening in the cliff. Blasted through the rock with dynamite and reinforced with wooden poles, it's known as **Grebes Nest** and leads to a quiet beach on the other side. While the safest option is to admire the tunnel opening from the shoreline, many make the trip through the tunnel to spend a day at the beach on the other side.

Returning to Wabana, follow Quigleys Line northeast to visit the lighthouse. Lighthouse Road leads to the tip of the island and the small **Bell Island Lighthouse**—benefiting from its natural elevation. Watch for sea birds, such as the sleek black guillemots.

But if the ferry lineups are long, it may be best to take your place in line as it snakes down the hill on the road shoulder. Although tedious, waiting in the line does create a great opportunity to visit the hillside **World War II gun battery** if you missed it when arriving on Bell Island.

29

Irish Loop

Bay Bulls to Ferryland to Cape Race to Salmonier

General Description: A 315-kilometer (196-mile) scenic drive follows the southeastern coast of the Avalon Peninsula, a route popularly known as the Irish Loop. From rocky but forested coves in Bay Bulls and Witless Bay, head south to the barren lands near Cape Race. Archaeological digs, fossil shores, and a hike to a community destroyed by a tidal wave feature along the route. Whale and puffin tours venture from the land to see the region's rich offshore wildlife, while moose and caribou herds inhabit the wilderness areas.

Special Features: Puffin and whale watching, East Coast Trail, La Manche Provincial Park, La Manche town site, Colony of Avalon, Ferryland Museum, Ferryland Lighthouse Picnics, Avalon Wilderness Reserve, Chance Cove Provincial Park, Mistaken Point Eco Reserve, Cape Race Lighthouse, Trepassey Area Museum, Holyrood Pond Interpretive Centre, St. Vincent's Fishermen's Museum, Riverhead Veterans' Museum, Salmonier Provincial Wildlife Park.

Location: Avalon Peninsula, Newfoundland.

Driving Route Numbers & Names: Irish Loop, Route 10, Route 90.

Travel Season: While the weather is usually fine and pleasant from June through September, avoid most bugs with a visit in August or early September.

Camping: La Manche Provincial Park provides the best camping facilities on the circuit. Comfort stations (with showers, washrooms, and laundry), drinking water, a playground, and fire pits provide solid services. The pretty valley park is also noted for bird-watching opportunities. Chance Cove Provincial Park offers only basic camping with pit toilets and drinking water, but the stunning shoreline location adds its own appeal.

Services: Fueling up in Bay Bulls and Trepassey will keep the gas tank full for this route. For major supplies or medical care, return to the St. John's area for the best options.

Nearby Points of Interest: Cape Spear National Historic Site, Cape St. Mary's, Castle Hill National Historic Site, O'Reilly House Museum.

Time Zone: Newfoundland time (GMT minus 3.5 hours).

The Drive

Embark on a 315-kilometer (196-mile) coastal drive from the forested rocky coves south of St. John's to the barren tip of the Avalon Peninsula. Wildlife sightings are the treat of the journey, from the whales and puffins in Witless Bay to the moose and caribou at Salmonier. A community swept away by a tidal wave, an archaeological dig, and one of the Atlantic's brightest lighthouses (which also first received the *Titanic* distress call) all create mysteries along the way.

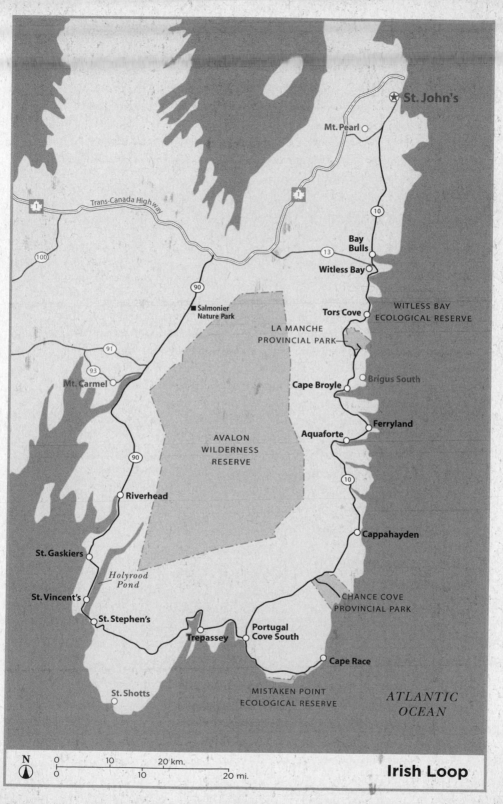

St. John's

Mt. Pearl

Trans-Canada Highway

Bay Bulls

Witless Bay

WITLESS BAY
ECOLOGICAL RESERVE

Tors Cove

LA MANCHE
PROVINCIAL PARK

Salmonier
Nature Park

Cape Broyle

Brigus South

Mt. Carmel

Ferryland

Aquaforte

AVALON
WILDERNESS
RESERVE

Riverhead

Cappahayden

St. Gaskiers

Holyrood
Pond

St. Vincent's

CHANCE COVE
PROVINCIAL PARK

St. Stephen's

Portugal
Cove South

Trepassey

Cape Race

St. Shotts

MISTAKEN POINT
ECOLOGICAL RESERVE

ATLANTIC
OCEAN

N

0   10   20 km.
0   10   20 mi.

Irish Loop

If traveling to Bay Bulls from Conception Bay or points farther west, cut across a glacier-raked landscape from exit 37 on the Trans-Canada Highway and along Route 13.

If traveling from St. John's, follow Route 10 as it parallels the **East Coast Trail,** a more than 200-kilometer (124-mile) mapped and signposted coastal hiking route that this drive will encounter a number of times. Perhaps start the drive with a side trip to the lighthouse and museum at **Cape Spear National Historic Site,** at the end of Route 11 or Cape Spear Drive, where you can see the sun rise at the easternmost point of North America.

Whales, Puffins & Wild Coasts

Arriving in **Bay Bulls** on Route 10, stop in at the visitor information center (alongside the grocery store) where you'll find hiking maps and plenty of brochures. North Side and South Side Roads lead around the harbor in Bay Bulls. Fishing vessels and wildlife-watching boats make it a busy spot. Allow a half day in Bay Bulls or Witless Bay if you plan to take a whale- and puffin-watching tour.

The **St. Peter and St. Paul Roman Catholic Church** in town is notable for its gateposts: cannons topped with saint statues. The cannons remain from the bay's fortifications, put in place by Governor David Kirke in 1638. Subsequent raids saw the Dutch land here and a final attack by the French in 1796.

About 2 kilometers (1.2 miles) after the Bay Bulls visitor center on Route 10, make a left onto Deans Road. The road is a scenic route to Witless Bay, becoming Harbour Road at Bear Cove Head and crossing Lower Pond.

As you arrive in **Witless Bay,** look out to Gull Island, the northernmost island in the **Witless Bay Ecological Reserve** chain. The reserve is home to the largest Atlantic puffin colony in North America, with more than 260,000 nesting pairs of the provincial bird. More than 600,000 breeding pairs of Leach's storm petrels as well as black-legged kittiwakes, common murres, razorbills, and northern fulmars also nest at the reserve.

As you travel along the coast you'll see the reserve's Gull, Green, Great, and Pee Pee Islands, as well as other rocky knolls. On each of the four islands in the reserve, puffins make their nests by burrowing into the grassy turf before laying a single egg. Leach's storm petrels also dig into the hillsides.

As the forest meets the ocean, the coniferous trees seem almost cemented to the shore in order to withstand the powerful storms.

From Witless Bay, the road reconnects with Route 10. Turn left to journey 8 kilometers (5 miles) south to **Tors Cove,** passing through Mobile Bay en route.

A lookout and interpretive sign with a history of the community lie alongside the main route for a quick stop and photo, but I prefer to venture down to explore this sheltered and picturesque spot. Follow Cove Road to the teal-painted **Five**

Island Art Gallery. The old school turned art gallery, at 7 Cove Rd., exhibits the works of talented local artists. Cove Road continues down to the shoreline, and a dirt road leads out past a fish plant to a crumbling wharf. Here, you'll have clear views of the bay's islands: Fox Island and Ship Island closest to the shore, and Great Island and Pee Pee Island that are part of the seabird reserve.

Leaving Tors Cove you'll see a large water pipe that runs from Tors Cove Pond to the community.

Past Tors Cove, a side road ventures off Route 10 along a residential coastline to East Bauline (pronounced like "Pauline" with a B). It's a one-way route, but it affords more coastal views for those on a relaxed time schedule. East Bauline is one of many trailheads for the East Coast Trail, which over this section follows the coast to the old La Manche village site.

Walk the trail or retrace the road to Route 10.

La Manche

From Tors Cove, Route 10 bends inland for good reason: It skirts the swath of valley and coast in **La Manche Provincial Park.** Hiking the trails, bird watching, swimming, and canoeing on the La Manche River are all popular park activities. A 70-site campground offers laundry, washrooms, and showers, making the park a comfortable camping destination.

Just south of the park boundaries, La Manche Road leads to a trailhead for an easy-to-moderate hour hike to the **old La Manche town site.** A forested trail passes ponds and rocky outcrops before reaching the former village. Within park boundaries find an inviting swimming hole and a suspension bridge that spans the harbor to form part of the East Coast Trail.

On both sides of the water, see concrete foundations that tell of the community washed away by a tidal wave on Jan. 18, 1966. No one was killed, and the community opted to resettle elsewhere following the destructive ocean swell. A commemorative plaque and coastal views add to the location's appeal. Allow about 1.5 hours for the return journey.

Back on Route 10, the road keeps inland through mostly forested scenery. About halfway between Tors Cove and Ferryland you'll pass the unassuming, dirt-surfaced Horse Chops Road. It leads to a special place, cutting into the heart of the peninsula to the **Avalon Provincial Wilderness Reserve.** The 1,070-square-kilometer (413-square-mile) tract of wilderness encompasses caribou migration lands and moose territory over rolling barrens, ponds, and forest. The caribou herd is the most southerly one in Canada.

Less than 2 kilometers (1.2 miles) farther, Brigus Road on the left makes a scenic detour to Brigus South for photos of a classic Newfoundland fishing village.

Passing through Cape Broyle (get gas and moose burgers here) and Calvert, the treed scenery ends abruptly in Ferryland.

Ferryland to Barren Land

Arriving in **Ferryland,** watch for the town building and visitor center on the right. But a stop is unnecessary unless seeking maps or accommodation information. Route 10 traces the coast, and the town's substantial attractions are easy to find.

Alongside the large stone **Holy Trinity Roman Catholic Church** (for which fishermen shipped the stone in from an island that is 2 kilometers [1.2 miles] offshore), find the **Ferryland Museum.** The museum, in the old courthouse building, houses exhibits ranging from a jail cell to details on shoreline shipwrecks.

Just past the museum, a road branches left out to Ferryland Head.

Sir George Calvert of England, who became the first Lord Baltimore, founded a colony here in 1621 to establish one of the first English settlements on the continent, the **colony of Avalon.**

The **Colony of Avalon Archaeological Dig Interpretive Centre** presents what Baltimore left behind. Gold rings, cannonballs, silver thimbles, pipes, glass windows, and gravestones have been unearthed by the dig, and some are on display at the interpretive center. Watch diggers in the site uncovering items and conservationists putting the pieces together like a jigsaw.

The area was first visited by the Beothuk and then migratory fishermen. Permanent settlement came when Sir George Calvert purchased title and established a colony on the lollipop-shaped land called the Downs. After one Newfoundland winter Calvert headed for warmer climes in Maryland in 1629, leaving the colony under a representative.

In 1638 Sir David Kirke arrived at Avalon. Having captured Nova Scotia and Quebec and been award Newfoundland when a treaty returned those regions to the French, Kirke deposed Calvert's representative and took residence at Ferryland as governor of Newfoundland.

Legal tensions between Kirke and Calvert ensued, but it is perhaps Sara Kirke who deserves the greatest attention: The widow ran a successful fish mercantile for decades after her husband died in prison.

Also on Ferryland Head sits the **Ferryland Head Lighthouse,** which is renowned for its **Lighthouse Picnics**—a gourmet picnic served on the rocky bluffs around the red metal lighthouse. Fresh molasses bread, homemade lemonade, and gingerbread with custard are just a selection from the tempting menu. It's a 25-minute hike out to the 1870 lighthouse.

The Ferryland community celebrates with the **South Shore Shamrock Festival** in late July, when Irish and Newfoundland musicians entertain the crowds.

Returning to Route 10, the road dips around the lovely **Aquaforte Harbour.** Watch for the power-generating wind turbines that sit on the far hill. Treed slopes lead down to a bay that has an almost turquoise hue on a fine day.

Past Aquaforte and Fermeuse—names which show that this coast was long visited by migratory French fishermen—a side road leads out to **Port Kirwan.** Even a short detour will take you to the odd complement of a huge boulder next to the **St. Charles Borromeo Church.** Farther down this road find an interpretive sign, picnic table, and then a fishing wharf.

Back on Route 10, another detour leads out to **Renews**—a small town with narrow streets to explore. Tales of shipwrecks and a daring rescue by Captain William Jackman show the resilient spirit of folk along the coast. The *Mayflower* stopped here in 1620 to resupply en route to its historic landing in Massachusetts.

As the barrenness of the land increases on the journey south through Cappahayden, the route bears southwest to follow the inland trajectory of the Southern Shore Highway.

Chance Cove to Cape Race

Flat lands, scattered boulders, waterlogged bogs, and hardy grasses reach from the road to the horizon along the 32-kilometer (20-mile) stretch from Cappahayden to Portugal Cove South. When there is forest, the trees are stunted and sparse. Off-the-grid hunting camps prompt musings about a disconnected life. Watch the barrens for wildlife.

For a break in the emptiness, 13 kilometers (8 miles) from Cappahayden turn into **Chance Cove Provincial Park.** Bump down the 6-kilometer (3.7-mile) dirt road to a parking lot where short trails lead to fabulous views. The day-use park has no attendant on-site and limited services, which include pit toilets, drinking water, and picnic tables. Although not a tended campground, camping is permitted in the parking area for RVs or by the picnic tables for tents.

The former village of Chance Cove once stood here, but was mysteriously abandoned by all its residents. Ghost tales recall the 1863 shipwreck of the steamer *Anglo Saxon* off Chance Cove. Of the 444 on board, only 97 were saved, and many of the dead were buried here. For the years following, screams were heard off the coast until the entire community left one night. No one knows where they went. Years later, after fishermen used the community as a summer camp, they torched the houses. At the very least it's a good campfire horror story, but maybe not for those who plan to camp here.

Back on Route 10, a rare sight in the barren landscape is the **Cape Race LORAN-C transmitter.** The original 411-meter (1,348-foot) tower has collapsed, but it was the tallest structure in Canada prior to the construction of the CN

Waves break at Chance Cove Provincial Park on the Irish Loop.

Tower in Toronto. The use of long-range transmission has been diminished by the popularity and easy use of GPS technology.

Finally arriving in **Portugal Cove South,** you'll first encounter the **Avalon Interpretive Centre.** The center provides details on the nearby attractions at Cape Race and Mistaken Point. From the center, head west to Trepassey or southeast to Cape Race.

Toward Cape Race, interpretive signs punctuate the 20-kilometer (12.4-mile) dirt road that skirts the inland side of the **Mistaken Point Provincial Ecological Reserve.** The reserve features fossils of the world's oldest creatures, which lived in the ocean 575 to 542 million years ago. The reserve is accessible by guided tour only, with information available at the Avalon Interpretive Centre.

At the end of the point find **Cape Race Lighthouse.** A national historical site, the lighthouse is known for its powerful light that has saved many a ship from being wrecked on the foggy point. Views are wide and flat, looking out at the Atlantic Ocean's expanse.

Also along the Cape Race road, get the long and the short of Morse code at the **Myrick Wireless Interpretation Centre.** The Marconi wireless station, originally built in 1904, received the first distress call from the RMS *Titanic* in 1912.

Return on the same road back to Portugal Cove to continue the journey through the south of Avalon.

The Portugal Cove South area celebrates its roots with the annual **Cape Race–PCS Heritage Days** in August. Beach bonfires, guided tours, and traditional tasks like butter churning cast a wide net for the festival.

In Portugal Cove pass the dunelike piles of rocks, washed ashore by powerful storms, and round the bend to Biscay Bay, where a flat sandy beach is a sheltered haven. The road then cuts across Cape Mutton toward Trepassey.

Spectacular barren bluffs, the Atlantic Ocean, and even a glimpse of Cape Pine Lighthouse treat visitors here. In the town, the squat blue-and-white **Trepassey Museum** features displays about Amelia Earhart's flight as the first female passenger to cross the Atlantic Ocean on the *Friendship* in 1928. Her better known solo flight across the Atlantic Ocean departed from Harbour Grace on Conception Bay in 1932.

For those driving the route over two days, **Trepassey** makes a good halfway point. Accommodations in town are limited, so inquire ahead for rooms during high season, July and August.

Holyrood Pond

As the road skirts Trepassey Harbour and passes through Daniels Point, the distances seem to lengthen with the emptiness of the scenery. The landscape is blown clean of trees. See ponds left from the scrape of glaciers and boulders deposited like litter.

Midway between Trepassey and St. Stephen's, St. Shott's Road presents a coastal detour to a fishing community. A dirt road also ventures out to **Cape Pine Lighthouse,** another dangerous point that has witnessed many shipwrecks in foggy conditions. The side trip to St. Shott's adds about 25 kilometers (15.5 miles) round trip from Route 10.

About 35 kilometers (22 miles) past Trepassey, the road dips into the pleasant discovery of Peter's River—a treed valley amid a clean-swept landscape.

Follow Route 10 to the **Holyrood Pond Interpretation Centre,** a sharp, red building sitting alongside the inland Holyrood Pond. Popular with anglers, the pond is a 21-kilometer (13-mile) landlocked fjord that provides habitat for 30 species of saltwater and freshwater fish.

On the west side of the pond, St. Vincent's tempts with tales of watching the whales from the shore. Stop in at the St. Vincent's **Fisheries Museum** on the main road to get tips on when and where.

For the next 8 kilometers (5 miles) of the route, now mapped as Route 90, the road climbs above Holyrood Pond and affords gentle views of the often calm waters. Heading north through Gaskiers, you may catch views of St. Mary's Bay, edged on the far side with Cape St. Mary's and a many-thousand-strong gannet colony at Bird Rock.

Trees, twisting roads, and more towns strike a contrast to the earlier barrens of the Avalon Peninsula. In Riverhead, there is a **Veterans' Museum** at the local legion.

A forested route with ponds and lots of moose territory continues to strike north to the wonderful **Salmonier Provincial Nature Park** off Route 90. The free attraction is great for families with its boardwalk, easy wildlife viewing, friendly staff, and good facilities. Watch for shy moose, hiding caribou, playful mink, and alert owls in the park. Arrive at morning feeding times to watch the animals devour their breakfasts.

From Salmonier, it's then just a short 9-kilometer (5.6-mile) journey to reconnect with the Trans-Canada Highway.

Side Trip: Cape St. Mary's

Although less of a scenic drive than the Irish Loop, a journey to **Cape St. Mary's** may be the headline highlight of a visit to the Avalon Peninsula. The **Cape St. Mary's Ecological Reserve,** off Cape St. Mary's Road at the southern end of Routes 92 and 100, features a huge gannet colony that nests on Bird Rock and the surrounding cliffs. A 1.4-kilometer (0.9-mile) hike leads down to a viewing cliff within meters of the birds, which numbered about 15,000 nesting pairs in 2010. Amid the gannets, with their 2-meter (6.5-foot) wingspan, try to spot common murres, cormorants, and seagulls.

This route pairs well with a return journey to the Maritimes via the Argentia–North Sydney ferry. The ferry makes the 16-hour crossing just twice a week, and reservations (particularly for bunks and cabins) are highly recommended.

If arriving in Placentia a day or two early, a series of historical museums and sites can fill the waiting time.

Castle Hill National Historic Site presents reenactments of the French and English conflicts over Newfoundland's rich fishing grounds. When the British blockaded the harbor, the French—given the little arable land in the area—were forced to abandon the fort. The 1713 Treaty of Utrecht made the fortress officially British territory, and the French moved south to build Fortress Louisbourg on Cape Breton Island.

Gannets nest by the thousand on Bird Rock at Cape St. Mary's.

Learn about more recent local history at the **O'Reilly House Museum,** including tales of the inshore fishery and the 1960s resettlement, when many who lived on island outports relocated to more central communities—sometimes by floating their house to the new location!

APPENDIX A:
MORE INFORMATION

Drive 1

Campobello Island ferry
East Coast Ferries
P.O. Box 301, Lords Cove
Deer Island, NB E5V 1W2
(506) 747-2159 or (877) 747-2159
www.eastcoastferries.nb.ca

Campobello Visitor Information Centre
44 Rte. 774
Welshpool, NB E5E 1A3
(506) 752-7043 (seasonal)

Deer Island ferry
511 or (888) 747-7006
www.gnb.ca/0113/ferries/ferries-e.asp

Head Harbour Lightstation
210 Lighthouse Rd.
Wilson's Beach, NB E5E 1M2
www.campobello.com/lighthouse

Herring Cove Provincial Park
136 Herring Cove Rd.
Campobello Island, NB E5E 1B8
(506) 752-7010
www.nbparks.ca/en-CA/01323

Roosevelt Campobello International Park
459 Hwy. 774
Campobello Island, NB E5E 1A4
(506) 752-2922 or (877) 851-6663
www.fdr.net

Drive 2

Atlantic Salmon Interpretive Centre
24 Chamcook Lake No. 1 Rd.
Chamcook, NB E5B 3S8
(506) 529-1384
www.salarstream.ca

Ministers Island Historic Site
199 Carriage Rd.
Ministers Island, NB E5B 0A4
(506) 529-5081 or (877) 386-3922
www.ministersisland.ca

St. Andrews Welcome Centre
24 Reed Ave.
St. Andrews, NB E5B 1A1
(506) 529-3556
www.standrewsbythesea.ca

Drive 3

Fundy Parkway
229 Main St. (mailing address)
St. Martins, NB E5R 1B7
(506) 833-2019 or (866) 386-3987
www.fundytrailparkway.com

Quaco Museum
236 Main St.
St. Martins, NB E5R 1B8
(506) 833-4740 (seasonal) or
(506) 833-4768
www.quaco.ca

St. Martins Visitor Information Centre
424 Main St.
St. Martins, NB E5R 1B9
(506) 833-2006 (seasonal)
www.stmartinscanada.com

Drive 4

Albert County Museum
3940 Rte. 114
Hopewell Cape, NB E4H 3J8
(506) 734-2003
www.albertcountymuseum.ca

Alma Visitor Information Centre
8584 Main St.
Alma, NB E4H 1N5
(506) 887-6127 (seasonal)
www.villageofalma.ca

Bank of New Brunswick Museum
5985 Rte. 114
Riverside-Albert, NB E4H 4B8
(506) 882-2100

Cape Enrage
650 Cape Enrage Rd.
Waterside, NB E4H 4Z4
(506) 887-2273 or (888) 423-5454
www.capenrage.com

Fundy National Park
P.O. Box 1001
Alma, NB E4H 1B4
(506) 887-6000
www.pc.gc.ca/fundy

Hillsborough Visitor Information Centre
2861 Main St.
Hillsborough, NB E4H 2X7
(506) 734-2240

Hopewell Rocks
131 Discovery Rd,
Hopewell Cape, NB E4H 4Z5
(877) 734-3429
www.thehopewellrocks.ca

New Brunswick Railway Museum
2847 Main St.
Hillsborough, NB E4H 2X7
(506) 734-3195
www.nbrm.ca

Steeves House Museum
40 Mill St.
Hillsborough, NB E4H 2Z8
(506) 734-3102
www.steeveshousemuseum.ca

Drive 5

Beaverbrook Art Gallery
703 Queen St.
Fredericton, NB E3B 5A6
(506) 458-2028 (reception)
www.beaverbrookartgallery.org

Canadian Military Engineers Museum
Mitchell Building (J-10), CFB/ASG Gagetown
Oromocto, NB E2V 4J5
(506) 422-2000 ext. 1897
www.cmemuseum.ca

Fredericton Visitor Information Centre (City Hall)
397 Queen St.
Fredericton, NB E3B 1B5
(506) 460-2129
www.tourismfredericton.ca

Gagetown Military Museum
Building A-5, CFB/ASG Gagetown
Oromocto, NB E2V 4J5
(506) 422-1304
www.museumgagetown.ca/index.htm

Gagetown Visitor Information Centre
50 Front St.
Gagetown, NB E5M 1A1
(506) 488-2999 (seasonal)

Government House
51 Woodstock Rd.
Fredericton, NB E3B 9L8
(506) 453-2505
www.gnb.ca/lg/ogh/index-e.asp

Kings Landing Historical Settlement
5804 Rte. 102
Prince William, NB E6K 0A5
(506) 363-4999
www.kingslanding.nb.ca

Legislative Assembly of New Brunswick
706 Queen St.
Fredericton, NB E3B 1C5
(506) 453-2527
www.gnb.ca/legis

Mactaquac Provincial Park
1265 Rte. 105
Mactaquac, NB E6L 1B5
(506) 363-4747
www.nbparks.ca

New Brunswick Sports Hall of Fame
503 Queen St.
Fredericton, NB E3B 5P4
(506) 453-3747
www.nbsportshalloffame.nb.ca

Oromocto Visitor Information Centre
Restigouche Rd. at Waasis Rd.
Oromocto, NB
(506) 446-5010
www.oromocto.ca

Queens County Court House Museum
16 Court House Rd.
Gagetown, NB E5M 1A4
(506) 488-2966 (Tilley House—seasonal)
www.queenscountyheritage.com/CourtHouse.html

Queens County Museum—Tilley House
69 Front St.
Gagetown, NB E5M 1A4
(506) 488-2966 (seasonal)
www.queenscountyheritage.com/TilleyHouse.html

Saint John River cable ferries
(888) 747-7006
www.gnb.ca/0113/ferries/ferries-e.asp

School Days Museums
Justice Building Annex, east entrance
Queen Street
Fredericton, NB
(506) 459-3738
http://museum.nbta.ca

York Sunbury Museum
571 Queen St.
Fredericton, NB E3B 1C3
(506) 455-6041
www.yorksunburymuseum.com

Drive 6

Atlantic Salmon Museum and Aquarium
263 Main St.
Doaktown, NB E9C 1A9
(506) 365-7787
www.atlanticsalmonmuseum.com

Beaubears Island Shipbuilding National Historic Site
35 St. Patrick's Dr., Nelson
Miramichi, NB E1N 4P6
(506) 622-8526
www.beaubearsisland.ca

Central New Brunswick Woodmen's Museum
6342 Hwy. 8
Boiestown, NB E6A 1Z5
(506) 369-7214
www.woodmensmuseum.com

Doak Historic Site
386 Main St.
Doaktown, NB E9C 1E4
(506) 365-2026
www.doaktown.com

Historic Beaverbrook House
518 King George Hwy.
Miramichi, NB E1V 1N1
(506) 622-5572
www.beaverbrookhouse.com

Metepenagiag Heritage Park
2156 MicMac Rd.
Red Bank, NB E9E 2P2
(506) 836-6118
www.metepenagiag.com

Miramichi Visitor Information Centre
199 King St.
Miramichi, NB E1N 6C5
(506) 778-8444
www.miramichirivertourism.com

Rankin House Museum
2224 King George Hwy. (Highway 8)
Miramichi, NB E1V 5Z5
(506) 773-3448

St. Michael's Museum
12 Howard St.
Miramichi, NB E1N 3A7
(506) 778-5159
www.saintmichaelsmuseum.com

W. S. Loggie House & Cultural Centre
222 Wellington St.
Miramichi, NB E1N 1M9

Drive 7

Caraquet Visitor Information Centre
39 West St-Pierre Blvd.
Caraquet, NB E1W 1B6
(506) 726-2676

Éco-musée de l'Huître (Oyster Museum)
675 West St-Pierre Blvd.
Caraquet, NB E1W 1A2
(506) 727-3226
www.rmne.ca/eco-musee-huitre

Ecological Park of the Acadian Peninsula
65 Du Ruisseau St.
Lamèque, NB E8T 1M2
(506) 344-3223
www.parcecologique.ca

Grande-Anse Visitor Information Centre
404 Acadie St.
Grande-Anse, NB E8N 1C9
(506) 732-3256

Musée Acadien de Caraquet (Acadian Museum)
15 East St-Pierre Blvd.
Caraquet, NB E1W 1B6
(506) 726-2682
www.museecaraquet.ca

**New Brunswick Aquarium and
Marine Center**
100 Aquarium St.
Shippagan, NB E8S 1H9
(506) 336-3013
www.aquariumnb.ca

Popes' Museum
184 Acadie St.
Grande-Anse, NB E0B 1R0
(506) 732-3003

Shippagan Visitor Information Centre
200 Hôtel-de-ville Ave.
Shippagan, NB E8S 1M1
(506) 336-3993
www.shippagan.ca

Village Historique Acadien
14311 Rte. 11
Rivière-du-Nord, NB E8N 2V6
(506) 726-2600
www.villagehistoriqueacadien.com

Drive 8

**Bouctouche Visitor Information
Centre**
4 Acadie St.
Bouctouche, NB E4S 2T2
(506) 743-8811
www.bouctouche.ca

Bonar Law Historic Site
31 Bonar Law Ave.
Rexton, NB E4W 1V6
(506) 523-7615 or (877) 731-7007
www.bonarlawcommon.com

**Grande-Digue Visitor Information
Centre**
468 Route 530
Grande-Digue, NB E4R 5K3
(506) 532-6823
www.grande-digue.net

Hudson Oddities
338 Bas De L'Allée Rd.
Richibucto-Village, NB E4W 1A5
(506) 523-6248
www.hudsonoddities.com

Irving Eco Nature Park
1932 Rte. 475
Bouctouche, NB E4S 4W9
(506) 743-2600 or (888) 640-3300
www.irvingecocenter.com

Kent Museum
150 Couvent Lane
Bouctouche, NB E4S 3C1
(506) 743-5005
www.museedekent.ca

Kouchibouguac National Park
186 Rte. 117
Kouchibouguac, NB E4X 2P1
(506) 876-2443
www.pc.gc.ca/kouchibouguac

Le Pays de la Sagouine
57 Acadie St.
Bouctouche, NB E4S 2T7
(506) 743-1400 or (800) 561-9188
http://sagouine.com

Musée des Pionniers de Grande-Digue
468 B Rte. 530
Grande-Digue NB E4R 5K3
(506) 576-6789 or (506) 532-1572

Olivier Soapery
831 Rte. 505
Sainte-Anne-de-Kent, NB E4S 1J9
(506) 743-8938
www.oliviersoaps.com

Parlee Beach Provincial Park
45 Parlee Beach Rd.
Pointe-du-Chêne, NB E4P 8V5
(506) 533-3363
www.nbparks.ca/en-CA/02074

Pascal-Poirier Historic House
399 Main St.
Shediac, NB E4P 2B7
(506) 532-7022 (town office)

Richibucto River Museum
31 Bonar Law Ave.
Rexton, NB E4W 1V6
(506) 523-7615 or (877) 731-7007
www.bonarlawcommon.com

Seawind Buffalo Ranch
136 St-Pierre Road
Bouctouche, NB E4S 2J2
(506) 743-6200
www.seawindbuffalo.com

Shediac Visitor Information Centre
229 Main St.
Shediac, NB E4P 2A5
(506) 532-7788
www.shediac.org

Drive 9

Age of Sail Heritage Centre
8334 Rte. 209
Port Greville, NS B0M 1T0
(902) 348-2030 (seasonal)
www.ageofsailmuseum.ca

Bass River Heritage Museum
5666 Hwy. 2
Bass River, NS B0M 1B0
(902) 647-2648
http://bassriver.ednet.ns.ca

Cape Chignecto Provincial Park
1108 West Advocate Rd.
Advocate Harbour, NS B0M 1A0
(902) 392-2085 or (888) 544-3434
www.capechignecto.net

Cape d'Or Scenic Area
Cape d'Or Road
Advocate Harbour, NS B0M 1A0
(902) 670-0534 (seasonal)
www.capedor.ca

Cobequid Interpretation Centre
3248 Hwy. 2
Economy, NS B0M 1J0
(902) 647-2600

Five Island Provincial Park
618 Bentley Rd.
Five Islands, NS
(888) 544-3434 (camping reservations)
http://parks.gov.ns.ca/parks/five
islands.asp

Fundy Geological Museum
162 Two Islands Rd.
Parrsboro, NS B0M 1S0
(902) 254-3814
http://museum.gov.ns.ca/fgm

Glooscap Country Bazaar
Highway 2
Economy, NS
(902) 647-2920

Joggins Fossil Cliffs
100 Main St.
Joggins, NS B0L 1A0
(902) 251-2727 or (888) 932-9766
www.jogginsfossilcliffs.net

Ottawa House
1155 Whitehall Rd.
Parrsboro, NS B0M 1S0
(902) 254-2376 (summer only)
www.ottawahouse.org

Ship's Company Theatre
18 Lower Main St.
Parrsboro, NS B0M 1S0
(902) 254-3000 (box office)
www.shipscompany.com

That Dutchman's Farm
112 Brown Rd.
Upper Economy, NS B0M 1J0
(902) 647-2751
www.thatdutchmansfarm.com

Thomas' Cove Coastal Reserve
Economy Point Road
Economy, NS
www.colchester.ca/thomas-cove-
coastal-reserve

Truro Tidal Bore Interpretive Centre
Tidal Bore Road, exit 14 on
Highway 102
Truro, NS B2N 5G6
(902) 893-8951 (Palliser Motel)

Truro Visitor Information Center
65 Treaty Trail
Truro, NS B2N 5A9
(902) 843-3493
www.truro.ca

Drive 10

Fort Edward Blockhouse National Historic Site
Fort Edward Street
Windsor, NS
(902) 532-2321
www.pc.gc.ca/fortedward

Grand Pré National Historic Site
2241 Grand-Pré Rd., P.O. Box 150
Grand-Pré, NS B0P 1M0
(902) 542-3631 or (866) 542-3631
www.pc.gc.ca/grandpre

Haliburton House
414 Clifton Ave.
Windsor, NS B0N 2T0
(902) 798-2915
http://museum.gov.ns.ca/hh

Howard Dill Enterprises
400 College Rd.
Windsor, NS B0N 2T0
(902) 798-2728
www.howarddill.com

Randall House
259 Main St.
Wolfville, NS B4P 1C6
(902) 542-9775 (seasonal)
http://wolfvillehs.ednet.ns.ca

Robie Tufts Nature Centre
Front Street and Elm Avenue
Wolfville, NS
www.wolfville.ca/robie-tufts-nature-
centre.html

Shand House Museum
389 Avon St.
Windsor, NS B0N 2T0
(902) 798-8213
http://museum.gov.ns.ca/sh

West Hants Historical Society Museum
281 King St.
Windsor, NS B0N 2T0
(902) 798-4706
www.westhantshistoricalsociety.ca

Windsor Hockey Heritage Centre
128 Gerrish St.
Windsor, NS B0N 2T0
(902) 798-1800

Windsor–West Hants Visitor Information Centre
Exit 6, Highway 101
Wolfville, NS
(902) 798-2690 (seasonal)
www.town.windsor.ns.ca

Town of Wolfville Tourist Bureau
11 Willow Ave.
Wolfville, NS B4P 2G5
(902) 542-7000
www.wolfville.ca

Drive 11

Admiral Digby Museum
95 Montague Row
Digby, NS B0V 1A0
(902) 245-6322
www.admuseum.ns.ca

Annapolis Royal Historic Gardens
441 St. George St.
Annapolis Royal, NS B0S 1A0
(902) 532-7018
www.historicgardens.com

Annapolis Royal Visitor Information Centre
209 St. George St.
Box 2, Annapolis Royal, NS B0S 1A0
(902) 532-5454
www.annapolisroyal.com

Annapolis Tidal Generating Station
236 Prince Albert Rd.
Annapolis Royal, NS B0S 1E0
(902) 532-0502 (seasonal)
www.nspower.ca/en/home/
environment/renewableenergy/tidal/
annapolis.aspx

Cornwallis Military Museum
726 Broadway, Cornwallis Industrial
Park
Cornwallis Park, NS
(902) 638-3118
www.cornwallismuseum.ca

Digby Visitor Information Centre
237 Shore Rd.
Digby, NS
(902) 245-2201 (seasonal)
www.digbyarea.com

Fort Anne National Historic Site
St. George Street
Annapolis Royal, NS B0S 1A0
(902) 532-2397
www.pc.gc.ca/fortanne

O'Dell House Museum
136 St. George St.
Annapolis Royal, NS
(902) 532-7754
www.annapolisheritagesociety.com/
odell.htm

Port-Royal National Historic Site of Canada
P.O. Box 9
Annapolis Royal, NS B0S 1A0
(902) 532-2898
www.pc.gc.ca/portroyal

Sinclair Inn Museum
230 St. George St.
Annapolis Royal, NS
(902) 532-7754
www.annapolisheritagesociety.com/
sinclair%20inn.htm

Upper Clements Parks
2931 Hwy. 1
Annapolis Royal, NS B0S 1A0
(902) 532-7557 or (888) 248-4567
www.upperclementsparks.com

Drive 12

Fort Point Museum
100 Fort Point Rd.
LaHave, NS B0R 1C0
(902) 688-1632
www.fortpointmuseum.com

Halifax & Southwestern Railway Museum
11188 Hwy. 3
Lunenburg, NS B0J 2C0
(902) 634-3184
www.hswmuseum.ednet.ns.ca

LaHave Islands Marine Museum
100 LaHave Islands Rd.
LaHave, NS B0R 1C0
(902) 688-2973
www.lahaveislandsmarinemuseum.ca

Ovens Natural Park
326 Ovens Rd.
Feltzen South, NS B0J 2W0
(902) 766-4621
www.ovenspark.com

Rissers Beach Provincial Park
5366 Hwy. 331
Petite Riviere, NS
(888) 544-3434 (camping reservations)
http://parks.gov.ns.ca/parks/rissers.asp

Drive 13

Amos Pewter
589 Main St.
Mahone Bay, NS B0J 2E0
(902) 624-9547
www.amospewter.com

Bluenose II
68 Bluenose Dr.
Lunenburg, NS B0J 2C0
(902) 634-4794 ext. 221 or
(902) 634-8483
http://museum.gov.ns.ca/bluenose

Chester Playhouse
22 Pleasant St.
Chester, NS B0J 1J0
(902) 275-3933
www.chesterplayhouse.ca

Chester Visitor Information Centre
20 Smith Rd., Highway 3
Chester, NS B0J 1J0
(902) 275-4616
www.chesterareans.ca

Fisheries Museum of the Atlantic
68 Bluenose Dr.
Lunenburg, NS B0J 2C0
(902) 634-4794
http://museum.gov.ns.ca/fma

Graves Island Provincial Park
230 Graves Island Rd.
East Chester, NS
(888) 544-3434 (camping reservations)
http://parks.gov.ns.ca/parks/
gravesisland.asp

Knaut-Rhuland House Museum
125 Pelham St.
Lunenburg, NS B0J 2C0
(902) 634-3498
www.lunenburgheritagesociety.ca/
krhouse.htm

Lunenburg Academy
97-101 Kaulback St.
Lunenburg, NS B0J 2C0
(902) 634-2220 (school office)
www.lunenburg.ednet.ns.ca

**Lunenburg Visitor Information
Centre**
11 Blockhouse Hill Rd.
Lunenburg, NS B0J 2C0
(902) 634-8100 or (902) 634-3656
www.lunenburgns.com

Mahone Bay Settlers Museum
578 Main St.
Mahone Bay, NS B0J 2E0
(902) 624-6263
www.settlersmuseum.ns.ca

**Mahone Bay Visitors Information
Centre**
165 Edgewater St.
Mahone Bay, NS
(902) 624-6151
www.mahonebay.com

Oak Island
6 Oak Island Dr., P.O. Box 136
Western Shore, NS B0J 3M0
www.friendsofoakisland.com

**Peggy's Cove Visitor Information
Centre**
109 Peggy's Point Rd.
Peggy's Cove, NS
(902) 823-2253 or (902) 823-2256
(deGarthe Gallery)

St. John's Anglican Church
81 Cumberland St.
Lunenburg, NS B0J 2C0
(902) 634-4994
www.stjohnslunenburg.org

SS *Atlantic* Memorial
180 Sandy Cove Rd.
Terence Bay, NS B3T 1Y5
(902) 852-1557
www.ssatlantic.com

Drive 14

Acadian House Museum
79 Hill Rd.
West Chezzetcook, NS B0J 1N0
(902) 827-5992

Cole Harbour Heritage Farm Museum
471 Poplar Dr.
Cole Harbour, NS B2W 4L2
(902) 434-0222
http://coleharbourfarmmuseum.ca

**Evergreen House, Dartmouth
Heritage Museum**
26 Newcastle St.
Dartmouth, NS B2Y 3M5
(902) 464-2300
www.dartmouthheritagemuseum.ns.ca/
dhmHistoricHousesEvergreen.html

Fisherman's Cove
30 Government Wharf Rd.
Eastern Passage, NS B3G 1M7
(902) 465-6093
www.fishermanscove.ns.ca

Lawrencetown Beach Provincial Park
4348 Lawrencetown Rd.
Lawrencetown, NS
http://parks.gov.ns.ca

Martinique Beach Provincial Park
2389 Petpeswick Rd.
East Petpeswick, NS
http://parks.gov.ns.ca

**McNabs and Lawlor Islands
Provincial Park**
Halifax Harbour
http://parks.gov.ns.ca/parks/
mcnabs.asp

Musquodoboit Railway Museum
Highway 7
Musquodoboit Harbour, NS B0J 2L0
(902) 889-2689

Porters Lake Provincial Park
1160 West Porters Lake Rd.
Porters Lake, NS
(888) 544-3434 (camping reservations)
http://parks.gov.ns.ca/parks/porters.asp

**Quaker House, Dartmouth Heritage
Museum**
55/57 Ochterloney St.
Dartmouth, NS
(902) 464-2300
www.dartmouthheritagemuseum.ns.ca/
dhmHistoricHousesQuaker.html

**Rainbow Haven Beach Provincial
Park**
2248 Cow Bay Rd.
Rainbow Haven
http://parks.gov.ns.ca

Shearwater Aviation Museum
34 Bonaventure St.
Shearwater, NS B0J 3A0
(902) 720-1083
www.shearwateraviationmuseum.ns.ca

**Shearwater Flyer, Salt Marsh, and
Altantic View trails**
http://visitors.halifax.ca/trails.shtml

Drive 15

Antigonish Heritage Museum
20 East Main St.
Antigonish, NS B2G 2E9
(902) 863-6160
www.parl.ns.ca/aheritage

Arisaig Provincial Park
5704 Hwy. 245
Arisaig, NS
http://parks.gov.ns.ca

**Ballantynes Cove Tuna Interpretive
Centre**
57 Ballantyne's Cove Wharf Rd.
Ballantyne's Cove, NS

**Cape George Heritage School
Museum**
5758 Hwy. 337
Cape George, NS

Cape George Point Lighthouse
152 Lighthouse Rd.
Cape George Point, NS
www.parl.ns.ca/lighthouse

Drive 16

Acadian Museum and Restaurant
15067 Main St.
Chéticamp, NS B0E 1H0
(902) 224-2170
cbmuseums.tripod.com/id59.html

Cabots Landing Provincial Park
1904 Bay St. Lawrence Rd.
Sugarloaf, NS
http://parks.gov.ns.ca

Cape Breton Highlands National Park
Ingonish Beach, NS B0C 1L0
(902) 224-2306
www.pc.gc.ca/capebreton

Cape Smokey Provincial Park
40301 Cabot Trail
Cape Smokey, NS
http://parks.gov.ns.ca

Giant MacAskill Museum
Route 312, P.O. Box 41
Englishtown, NS B0C 1H0
(902) 929-2875

Les Trois Pignons: Museum of Hooked Rug and Home Life
15584 Cabot Trail
Chéticamp, NS B0E 1H0
(902) 224-2642
www.lestroispignons.com

North Highlands Community Museum
29243 Cabot Trail
Cape North, NS B0C 1G0
(902) 383-2579
www.northhighlandsmuseum.ca

Whale Interpretive Centre
104 Harbour Way
Pleasant Bay, NS B0E 2P0
(902) 224-1411 (seasonal)

Drive 17

Argyle Shore Provincial Park
Route 19
(902) 859-8790
www.tourismpei.com/argyle-shore

Borden-Carleton Visitor Information Centre
100 Abegweit Dr., Gateway Village
Borden-Carleton, PE C0B 1X0
(902) 437-8570
www.gentleisland.com

Cape Jourimain Nature Centre
5039 Rte. 16
Bayfield, NB E4M 3Z8
(506) 538-2220 or (866) 538-2220
www.capejourimain.ca

Fort Amherst/Port-la-Joye National Historic Site
Hache Gallant Drive, off Route 19
Rocky Point, PE
(902) 566-7626 (Province House)
www.pc.gc.ca/fortamherst

Victoria Seaport Lighthouse Museum
Water Street
Victoria, PE

Drive 18

Acadian Museum
23 Main Dr., Highway 2
Miscouche, PE C0B 1T0
(902) 432-2880
www.gov.pe.ca/peimhf
www.teleco.org/museeacadien

Bideford Parsonage Museum
784 Bideford Rd., Route 166
Bideford, PE C0B 1J0
(902) 831-3133
www.bidefordparsonagemuseum.com

The Bottle Houses
6891 Rte. 11
Cap-Egmont, PE C0B 2E0
(902) 854-2987
www.bottlehouses.com

College of Piping
619 Water St. East
Summerside, PE C1N 4H8
(902) 436-5377
www.collegeofpiping.com

Eptek Art & Culture Centre
130 Harbour Dr.
Summerside, PE
(902) 888-8373
www.gov.pe.ca/peimhf

Green Park Provincial Park
364 Green Park Rd., Route 12
Port Hill, PE
(902) 831-7912
www.tourismpei.com/green-park

Indian Art & Crafts of North America
4 Eagle Feather Trail
Lennox Island First Nation, PE
(902) 831-2653
www.indianartpei.com

International Fox Museum
33 Summer St.
Summerside, PE
(902) 432-1296
www.wyattheritage.com

Lennox Island Mi'kmaq Cultural Centre
Sweetgrass Trail
Lennox Island, PE
www.lennoxisland.com

Linkletter Provincial Park
437 Linkletter Rd, Route 11
Linkletter, PE
(902) 888-8366
www.tourismpei.com/linkletter

Mont-Carmel Museum of Religious Art
Le Club d'age d'or, Route 11
Mont-Carmel, PE

PEI Shellfish Museum
156 Bideford Rd.
Ellerslie, PE
(902) 831-3225

PEI Sports Hall of Fame
124 Harbour Dr.
Summerside, PE C1N 5P5
(902) 436-0423
www.peisportshalloffame.ca

Shipbuilding Museum & Yeo House
Green Park Provincial Park
364 Green Park Rd., Route 12
Port Hill, PE
(902) 831-7947
www.gov.pe.ca/peimhf

Summerside Visitor Information Centre
150 Harbour Dr.
Summerside, PE
(902) 436-6692

Union Corner Provincial Park and Schoolhouse Museum
Route 11
Union Corner, PE
(902) 859-8790
www.tourismpei.com/union-corner

Wyatt House Museum
85 Spring St.
Summerside, PE
(902) 432-1296
www.wyattheritage.com

Drive 19

Cedar Dunes Provincial Park
265 Cedar Dunes Park Rd., Route 14
West Point, PE
(902) 859-8785
www.tourismpei.com/cedar-dunes

Irish Moss Interpretive Centre
11318 Rte. 14
Miminegash, PE C0B 1S0
(902) 882-4313

North Cape Interpretive Centre
21817 Route 12
North Cape, PE C0B 2B0
(902) 882-2991
www.northcape.ca

West Point Lighthouse Museum
364 Cedar Dunes Park Rd. Lot 8
West Point, PE C0B 1V0
(902) 859-3605 or (800) 764-6854
www.westpointlighthouse.com

Drive 20

Cavendish Visitor Information Centre
7591 Cawnpore Lane
Cavendish, PE
(902) 963-7830

Dalvay-by-the-Sea National Historic Site
16 Cottage Crescent
PEI National Park
Grand Tracadie, PE C0A 1P0
(902) 672-2048
www.dalvaybythesea.com

The Dunes Studio Gallery and Café
RR#9
Brackley Beach, PE C1E 1Z3
(902) 672-2586 or (902) 672-1883
(restaurant)
www.dunesgallery.com

Farmers' Bank Museum and Doucet House
2188 Church Rd.
Hunter River, PE C0A 1N0
(902) 963-3168
www.farmersbank.ca

Green Gables House
Route 6
Cavendish, PE
(902) 963-7874
www.pc.gc.ca/greengables

Lucy Maud Montgomery Birthplace
6461, junction of Routes 6 and 20
New London, PE
(902) 886-2099

Prince Edward Island National Park
North-central coast of PEI
(902) 672-6350
www.pc.gc.ca/pei

Rustico Harbour Fishery Museum
318 Harbourview Dr.
North Rustico, PE C1A 1M6
(902) 963-3799

Site of Lucy Maud Montgomery's Cavendish Home
8521 Cavendish Rd.
Cavendish, PE
(902) 963-2231
www.peisland.com/lmm

Stanley Bridge Marine Aquarium
32 Campbellton Rd., Route 6
Stanley Bridge, PE C0A 1E0
(902) 886-3355

Drive 21

Cape Bear Lighthouse
Route 18
Cape Bear, PE
(902) 962-2917 (seasonal) or
(902) 962-2469

Kings Castle Provincial Park
1887 Gladstone Rd., Route 348
Gladstone, PE
(902) 962-7422
www.tourismpei.com/kings-castle

Northumberland Provincial Park
12547 Shore Rd., Route 4
Wood Islands, PE
(902) 962-7418
www.tourismpei.com/northumberland

Panmure Island Lighthouse
62 Lighthouse Rd., Route 347
Panmure Island, PE
(902) 838-3568

Panmure Island Provincial Park
350 Panmure Island Rd., Route 347
Panmure Island, PE
(902) 838-0668
www.tourismpei.com/panmure-island

Plough the Waves
13056 Shore Rd., Route 4
Wood Islands, PE
(902) 962-3761
www.woodislands.ca

Rossignol Estate Winery
11147 Shore Rd., Route 4
Little Sands, PE
(902) 962-4193
www.rossignolwinery.com

Wood Islands Ferry
NFL Ferries
94 Water St.
Charlottetown, PE C1A 7L3
(902) 566-3838 or (877) 635-7245
www.peiferry.com

Wood Islands Lighthouse
173 Lighthouse Rd.
Wood Islands, PE C0A 1B0
(902) 962-3110
www.woodislandslighthouse.com

Drive 22

Basin Head Provincial Park and Basin Head Fisheries Museum
336 Basin Head Rd.
Kingsboro, PE
(902) 357-7233 (museum)
www.tourismpei.com/basin-head (park)
www.gov.pe.ca/peimhf (museum)

East Point Lighthouse
Lighthouse Rd.
East Point, PE
(902) 357-2106 (seasonal)
www.eastpointlighthouse.com

Elmira Railway Museum
457 Elmira Rd., Route 16A
Elmira, PE
(902) 357-7234 (seasonal)
www.elmirastation.com

Magdalen Islands ferry
435 Chemin Avila Arseneau
Cap-aux-Meules, QC G4T 1J3
(418) 986-3278 or (888) 986-3278
www.ctma.ca

Red Point Provincial Park
249 Red Point Park Rd., Route 16
Red Point, PE
(902) 357-3075
www.tourismpei.com/red-point

Souris Beach Provincial Park
8 Main St.
Souris, PE
www.tourismpei.com/souris-beach

Souris East Lighthouse
134 Breakwater St.
Souris, PE
(902) 687-2251 (seasonal)
www.sourislighthouse.com

Souris Visitor Information Centre
95 Main St.
Souris, PE
(902) 687-7030 (seasonal)

Drive 23

Gros Morne National Park
P.O. Box 130
Rocky Harbour, NL A0K 4N0
(709) 458-2417
www.pc.gc.ca/grosmorne

Jacob A. Crocker House
221 Main St.
Trout River, NL
(709) 451-5376 (town office)

Trout River Fishermen's Museum
Main wharf
Trout River, NL
(709) 451-5376 (town office)

Trout River Interpretation Centre
245–257 Main St.
Trout River, NL
(709) 451-5376 (town office)

Drive 24

Gateway to Labrador
Route 510
L'Anse Au Clair, NL A0K 3K0
(709) 931-2013
www.labradorcoastaldrive.com

Labrador Marine
(709) 535-0810 or (866) 535-2567
www.gov.nf.ca/ferryservices
www.labradormarine.com

Pinware River Provincial Park
Route 510
Pinware, NL
(709) 927-5516
www.env.gov.nl.ca/env/parks

Point Amour Lighthouse
L'Anse Amour Road
L'Anse Amour, NL
(709) 927-5825 (seasonal)
www.pointamourlighthouse.ca

Red Bay National Historic Site
P.O. Box 103
Red Bay, NL A0K 4K0
(709) 920-2142
www.pc.gc.ca/redbay

Right Whale Exhibit Museum
Main Hwy.
Red Bay, NL
(709) 920-2197 (town)

Straits Museum
P.O. Box 15
West St. Modeste, NL A0K 5S0
(709) 931-2067 or (709) 920-2025
www.labradorstraitsmuseum.ca

Drive 25

Dark Tickle Economuseum
75 Main St., P.O. Box 29
St. Lunaire-Griquet, NL A0K 2X0
(709) 623-2354
www.darktickle.com

L'Anse aux Meadows National Historic Site
P.O. Box 70
St-Lunaire-Griquet, NL A0K 2X0
(709) 458-2417
www.pc.gc.ca/meadows

Norstead: A Viking Port of Trade
Route 436
L'Anse aux Meadows, NL
(709) 623-2828 or (877) 620-2828
www.norstead.com

Drive 26

Beothuk Interpretation Centre
Boyd's Cove South Road, off Route 340
P.O. Box 131
Boyd's Cove, NL A0G 1G0
(709) 656-3114
www.seethesites.ca

By the Bay Museum
235 Main St.
Lewisporte, NL A0G 3A0
(709) 535-3900

Dildo Run Provincial Park
Route 340
Virgin Arm, NL
(709) 635-4520 (general)
www.env.gov.nl.ca/env/parks

Durrell Museum
17 Museum Rd.
Durrell, NL A0G 1Y0
(709) 884-2780 (seasonal) or
(709) 884-5537

Lewisporte Train Park
Main Street West
P.O. Box 219
Lewisporte, NL A0G 3A0
(709) 535-2737 or (709) 535-6696

Notre Dame Junction Visitor Information Centre
P.O. Box 510
Gander, NL A1V 2EI
(709) 535-8547 (seasonal)

Prime Berth—Twillingate Fishery Museum
Twillingate Island
(709) 884-5925 (seasonal) or
(709) 884-2485

Twillingate Museum
Route 340
P.O. Box 369
Twillingate, NL
(709) 884-2825
www.tmacs.ca

Drive 27

Burnside Archaeology Centre
Burnside Road
Burnside, NL
(709) 677-2474 (seasonal)
www.burnsideheritage.ca

Eastport Heritage Centre
P.O. Box 136
Eastport, NL A0G 1Z0
(709) 677-2360
www.beachesheritagecentre.ca

Glovertown Museum
11 Memorial St.
P.O. Box 457
Glovertown, NL A0G 2L0
(709) 533-6004
www.glovertown.net/attractions/janes-house-museum

Salvage Fishermen's Museum
General Delivery
Salvage, NL A0G 3X0
(709) 677-2414

Terra Nova National Park
Off the Trans-Canada Highway
General Delivery
Glovertown, NL A0G 2L0
(709) 533-2801
www.pc.gc.ca/terranova

Drive 28

Bell Island Ferry
(709) 895-6931 or (888) 638-5454
www.tw.gov.nl.ca/ferryservices

Bell Island Mine Museum and No. 2 Mine Tours
1 Compressor Hill
Wabana, Bell Island, NL
(709) 488-2880
www.bellisland.net/no2mine

Bell Island Sports Hall of Fame
Petrie's Hill, No. 2 Road
Wabana, Bell Island, NL A0A 4H0
(709) 488-2326

Drive 29

Avalon Wilderness Reserve
(709) 685-1853
www.env.gov.nl.ca/env/parks/wer/r_aw/index.html

Chance Cove Provincial Park
Route 10
Chance Cove, NL
(709) 635-4520 (general)

Colony of Avalon
P.O. Box 119
Ferryland, NL A0A 2H0
(709) 432-3200 or (877) 326-5669
www.colonyofavalon.ca

East Coast Trail
P.O. Box 8034
St. John's, NL A1B
(709) 738-4453
www.eastcoasttrail.ca

Ferryland Lighthouse Picnics
Ferryland Head
Ferryland, NL A0A 2H0
(709) 363-7456
www.lighthousepicnics.ca

Ferryland Museum
P.O. Box 3
Ferryland, NL A0A 2H0
(709) 432-2711

Five Island Art Gallery
7 Cove Rd.
Tors Cove, NL A0A 4A0
(709) 334-3645
www.fiveisland.ca

Holyrood Pond Interpretive Centre
St. Stephen's, NL
(709) 525-3100 (seasonal) or (709) 525-2306

Irish Loop Tourism Visitor Information Centre
Foodland Plaza
Bay Bulls, NL A0A 1C0
(709) 334-2609

La Manche Provincial Park
Route 10
La Manche, NL
(709) 685-1823 (seasonal) or
(709) 635-4520
www.env.gov.nl.ca/env/parks

Mistaken Point Eco Reserve
(709) 438-1100 (ask for a reserve interpreter)
www.env.gov.nl.ca/env/parks

onier Provincial Wildlife Park
J. Box 190
Holyrood, NL A0A 2R0
(709) 229-3915 or (709) 229-7888
www.env.gov.nl.ca/env/snp

St. Vincent's Fishermen's Museum
Off Cemetery Road
St. Vincent's, NL
(709) 525-2540

Trepassey Area Museum
Main Road
Trepassey, NL A0A 4B0
(709) 438-2044

Additional Reading

Barrett, Wayne, and Harry Thurston. *Atlantic Canada Nature Guide.* Toronto: Key Porter, 1998.

Creighton, Helen. *Bluenose Ghosts.* Halifax, NS: Nimbus Publishing, 2009.

Day, Frank Parker. *Rockbound.* Toronto: University of Toronto, 2005.

Grenfell, Wilfred Thomason. *Adrift on an Ice Pan.* St. John's, NL.: Creative, 1992.

Hubbard, Mina, Roberta Buchanan, Anne Hart, and B. A. Greene. *The Woman Who Mapped Labrador: The Life and Expedition Diary of Mina Hubbard.* Montreal: McGill-Queen's University Press, 2005.

Montgomery, L. M. *Anne of Green Gables.* Oxford, UK: Oxford University Press, 2007.

Proulx, Annie. *The Shipping News.* New York: Scribner, 2003.

Running Wolf, Michael B., and Patricia Clark Smith. *On the Trail of Elder Brother: Glous'gap Stories of the Micmac Indians.* New York: Persea Books, 2003.

Young, Ron. *Dictionary of Newfoundland and Labrador: A Unique Collection of Language and Lore.* St. John's, NL: Downhome, 2006.

New Brunswick

New Brunswick Provincial Parks
www.nbparks.ca

Tourism New Brunswick
Department of Tourism and Parks
P.O. Box 12345
Campbellton, NB E3N 3T6
(800) 561-0123
www.tourismnewbrunswick.ca

Nova Scotia

Nova Scotia Provincial Parks
(888) 544-3434 (camping reservations)
http://parks.gov.ns.ca

Nova Scotia Tourism
P.O. Box 456
Halifax, NS B3J 2R5
(902) 425-5781 or (800) 565-0000
www.novascotia.com

Prince Edward Island

Prince Edward Island Provincial Parks
www.tourismpei.com/pei-provincial-park

Tourism Prince Edward Island
P.O. Box 2000
Charlottetown, PE C1A 7N8
(902) 368-4444 or (800) 463-4734
www.tourismpei.com

Newfoundland & Labrador

East Coast Trail
P.O. Box 8034
St. John's, NL A1B 3M7
(709) 738-4453
www.eastcoasttrail.ca

Newfoundland and Labrador Heritage
www.heritage.nf.ca

Newfoundland and Labrador Provincial Parks (camping)
(905) 280-2248 or (877) 214-2267
www.nlcamping.ca

Newfoundland and Labrador Tourism
P.O. Box 8700
St. John's, NL A1B 4J6
(709) 729-2830 or (800) 563-6353
www.newfoundlandlabrador.com